Understand Counselling

D0199093

Teach Yourself®

Understand Counselling

Aileen Milne

For UK order enquiries: please contact Bookpoint Ltd, 130 Milton Park, Abingdon, Oxon OX14 4SB. Telephone: +44 (0) 1235 827720. Fax: +44 (0) 1235 400454. Lines are open 09.00–17.00, Monday to Saturday, with a 24-hour message answering service. Details about our titles and how to order are available at www.teachyourself.com

For USA order enquiries: please contact McGraw-Hill Customer Services, PO Box 545, Blacklick, OH 43004-0545, USA. Telephone: 1-800-722-4726. Fax: 1-614-755-5645.

For Canada order enquiries: please contact McGraw-Hill Ryerson Ltd, 300 Water St, Whitby, Ontario L1N 9B6, Canada. Telephone: 905 430 5000. Fax: 905 430 5020.

Long renowned as the authoritative source for self-guided learning – with more than 50 million copies sold worldwide – the Teach Yourself series includes over 500 titles in the fields of languages, crafts, hobbies, business, computing and education.

British Library Cataloguing in Publication Data: a catalogue record for this title is available from the British Library.

Library of Congress Catalog Card Number: on file.

First published in UK 1999 by Hodder Education, part of Hachette UK, 338 Euston Road, London NW1 3BH.

First published in US 1999 by The McGraw-Hill Companies, Inc.

This edition published 2010.

Previously published as *Teach Yourself Counselling.*

The Teach Yourself name is a registered trade mark of Hodder Headline.

Typeset by Macmillan Publishing Solutions.

Printed in Great Britain for Hodder Education, an Hachette UK Company, 338 Euston Road, London NW1 3BH, by CPI Cox & Wyman, Reading, Berkshire RG1 8EX.

The publisher has used its best endeavours to ensure that the URLs for external websites referred to in this book are correct and active at the time of going to press. However, the publisher and the author have no responsibility for the websites and can make no guarantee that a site will remain live or that the content will remain relevant, decent or appropriate.

Hachette UK's policy is to use papers that are natural, renewable and recyclable products and made from wood grown in sustainable forests. The logging and manufacturing processes are expected to conform to the environmental regulations of the country of origin.

Impression number   10 9 8 7 6 5 4 3 2 1

Year   2014 2013 2012 2011 2010

Acknowledgements

Thanks to the following publishers for granting permission to use material for which they hold copyright: Constable & Co. Ltd for extracts from text by Carl Rogers: *The Carl Rogers Reader*, edited by Howard Kirschenbaum and Valerie Land Henderson; Butterworths for permission to use extracts from *Individual Psychotherapy and the Science of Psychodynamics* by David H. Malan; Hodder Education for the use of material from *Teach Yourself Visualization* by Pauline Wills and *Teach Yourself Meditation* by Naomi Ozaniec; Sage Publications Ltd for material used from *Transcultural Counselling in Action* by Patricia d'Ardenne and Aruna Mahtani (1989) and from Dr Patricia d'Ardenne for same; Ubaldini Editore for permission to reproduce material from *Transpersonal Development: The Dimension Beyond Psychosynthesis* by Roberto Assagioli MD; The University of California Press for material from *The Johari Window: A Graphic Model of Interpersonal Relations* by Jo Luft and Harry Ingham; Open University Press for material from *An Introduction to Counselling* by John McLeod.

Every effort has been made to trace the correct copyright holder, but if any have been inadvertently overlooked the publisher will be pleased to make the necessary arrangements at the first opportunity.

Many thanks to Morowa Selassie, Roy Radcliffe and Diane Harrison for their contributions.

Thanks also to family and friends for the love and support they gave me during the writing of this book. They include Anita Jeffery, Heather Minton, Joe Jenkins, Helen Johnson, Sue Edwards, David Roberts and my sons, Dylan and Jamie. A special thanks also to Trisha Ledeboer and Sylvia Williams.

Contents

Meet the author

Welcome to *Understand Counselling*!

Let me introduce myself as the author of *Understand Counselling* and tell you something about my work and what has led me to write about counselling.

My name is Aileen. I am a practising counsellor and I have been working as a counsellor in Gloucestershire in various settings for the past 15 years or so. Writing this I can't believe that it has been so long – but it has. I think that it would be fair to say that during these 15 years I have accrued considerable counselling experience. I have worked with both young and elderly clients, male and female, and people of different nationalities and cultures, gaining experience by working with the myriad variety of issues people present – problems both individual and universal in their themes. I have counselled over the telephone, face to face and online. I enjoy ongoing training and have read extensively about old, well-established theories as well as new ideas on a whole range of subjects such as bereavement, developmental stages, stress management, anxiety disorders, anger management, depression, post-traumatic stress disorder, obsessive compulsive disorder and many more.

I initially trained in one model of counselling called *psychodynamic* and then went on to train in other methods of counselling, adding to my repertoire. In my current employment with an employee assistance programme (EAP) provider – where the company provides counselling for employees of companies and organisations throughout the UK – I primarily use *cognitive behavioural therapy* techniques and other solution-focused methods to do my job. However, don't let titles like 'psychodynamic' or 'cognitive behavioural therapy' intimidate you; basically the aim of all the different counselling approaches is the same – to help people overcome whatever it is that they're going through that is causing them psychological distress. I have enjoyed running workshops and training for young mothers for a local educational authority and have counselled in schools and I practice privately from time to time.

I began counselling in a young people's counselling service in Gloucester where the clients were between the ages of 14 and 25. It was a valuable learning environment and I feel very lucky that I started off my practical training by working with young people – it is a challenging age group, not always willing to open up and trust intimate details to a stranger (quite right too). It called for an inventive approach. It taught me a valuable lesson as a novice – that being genuinely yourself and relaxed in your role as counsellor goes a long way; far more than doggedly adhering to set theories and practices. When the counsellor appears human – friendly and approachable and genuinely interested in the client – it encourages the other person to unburden.

I am an advocate of counselling and therapy in general. I believe in its value. Because I have seen again and again how people have benefited from counselling, from being listened to, encouraged to talk and explore their problems, and find more positive ways of looking at life situations and lessening the impact of difficulties. I have personally been helped by counselling and regard it as potentially a fantastic vehicle of self-empowerment.

When I started writing *Understand Counselling* it felt like a huge topic and, perhaps to make it easier for myself as well as the reader, I tried to make the coverage as simple and straightforward as possible. I also tried to get as much general information about counselling packed into the book, which hopefully I have achieved.

More details follow about the contents and structure of the book in a further introduction. I really hope that you find the book interesting as well as useful, whether your interests lie in training as a counsellor, you picked up the book because you're considering having counselling, or you just want to learn more about the subject.

With my very best wishes,

Aileen

Only got a minute?

The use of counselling has become widespread.

Why? The bottom line is that if something is

seriously diminishing a person's quality of life

and affecting their general functioning then it

is worth taking steps to sort it out. Counselling

is somewhere where we can deal with our

troubles when they feel like they are taking over

and getting out of hand. This might be because

of issues such as: grief over the loss of a loved

one, feeling out of our depth or swamped by

responsibilities at work, problems in relationships

with other people, drug or alcohol dependency or

just feeling generally anxious and stressed.

The list is endless because people are complex

and therefore the difficulties they experience are

also complex and somewhat idiosyncratic. This

book aims to explore some of those complexities

and show how counselling can help us deal with

our problems.

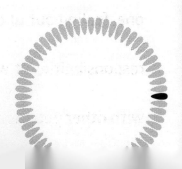

5 Only got five minutes?

So what are the strengths of counselling and why do people find it invaluable in overcoming their problems? Something of a small miracle can happen in counselling. Take two people who are complete strangers to each other, place them in a room, and within a short time one person is telling the other all the intimate business of their lives, confiding, trusting and opening up to the other like a flower to the sunshine and rain. The result, more often than not, is that in a short time the person having counselling feels relieved of their burdens or at least feels a whole lot better, not only about their problems but also about themselves.

Spending time with a counsellor – someone who is completely outside our problems – offers respite from ordinary life where, out of necessity, we bypass many of our fundamental needs. Counselling gives the opportunity for 'me time'. It's a place where we can talk about what we choose for a whole hour, in fact Freud defined psychoanalysis as 'the talking cure'. Outside of counselling when and where can we count on this happening without us feeling self-indulgent or fearing we are boring someone? We know that it is the counsellor's job to listen, to be attentive, be on our side, yet maintain professionalism.

Counselling provides a time and a place in our busy lives where we can take a long honest look at what's distressing us. It is somewhere we can explore issues, raise our awareness, develop powers of self-reflection and feel encouraged to generate new understanding. With the support of a counsellor, we can find ways to accept and make peace with things we can't change and make positive changes where we can. *We become aware that we have choices in life.*

Gradually we get a sense that we can be whoever and however we want to be. This may sound like a form of escapism or delusion but it is rooted in the findings of psychology which attest the theory that the way people think determines their sense of self, other people and the world around them as well as their abilities to cope with stressful problems. Neuroscience has proved the human ability to build new neural pathways in the brain as a method of developing a more creative and expansive view of our lives and coping with the world around us.

We can question and challenge things that feel fixed in stone. We can, with the counsellor's guidance, explore what *really* matters to us, what and who we value, our beliefs, hopes and needs. In other words, counselling helps people to discover and express their authentic, true self rather than the self they think they need to put forward for other people's approval. It purports the idea that we have a right to feel what we feel and think what we think.

Speaking as an experienced counsellor, I believe that another very important component is that not only do we feel listened to and heard by the counsellor but we also have the opportunity to articulate our thoughts and *hear ourselves* say them out loud. Telling another uninvolved person material that might feel very personal has been likened to the confessional element in religion; you are left with a sense of having shared the burden. Counsellors are witnesses to the client's suffering and it is the feeling that someone is there with us in the struggle to make sense of and take charge of what seems to the client, at the onset of counselling, insurmountable troubles. The counsellor isn't critical of what they hear, which encourages us to open up and trust in the counselling process. Yet counsellors are challenging at times and will help us focus on how we can change negative life patterns.

Putting difficult thoughts and emotions into words, bringing them out into the open, can bring tremendous relief. What we discover is often revelatory. Working as a counsellor, I have frequently heard people say things like: 'I wasn't aware I thought that', 'I didn't know that was still bothering me – I thought I'd put that behind me', 'It feels so good to get that off my chest.'

When talking with a counsellor we have the opportunity, if we choose, to be different than we would normally be. We don't have to pretend that we are on top of things. For example, if we relate a story about a past experience or something we are currently going through and we feel sad or embarrassed, we can be frank about it and examine these emotions with the counsellor. We don't have to worry that the counsellor will be dismissive, or that we will hurt their feelings or they'll take offence and become defensive, as we might with other people. The counselling situation gives us the opportunity to express ourselves more freely, for example a person might cry and talk for the first time in a while about a person who has died, having stopped themselves from showing emotion for the sake of others.

People cry and get in touch with powerful emotions in counselling, which in itself can bring cathartic release, especially when a person has reined in their emotions for some time. Pent-up emotion can lead to anxiety, stress and depression, and in many cases being able to express strong emotion can alleviate such symptoms.

In counselling we can: uncover our true feelings, discover new ways to express ourselves, reconnect with our strengths, look at our values, our short comings, personality traits and who and what is important to us in our lives. We can learn how to relate more productively with other people, develop coping strategies, skills and techniques to help us cope at difficult times in our lives. We come to appreciate our strengths and competencies and also accept that it is OK to be imperfect because being imperfect is part of the human condition. Counselling is also, most importantly, a place that we learn to respect and care for ourselves.

Introduction

Understand Counselling aims to present the reader with an overview of the main theories, skills and applications of one-to-one counselling. There is a large amount of literature available on the subject of counselling and it can be intimidating to those who are interested in learning about counselling but aren't sure where to start. With this in mind, the book addresses the basics of counselling, for example its origins, the role of the counsellor, the practical use of counselling skills and the training involved in becoming a professional counsellor. A chapter is also set aside to deal with the different counselling orientations.

Who will benefit from this book?

Understand Counselling will be useful for those interested in training or those who have already begun training as a counsellor. The book will also inform the individual who is interested in learning about counselling skills with a view to communicating with others more effectively, both in the workplace and in their private lives.

The material covers a broad spectrum and comprises two parts. The first section begins by focusing on the roles of counselling and on the counsellor. Skills and the core conditions of the person-centred approach are introduced and discussed in relation to their use in other areas of life outside counselling. The first section concludes with Enjoying the exploration (Chapter 5), which suggests methods of self-development and reflection to complement the aims and beliefs of counselling and prepare the individual for helping others.

The second part of the book takes the reader a stage further into the theories, concepts and techniques of counselling. It addresses the person who has embarked on training or who is interested in becoming a counsellor in a voluntary or professional capacity and begins by looking at course components. Material in this section includes an outline of the three main approaches to counselling; that is, the psychodynamic approach that originates from the psychoanalytical model; the person-centred approach that represents the humanistic model, and the behavioural/cognitive behavioural approach. Therapeutic jargon is highlighted and explained in the glossary and technical terms are explained in context throughout the text. Other titles are suggested in the Taking it further section to enable the reader to follow up his or her interest and build a deeper, richer understanding.

Sometimes newly trained counsellors are thrown in at the deep end and find themselves working with issues that they are unprepared for: the angry client, the client who discloses they have suffered abuse, the client who feels suicidal, the grieving client, or the person who self-harms. Chapters 9 and 10 deal with these subjects and Chapter 11 looks at the particular concerns of working with cultural difference.

The intention is that these chapters will go some way towards demonstrating that we learn fundamentally how to be with our clients (or people we hope to help) from the clients themselves – if we listen, attend and respond in a skilled way. These subjects are introduced to provide insight into the challenges that are inherent to the work. Self-responsibility and the development of personal resources are central themes and goals of counselling that apply equally to the counsellor. The later chapters refer to how experienced counsellors work with their clients and offer guidelines. As we'll explore in the book, many counsellors work integratively – blending two or more approaches.

Finally, where case studies have been included, care has been taken to protect the anonymity of the client.

Recommendation by Phillip Hodson

I am very happy to be asked to write a few words of introduction to the new edition of Aileen Milne's *Understand Counselling*. This book seems to me to fill a vital gap in the literature on counselling and I am really glad the publishers have decided on a reissue. The text serves to help both the layman and the student. Although I have been a practitioner for 25 years, I find that this is the book I refer to when in need of a quick piece of information or to remind myself of a crux in counselling theory. Let me add, I am writing about a book I have actually read – several times – as my battered copy of the first edition demonstrates.

Counselling and psychotherapy are huge subjects for the non-professionals. There are several dozen different schools of approach. Many therapists speak in a specialized language. As a member of the public, it is sometimes difficult to know how you are supposed to behave as a client. At the very least, will you be vertical or horizontal when doing your talking? Aileen explains what the three main schools of approach are trying to achieve and how you can turn the therapist into YOUR therapist.

Counselling and psychotherapy are hugely successful but relatively new disciplines. Many thousands of people have found a calling and wish to become practitioners. Aileen's book is an exemplary introduction to what you might be taking on and where to start looking for the best training courses in your area. At the same time, as Aileen shows, the field of therapy remains unregulated by the government despite the fervent wishes of all responsible therapists. Anyone can call himself or herself a 'counsellor', 'psychologist' or 'psychotherapist' and start practising this afternoon. They won't know what they are doing and won't be any good at it. But the fact remains. All the more reason, therefore, to seek out a practitioner or training institute registered with an in-house regulator such as the British Association for Counselling and Psychotherapy (www.counselling.co.uk).

There are a plethora of counselling styles but only one correct approach to practice: a therapist needs to be accountable, ethical, trained, supervised, client-centred and insured. If you take nothing else from this book, remember that good practice is more important in the healing process, exploring difficult emotions or helping people to extend their emotional range than any petty differences of theory. I happily recommend Aileen's work.

Phillip Hodson
Author and broadcaster
Fellow, the British Association for
Counselling and Psychotherapy

Part one

The fundamentals

1

The counselling role

In this chapter you will learn:
- *the differences and similarities between counselling and psychotherapy*
- *what counselling involves*
- *about the counsellor–client relationship*
- *the importance of confidentiality in the counselling setting.*

Counselling can take many forms: people receive counselling individually, or have couple counselling or family counselling – when the dynamics between family members will be the focus of the work. The capacity and setting in which counsellors work also varies, ranging from a few hours a week doing voluntary work with an agency or organization to working privately in a professional practice. Some counselling involves working with particular client groups – examples are student counselling and marriage counselling; and some focus on particular problems – for example, medical conditions such as cancer or AIDS, or social problems such as alcohol or drug abuse. To add to the complexity, there are many 'schools' of counselling which are informed by their own particular theoretical frameworks. These can, however, be identified and understood by the three core approaches of **analytical, humanistic** and **behavioural** perspectives and these will be explored in later chapters.

Given that there has been a proliferation of counselling activity in the past 20 years or so in Western societies, it seems likely that counselling is fulfilling a need that was in the past met by other means. People in the community – family members, neighbours, friends, local doctors and clergy – formed emotional and social support systems for individuals.

Many of us no longer live in supportive communities bound together by religious faith and beliefs. Our world horizons have expanded; the cities where many of us live can feel large and impersonal. Perhaps in seeking counselling we attempt to repersonalize our lives. We take our problems to a place where we feel we will be listened to and where our thoughts and feelings are regarded as important. The role of counselling is ever evolving to meet the challenges of modern social pressures and demands which we often attempt to deal with at cost to our inner world. The role of counselling has been defined by its aims and values. Aims include providing an environment that enables the client to work towards living in a more resourceful and personally fulfilling way. Integrity, respect and impartiality are basic values that are demonstrated throughout the counselling process.

We enter into a counselling relationship when we engage the help of a counsellor in mutual agreement. No one can be forced into a counselling–client relationship; a person chooses to have counselling, otherwise it isn't counselling at all. The activity of counselling has been defined in many ways. The following are some of the ways that counselling can help people resolve problems or help people live their lives in a more insightful, fulfilling way. Counselling can help people:

- ▶ *to clarify what's important in their lives*
- ▶ *to get in touch with their inner resources*
- ▶ *in the exploration of feelings, thoughts and meanings particular to them*
- ▶ *by offering support at times of crisis*
- ▶ *by offering support during developmental and transitional periods*
- ▶ *to work through 'stuck' issues – this might involve integrating childhood experiences*
- ▶ *to reach a resolution of problems.*

Insight

> People are a lot more resourceful and resilient than they
> think and counselling can help them reconnect with their
> coping side.

Psychotherapy and counselling: where they converge and where they differ

The terms **counselling, psychotherapy** and **therapy** often seem to
be used in an interchangeable way, their differences unclear to the
uninitiated. In particular, the use of the term 'therapy' is widespread.
A dictionary of psychology would define therapy using the words:
'treatment of disease or disorder' and 'to make better'. If we look
at the word 'disease' in two parts, *dis* and *ease*, we see that it refers
to the state of a person who is no longer at ease with themselves in
their physical and/or psychological state. Therapy, or counselling, is
a process that helps the client make their life better by focusing on
the areas of their lives that cause them problems or distress.

The word 'therapy' has come to be a generic term used to describe
something that is helpful or nurturing in some way or that gives
relief from the strains of everyday life, hence such terms as 'retail
therapy'. It's also used as an abbreviated form of 'psychotherapy'.
The word 'therapist' is used likewise as an abbreviated form of
'psychotherapist', but many counsellors also refer to themselves
as therapists.

SIMILARITIES BETWEEN PSYCHOTHERAPY AND COUNSELLING

Psychotherapy and counselling are regarded as separate
professions. They sometimes have their own, and sometimes share,
professional associations that safeguard the interests of both clients
and practitioners. Among the functions that these professional
associations serve is the accreditation of training courses and the
accreditation of individual practitioners.

Although they have separate identities in the field of therapy, it's a widely held view that there's a lot of overlap between the two. Both use a similar theoretical framework of reference; the same training materials, books and resources are used on courses. This is particularly true when courses are based around the same theoretical 'school' or approach; for example, person-centred or psychodynamic. A person may reach professional status as either a person-centred counsellor or psychotherapist, yet their fundamental differences are unclear. The **humanistic psychologist** Carl Rogers made no clear distinction between the two titles, sometimes referring to himself as a counsellor and at other times as a psychotherapist. Members of both professions work in similar settings, in medical and health centres, doctors' surgeries and clinics, and this can add to the confusion. The therapist and writer Windy Dryden, discussing the difference between the two titles in *Self and Society*, a humanistic psychology journal, jokes that the main difference is 'about £8,000 a year'. He states that he finds difficulty in making clear distinctions between the two activities.

In his book *Ordinary Ecstasy*, John Rowan, a humanistic therapist, states, 'Every technique which is used in personal growth and in counselling is also used in psychotherapy and vice versa,' and in 2001 he wrote an article again discussing the subject of difference. He draws attention to the paradox when he writes:

> **On the one hand psychotherapy and counselling are different – they have different histories and associations, for example; while on the other hand they are the same – for example; they have many identical interventions and involvements. This contradiction – they are the same and they are different – has to be held and maintained.**
>
> (*CPJ: Counselling and Psychotherapy Journal*, August 2001)

DIFFERENCES BETWEEN PSYCHOTHERAPY AND COUNSELLING

Length and depth of training
There are a few differences that can be identified at training level. Psychotherapy usually involves longer training. It's possible to

obtain a certificate in counselling within a few months and a diploma in a year. There's a lack of regularity in awarding such titles; many courses demand two or three years' part-time study to reach diploma level. The varied length, and presumably depth, of training to reach the same status of qualification brings up ethical issues of standards. It's obviously important for the consumer – the client – to check out what the counsellor's qualifications and experience are when embarking on therapy.

Whereas to reach a professional level a counsellor would most likely be expected to train for a period of two to three years part-time, a psychotherapist would have spent a minimum of three years and often longer in training. Psychotherapy training often incorporates a year of working in a health care setting or private practice towards the end of the course, providing case study material for assessment.

Origins

Psychotherapy has been a branch of medicine from the late nineteenth century and **psychoanalysis** was a major development in psychotherapy in the twentieth century. In the early 1900s another type of psychotherapy called **behaviourism** associated therapy with psychology and science, mainly because its theories were developed from behavioural experiments. In contrast, counselling is a comparatively new discipline which was developed by psychotherapists such as Carl Rogers in America in the late 1950s. Counselling began in educational settings and was widely applied in marriage guidance, pastoral care and voluntary organizations. It subsequently developed into private practice.

Length of treatment

It's generally thought that psychotherapists work long term with clients while counsellors work short term, or in crisis situations. There are no hard and fast rules. Counselling can incorporate both short-term and long-term ways of working; it sometimes begins with a short-term focus and for various reasons results in long-term therapy. Long-term counselling is common and, conversely, it's not uncommon for psychotherapists to offer brief psychotherapy.

Often the two activities are indistinguishable from each other, especially when the practitioners are very experienced. In some situations practitioners are restricted by the limited resources of their workplace; it might be deemed more satisfactory to offer six to eight weeks' therapy to a greater number of people rather than long-term therapy to only a few.

Depth of work

The extended training of the psychotherapist is designed to equip them to work in more depth with clients. However, although this is used as a focus of training, it's not always the case that psychotherapists exclusively cater for the client with more difficulties. It does seem true to say, as a general rule, that while the counsellor sees a client once a week for a single session, the psychotherapist might see a client two or more times in a week.

Personal therapy for trainees

Both professions require trainees to have personal therapy for the duration of the course. A psychotherapist in training, who is expecting to see individual clients two or more times a week, is usually required by the conditions of their course to have the corresponding amount of personal therapy throughout the training. The same applies to the counsellor who's training with a view to seeing individuals once a week; they too will require personal therapy once a week for the duration of the course, although this requirement doesn't necessarily apply to shorter courses.

The counselling role

Counselling can take many forms:

- *doctors refer patients to counsellors who practise alongside them in their surgeries*
- *teachers and youth workers will often direct young people to counselling agencies for help*

- *counsellors are called to accidents and disaster areas to counsel the victims and their families*
- *individuals seek counselling for themselves for all kinds of reasons*
- *counselling is used in a variety of settings: in education, in pastoral care and increasingly in industry.*

The role counselling plays in society is increasingly multifaceted and always supportive. Counselling now seems to be very much a part of our lives, no longer regarded as a luxury or indulgence. Therapy is seen for the most part as a sensible move towards self-care and healing. The majority of us are open-minded about it, taking the view that anything that is nurturing, supportive and self-enlightening is bound to be useful.

Roles within roles
So that we can make informed choices about how we would like to get involved in counselling, it's important to make distinctions between the different roles of counselling. What has been described previously, in relation to psychotherapy, was the counsellor who has trained to a professional level. This is the counsellor who works alongside doctors, or who counsels students in an educational establishment or a social services setting. These counsellors are most likely to be accredited by a national professional counselling association; for example, the British Association for Counselling and Psychotherapy (BACP), the American Counselling Association (ACA) or the Australian Institute of Professional Counsellors (AIPC). Accreditation is awarded to counsellors who reach a certain standard of qualification and experience and is often required for jobs. Counselling association members will be required to work within the association's codes of ethics and practice.

Other counsellors, who aren't working at a professional level but nevertheless provide a very valuable service, are trained by agencies to offer help in specialized areas such as bereavement, alcohol abuse, drug abuse and race issues. The initial training (given before the helpers begin to counsel clients) is likely to be of a comparatively short duration. However, specialist agencies usually provide their counsellors with excellent ongoing training and supervision. These counsellors are likely to be working in the voluntary sector, usually offering one or two days' help to the agency per week. Many people whose interest in counselling began in this way go on to further training to a professional level. Social workers, teachers, youth workers, managers and probation officers who want to be more attuned to the needs of the people they work with are among those who learn counselling skills as an enhancement to their work.

Ways to participate in counselling
To recap, there are three different ways to work in counselling:

1 *As a professional, which will usually require two to three years of study to acquire knowledge of skills, theory and practical experience.*
2 *By working in the voluntary sector within an organization that will offer training, sometimes in a specialist area.*
3 *As part of a job, probably using basic skills to enhance communication and listening/responding abilities.*

Other uses for acquired counselling skills are in personal development and learning how to be an effective supporter of colleagues, family and friends.

Those who have counselling

Who has counselling?

▶ *From a counsellor's perspective, are they different from you or me?*
▶ *Are they a certain type of person who is unable to cope as the rest of us do?*

The answer to both these questions is usually 'No'. Often the problems clients bring to session are not outside our own life experiences. When they are, the counsellor would be wise to find out as much as possible about the subject or guide the client to an agency or a counsellor with expertise in the particular problem – for example, sexual abuse, a serious case of self-harming or a drug habit. There are often underlying problems and issues that aren't obvious at first and they might not arise until some time into the therapy when trust and support have been established. Sometimes an ethical judgement has to be made about whether or not we're equipped, through our training and experience, to work at the level required by the severity of the client's problems or the state of their mental health.

The counsellor enters the counselling role as a professional or skilled helper, sufficiently trained, sufficiently self-aware and experienced in the job at hand. It's this efficiency that will allow the client to accept their role and trust the therapeutic counselling relationship.

Insight

People aren't generally used to speaking about themselves at length and may, at first, worry that they're being self-indulgent or that their problem will be considered too small to warrant attention.

PROBLEMS PEOPLE TAKE TO COUNSELLING

As a counsellor I am often asked: 'What kind of problems do people bring to counselling?' I've sometimes wondered if those posing the question ask because they would like to have counselling for themselves but feel that their problem is not somehow 'big enough' to warrant the attention.

People go to counselling for all kinds of reasons: following a bereavement or divorce, stress at work or school, depression or low self-esteem. There are many other factors that can leave people feeling alone and overwhelmed with hopelessness.

Some people want help with a life transition – for example, both men and women can find moving into the second part of their lives difficult. We are often told 'Life begins at 40', but many people in their forties and fifties, feeling middle aged, reach a crisis of identity or purpose. They feel panic-stricken that the dreams of their youth may never be fulfilled. This can be a time, like other times of transition, to take stock, examine and re-evaluate ourselves and aspects of our lives. Another difficult time is the teenage years when we make the transition from childhood into the grown-up world of decision-making and responsibility. When an individual seeks counselling it's because they have internal conflicts and pent-up feelings of some form that are spoiling their enjoyment of life.

Insight

Counselling is sometimes dismissed as 'just listening' and money for old rope, and therefore as not having much value. While it's true that an experienced counsellor can make it look fairly effortless they will be working hard – I know I do!

The active listener

Counsellors are commonly thought of as sympathetic professional 'listening ears' but, as I hope will become apparent, there are many skills involved. A trained and experienced counsellor is adept at *active* listening. The skills this requires will be covered in a later chapter but, suffice to say at the moment, the counsellor is far from passive or only receptive. They're actively involved in giving the client full attention and appropriate responses. This is a lot more complex than it first sounds. Basically, effective counselling employs active listening and empathic responding.

The counsellor–client relationship

Increasingly it's the relationship between the counsellor and client that's seen as crucial to a successful therapeutic process, more so than the counsellor's choice of theoretical background. Therapists such as Petruska Clarkson and Michael Khan see this working relationship as a fundamental determining factor in how much a client is able to benefit from therapy. In *Between Therapist and Client: The New Relationship*, Khan promotes the integration of the psychodynamic and humanistic models; and Clarkson's *The Therapeutic Relationship* explores 'five modalities' of relationship.

Generally speaking, whatever theories the counsellor is familiar with – many favour an integrated or eclectic approach, working with a few or many theoretical models (see Integrationism in Chapter 6) – the basic requisites are the same. These are that the counsellor provides an environment of privacy, safety and assured confidentiality, is non-defensive and shows respect for the client at all times.

A non-judgemental stance encourages an openness and an understanding to develop. Acceptance and empathy from the counsellor helps the client access their innermost feelings and inner resources. No therapist can ever take away painful experiences that have happened in a person's life but they can help them to acknowledge and understand what they have gone through and work through complex associated feelings. By their warm, accepting attitude towards clients, counsellors are conveying: 'I accept you; given what has happened to you in your life, it's understandable that you should feel the way you do or that you have behaved the way you have.' This is not token blanket approval of everything a client has felt or done, but is an empathic response, as if having walked in their shoes and felt what they have felt. The 'as if' stance is necessary to sustain because the counsellor would be little help if they couldn't maintain a separate self from the client in the professional 'holding' role.

NON-DIRECTIVE COUNSELLING

Most counsellors won't offer advice or tell the client what they should do, or take advantage in any way of the client, who is, after all, in a vulnerable position. Some forms of counselling are more directive or goal oriented than others but nevertheless the counsellor would never tell the client what to do; rather they would help clients to identify and clarify areas in their lives that they want to change and also help clients to tap into their own resources to find solutions.

This is different from giving advice or setting an agenda designed by the counsellor. The non-directive position respects the autonomy of the individual and their innate ability to find their own solutions.

THE WORKING ALLIANCE

The **working alliance** is the agreement and established framework of the work that's mutually undertaken. A framework needs to be established at the onset in which both client and counsellor are in agreement about the ways they'll work together. This helps establish trust. When the counsellor and the client agree to enter into a working relationship, they enter into a contract (which can be either verbal or written). The client is asked at the onset what they're hoping for from the counselling and what their expectations might be. The counsellor will inform the prospective client of the service they offer and give details of their training and way of working. The initial meeting is very important; both the client and counsellor are assessing whether or not they think they could work together.

THE 50-MINUTE THERAPY HOUR

Usually a counsellor will agree to see a client for 50 minutes once a week at their work premises. Why 50 minutes, as opposed to an hour? The 50-minute session is common to agencies where a counsellor could be seeing quite a few clients in a day. It has become a tradition, to allow 50 minutes of undivided attention for the client followed by ten minutes' break for the counsellor, during which they can make a few notes about the session or to have a few minutes to relax between seeing clients. Some counsellors, however, prefer one-hour sessions.

Insight

In my experience, clients are often concerned that their intimate details are safe with the counsellor and need information from the start about when (in rare circumstances) disclosure may be necessary.

CONFIDENTIALITY

A confidential setting provides the client with safety and privacy. In usual circumstances confidentiality is upheld. Brief case notes might be written during or after a session but these will be destroyed in time. However, if a client tells the counsellor something that puts them or others in danger or is illegal, it would be irresponsible for the counsellor to hold on to this. Counsellors need to be aware of legal obligations and agency policies regarding, for example, disclosure of physical or sexual child abuse, when legal requirements demand that confidential information is made available. Law, regulations or institution procedures could require counsellors to create and maintain records, and they need to be aware of the inherent responsibilities, whether records are written, computerized or stored in any other form. The client needs to be informed of any conditions and limitations of confidentiality at the onset of counselling. It's also advisable to inform a client of the procedures in effect to ensure their anonymity. Generally the practice of agencies is that when a client ceases to have counselling, any notes the counsellor has made during the therapy are destroyed; however, records could be stored for a specified period of time before this is done. To ensure the privacy of the client, they are often given a number or their initials are used rather than the full name. Procedures like these can be agreed in the initial intake sessions where counsellors work privately.

The difference between a counsellor's role and that of a friend

A friend, by the very nature of the relationship, has a vested interest. Something told to a friend could be embarrassing, shocking or hurtful to them. It might be something they feel ill-equipped to deal with, or involve mixed loyalties. Also, with friends we sometimes assume a persona that we feel is acceptable to them; for example, a mask that says, 'I'm a person who can cope with anything life throws at me,' when we wish others to believe that nothing fazes us; or another – which can be the most detrimental of all to our self-awareness and development – 'I'm always a helpful and kind person.' How can we then confide in a friend that we're not coping at all, or tell them that we're feeling annoyed with some people at the moment, including them?

CONFIDENTIALITY AND A FRIEND

A friend could agree not to tell anyone else something that's said in confidence but later, in a moment of weakness, or because they think it might be best to tell, for whatever reason, might go ahead and divulge a secret. The feelings of betrayal can be damaging to both individuals and their friendship.

To be in a position to help, a friend or family member needs to be aware of these and other possible pitfalls. The danger is that, as an unskilled helper, we leap in at times, realizing too late that we're ill-equipped and unable to cope with such a responsible position. The fact that we're emotionally involved with the person need not, however, be a drawback, as we'll explore in Chapter 4.

But first, in order that we can appreciate:

> ▶ *what can go wrong when unskilled helpers take on the task of helping;*

▶ *what a counsellor can offer someone who can't confide in those close to them*

let's look at a couple of hypothetical case studies.

Case study 1

A young woman, whom I'll call Donna, has recently discovered that she's pregnant. She is 17. Her relationship with her boyfriend, the father of her unborn child, isn't stable. He has been violent towards her on more than one occasion and although he's very young himself he's a married man. Donna is beside herself with worry and confides in a close friend one night when she has had a drink. Donna hasn't told anyone else. Her parents don't know about her relationship with this man. The friend promises not to tell anyone, but tells Donna she should have an abortion or her life will be ruined, and that she should ditch the man as soon as possible. These comments, although said out of genuine concern and affection for the girl, have the effect of panicking her even more. Donna's friend, seeing her increasingly upset, confides in another friend, who tells her own mother, who then tells Donna's mother. All those concerned are well meaning but such snowballing effects can limit a person's choices. When confronted by her mother, Donna feels embarrassed, guilty and ashamed. She wants to end her parents' anguish and therefore is more likely to do anything those close to her want her to, including having an abortion, than thinking and feeling what the best plan of action is for her.

This is not suggesting that all parents would automatically be dictatorial and insist on their daughter having an abortion in this situation or that they would ignore the girl's needs. Remember, this example is chosen to differentiate between confiding in someone close to us (and the associated pitfalls), and taking our problems to a counsellor.

Insight

It is a common misconception that a counsellor's job is to advise people and tell them what they should do about their problems.

CASE STUDY

WORKING WITH A COUNSELLOR

The counsellor might be emotionally attuned to the client within the therapeutic relationship but not emotionally involved in the sense that their emotions interfere with the process. They're not there to offer advice or tell them what to do but to help the client find out what they want to do; what will work for them. In Donna's situation, the issues that the counsellor might help her focus on are: her thoughts and feelings about being pregnant, how she feels about the possibility of becoming a mother, the impact this could have on her life, what she feels towards her boyfriend and the sense of loneliness and other emotions she might presently be experiencing, as well as looking at the various options open to her. Obviously, in this case some information and guidance might be appropriate as Donna has only a few weeks to decide what would be the best outcome for her.

Case study 2

A middle-aged man, whom I'll call Colin, has come to counselling because he feels that he's not coping at the moment. He hasn't told anyone that he's sought help for himself in the form of counselling because it's a source of shame for him to admit that he doesn't feel in control of his life and he needs help. Colin was made redundant six months ago and, although he's been trying to establish himself as a freelance worker, prospective clients are prejudiced towards his age. At 52 years old Colin is feeling a failure – a 'has-been' with no useful future. His son too has his own problems with his marriage. Colin has never been one to confide in others, friends or family. He's always been the stoic provider, the reliable father and husband, and he's now feeling without a role in life. As a person who has rarely shown his emotions, he is now feeling 'all at sea'. In this frame of mind there really isn't anyone Colin feels he can share his feelings of inadequacy with. The image he thought others had of him was virtually all he had left to bolster his sinking self-esteem.

Presenting these problems to counselling

Colin felt that he'd nothing to lose by going to counselling. He had no image to live up to there. He could explore his feelings of inadequacy, shame and depression and growing sense of hopelessness. With the help of his counsellor he was able to talk about his fears: of ageing, of feeling that he was of no use to anyone, of perhaps in the future being unable to look after himself or his family. Many issues came to the fore for Colin as he thought about his childhood and his overbearing father's expectations of him. He began to be aware of patterns in his life. He understood why he had always felt compelled to be an achiever and why he couldn't express or even access his emotions readily.

Acquiring skills for personal use

An understanding of basic counselling skills can be useful to any relationship. This doesn't mean that by acquiring a few skills you'll be able to solve all the problems you have with those you care about or be equipped to work at the same depth as an experienced counsellor, but, by learning simple listening and responding techniques, you can improve how you communicate with others. The probable outcome of this is that relationships will improve.

Had Colin's wife, for example, had a usable knowledge of basic counselling skills, of **Rogerian** core conditions (read about these in Chapter 7), she would have been more likely to sit back a little from her husband's situation and be less overwhelmed by her fear of it. She would have been able to understand her own feelings and her requirements of him. She would also have been able to listen more actively, entering into an exploration of his thoughts and feelings.

The success of this kind of activity, to a certain extent, depends on our ability to put our own needs aside, but this can be viewed as a temporary situation. When we're able to listen to the distress of another human being and not heavily identify with, resist or take offence in relation to that distress in some way, we open channels of greater communication and in time it benefits everybody.

THINGS TO REMEMBER

1 *Counselling and psychotherapy are similar in both training and practice but generally psychotherapy training is longer and the trainee psychotherapist usually enters into extensive personal therapy during training.*

2 *As a 'talking cure' counselling is about providing a place where people can talk openly about their problems and, with the help of a counsellor, find ways to resolve them.*

3 *Professional counsellors work in many different settings; for example, in schools, doctor's surgeries and in agencies.*

4 *The counsellor–client relationship is very important. To assure a good working relationship or 'working alliance' the counsellor is required to provide a safe, empathic and confidential environment. The counsellor's role is both more searching and objective than that of a friend.*

5 *Professional associations such as the British Association for Counsellors and Psychotherapists (BACP) provide standards and ethics guidelines for counselling which protect clients and counsellors alike.*

2

....

The counsellor's role

In this chapter you will learn:
- *which personal qualities help the would-be counsellor*
- *about the core conditions of person-centred counselling*
- *the emphasis on life experience and self-development.*

Perhaps you're interested in getting involved with counselling in some capacity but aren't sure what it involves. You might doubt that you have the right qualities, or perhaps you're unsure how much you would be able to commit in terms of training and counselling hours, realizing how demanding this kind of work can be.

....

Insight

It can be hugely gratifying for a counsellor to see clients grow in confidence and make positive changes in their lives.

....

Qualities of a counsellor

Kahlil Gibran wrote in *The Prophet*: 'No man can reveal to you aught but that which already lies half asleep in the dawning of your knowledge.' These words speak to the would-be counsellor and client alike. Potentially we're our own healers and problem solvers. Counsellors are not super-beings who have a monopoly on emotional strength and wisdom. Although people often have the expectation that counsellors will 'sort out' their problems, it's the clients themselves, guided and encouraged by the counsellor, who do the work.

While a practising counsellor will retain theoretical knowledge as a backdrop, the most important factor is likely to be the time and attention they give to a client. Psychologist Carl Jung advised the therapist: 'Learn your theories as well as you can, but put them aside when you touch the miracle of the living soul.' This reminds us of the uniqueness of each one of us and suggests to us that no encounter with one person will be quite the same as with another. Clients, as individuals with individual problems, are the counsellor's primary concern.

While brainstorming in a training session, the trainer asked the participants what qualities we might expect in a counsellor and the following words and phrases were suggested. Some of the suggestions demonstrate the high expectations that the prospective counsellors had of themselves. They included:

> *Integrity, an ability to look at oneself, knowledge of theory, humility, empathy, a liking of others, an interest in people, kindness, non-judgemental attitude, respect for others, a good memory for detail, being a good listener, patience, sensitivity, in control of own emotions, professionalism, ethical behaviour.*

To have all of these attributes is a tall order. These are ideals that we probably feel we fall short of. As an afterthought, someone added: 'being courageous'. That seemed to resonate with the trainer, who smiled in agreement and commented that a counsellor does need courage to face the problems a client brings and to be in the experience with them.

A VIEW OF THE 'SKILLED HELPER'

In an early edition of *The Skilled Helper*, Gerard Egan suggests an effective 'skilled helper' is committed to his or her own growth – intellectual, social, emotional and spiritual – and that such helpers need to become 'potent human beings'. Egan sees potent human beings as 'people with both the resources and the will to act'.

The founder of person-centred counselling, Carl Rogers, regarded the ability to express ourselves freely and spontaneously as important to our well-being, and the psychoanalyst Sigmund Freud, expressing it differently but with similar meaning, talked of having the 'freedom to love and work'. The skilled helper doesn't necessarily work as a professional counsellor but is familiar with and competent at using counselling skills.

According to Egan, the following factors will contribute to the effectiveness of a skilled helper, who ideally:

▶ *has basic intelligence, with respect for ideas*
▶ *reads, learns, is familiar with theory and is adept at making good use of it*
▶ *has skills of evaluation*
▶ *has common sense and social adeptness/intelligence*
▶ *has a certain easiness with others*
▶ *is at home in the social emotional world, their own and that of others*
▶ *is able to respond effectively to a wide range of human needs*
▶ *is not afraid of deep human emotions, their own and others, and is willing to work at the level of distress*
▶ *is willing to explore their own feelings and behaviour and work at recognizing and integrating all aspects of self*
▶ *can read non-verbal messages.*

Insight

Counsellors are like everyone else – they have problems and preoccupations – only they learn to put these aside when they are counselling. Similarly, a doctor won't tell us about their ailments when we visit them with ours!

CAN THESE PERSONAL QUALITIES BE ACQUIRED?

Do you recognize yourself in any of these descriptions? While most of the qualities named can be developed as skills, others are definite aspects of character that some people have more leaning towards than others; for example, not everyone is comfortable at working with strong emotions or high levels of distress, or has an easiness around the majority of people. A widely held view among therapists is that, to a large extent, qualities that are beneficial to the counsellor can be developed through training and personal therapy.

Not everyone will be considered to be suitable counsellor material by those who select for organizations or training courses. Selection procedures are usually thorough at all levels. Selection might take place over one or a number of days. Selectors use various assessment techniques. The qualities they will be looking for include:

1 *an ability to mix with others in an assessment situation (self-esteem and boundary issues)*
2 *an adaptability/spontaneity – able to respond to various set 'tasks'*
3 *an ability to self-assess*
4 *observational qualities – insightfulness*
5 *an ability to be themselves, e.g. what Carl Rogers called being 'real' – genuine and congruent*
6 *evidence of warmth of character, e.g. empathic responding*
7 *the nominee being in a position in their life that isn't at odds with the demands of training, which involves embarking on a self-growth programme and working with others in various levels of intimacy. (If a person is in the middle of a divorce, or has been recently bereaved, it might not be a good time to begin something as challenging and demanding as counselling training.)*

The methods usually used to assess the above include exercises, role-plays and games. Sometimes painting or drawing or elements of psychodrama are used. Individuals also have interviews with staff members or experienced counsellors from the organization, agency or educational establishment.

Individuals assess their own suitability – some drop out of counselling at selection stage, deciding that it's not for them. Others leave at various stages of training. Still others choose to train in gradual stages in correlation with their own personal development.

Creating core conditions

Of all the positive qualities already mentioned, the most important are generally considered to be encapsulated in the core conditions or values that originated from Carl Rogers' ideas of client-centred therapy, now more commonly referred to as person-centred therapy. These are congruence, **unconditional positive regard** and **empathy**; they can be abbreviated to CUE – a form that is easily remembered. (These and other details of person-centred therapy are the subject of a later chapter.) Other terms that are sometimes used in connection with the core conditions are: non-possessive warmth, acceptance and a **non-judgemental attitude. Genuineness** is sometimes used instead of 'congruence'.

Insight

Training, the counsellor's own life experience and counselling work experience – not least hearing all the different people's life stories – all give us counsellors a broad understanding of the complexities of human nature and how difficulties develop, which helps us to be less inclined towards being judgemental.

BEING NON-JUDGEMENTAL

What does it mean to be non-judgemental towards another? Is it even possible, considering that we make decisions all the time about what we like, dislike, tolerate or enjoy about other people? To judge a person can mean to have an opinion about whether they're a good or bad person or whether we approve or disapprove of their behaviour. The stance we take towards others is often strongly related to our own conditioning and life experiences. We might consider a person 'right' in their thoughts, emotions and behaviour because those are similar to our own. We can identify with their experiences. We might despise and reject in others aspects of character that we reject in ourselves.

How then can a counsellor be any different? This can be more easily understood if we view the non-judgemental approach as a position taken outside ordinary social interaction. Rather than rigidly classifying someone's behaviour or opinions as 'good' or 'bad', we need to consider the whole person. We can then understand the privilege of our position and adopt a receptive, supportive attitude. An empathic response to the client would be for the counsellor to understand that, given the circumstances and the experiences of the client's life, it's little wonder that they think, feel or behave in a certain way.

It's debatable whether we can ever truly sustain a non-judgemental approach with our clients. I personally see it as an ideal. When I find I am judging a client on some level I ask myself what I am feeling, what's going on for both myself and the client at the time, and I make sure I address the issues in supervision. A counsellor would have grounds for concern if a client is in danger of seriously harming either themselves or anyone else. Some kind of judgement might need to be made about what steps to take and the first step is usually to talk to a supervisor. Any judgement would be based on the client's behaviour and how the situation can be made safe.

Acceptance and self-development

It's considered important for counsellors to have personal therapy or counselling so that they can explore their own prejudices and unresolved emotional issues, which might otherwise get in the way of constructive work with a client. The much quoted words over the temple of Delphi, 'Know Thyself', have significance for any therapist. None of us is without human failings. We're all flawed and it helps if a counsellor gets to know themselves and acknowledge, what Carl Jung termed, their 'shadow side' (see Chapter 7). If we're aware of our own strengths and weaknesses, then we're more likely to understand the complexities and flaws of clients.

Personal therapy gradually helps us to become more comfortable around distress and strong emotions. How can we expect ourselves to be capable of 'holding' a client through their angry feelings if we haven't to some extent come to terms with our own anger?

Life experience

The most useful experience of all for preparation as a counsellor is to have lived and learned. Our own life experience obviously gives us insight into the situations of others, although there's a dichotomy in this. It would be a mistake to assume that because we have had a similar experience – for example, a divorce or the death of a loved one – our responses would be exactly the same as another person's. This example illustrates the point:

Example

I witnessed a relevant incident on a selection day at a counselling agency, at an early stage of my interest in counselling. In one of the exercises the nominees were given a piece of paper with a brief outline of a case study written on it. They were asked to think for a few minutes about how they might respond to their particular case. One example read: 'A 16-year-old girl has come for counselling. She has recently discovered that she was adopted as a baby. Although she wants to find out about her biological parents and possibly at some stage meet her mother, she is extremely anxious about this prospect.'

The nominee who received these details had by coincidence also been adopted. She responded by saying that she would tell the girl that she also had been adopted, say that her biological mother would most certainly be delighted to hear from her (as her own mother had been) and assure her that everything would be all right. This answer obviously reflected her particular experiences.

While this response was well meaning and no doubt in the spirit of 'openness', it was misguided. No two people will have exactly the same experience and this amount of self-disclosure on the part of the counsellor would take the focus away from the girl's underlying feelings. The counsellor appears to want to solve

(Contd)

any problems before they arise and make the girl optimistic. On realizing that she isn't being listened to, and is being required to adopt a positive attitude by the counsellor, she wouldn't be able to express her fears and anxieties, let alone explore them.

When we give people our subjective views, we sometimes assume an authority and then we're unable to explore different options. As counsellors we might try to salve a situation by reassurance. I felt I had witnessed an incident that was a very valuable lesson: that the therapist's role is not to reassure and thereby avoid difficult feelings, but rather to help the client get in touch with their feelings and stay with them.

Counselling is one of the few vocations where getting older is not a problem. To come to counselling in our thirties, forties or at a greater age means we come with an abundance of life experience. Hopefully we have learned from experiences, good and bad. We've gone through difficult times that stretched our emotional and psychological resources and survived the trauma. Tutors and trainers in counselling look for evidence of resilience in prospective trainees. Generally speaking, the amount of life experience in the young is much less than in those who are older. That's why the majority of counselling and psychotherapy courses require the trainee counsellor to be a specified age, usually 25 years or over.

What do you want to get out of counselling?

Teaching, social work and nursing are examples of the more obvious types of occupations that benefit from knowledge of counselling skills but any work that involves interactional communication would also benefit.

You might be interested in changing your career. People who become counsellors come from diverse backgrounds, such as business, teaching, nursing and social work. Some have initially taken up counselling on a voluntary basis or as an enhancement to their work. They become inspired by what they've learned, change track altogether and decide to train further to become professional counsellors or psychotherapists. Many people who become interested in counselling have had intensive therapy themselves. They've had first-hand experience as a client. They feel that therapy has been a positive experience and are consequently interested in pursuing counselling as a career. Others choose to work in areas where they themselves have suffered trauma; for example, a woman who has been physically abused might choose to counsel in a woman's refuge, and a former drug user may train to work in an agency as a drugs counsellor.

COMMITMENTS

Training as a professional counsellor can be a lengthy business. The more thoroughly we train the more commitment is involved in terms of time, finance and energy. Many people receive initial training through a counselling agency. Agencies usually offer training over a relatively short period of 10–12 weeks and after this the trainees begin to counsel clients in a voluntary capacity. Before embarking on the training, which is usually free, the trainees could be required to commit themselves to working a minimum of a few hours per week for a year or more. This is a good way to start counselling because it gives experience in both theory and practice. Agencies and organizations that enlist volunteer counsellors usually provide excellent ongoing training and supervision for their helpers. Good supervision is essential in any form of counselling.

It could be useful to ask yourself a few questions:

▶ *Why do I want to counsel other people?*
▶ *What do I want to get out of counselling?*
▶ *How much time can I give on a voluntary basis?*

- *Am I hoping to make a career out of counselling?*
- *Have I the financial resources to embark on a lengthy programme of learning?*
- *Am I willing to be personally challenged?*

COUNSELLING OR USING COUNSELLING SKILLS?

When visiting a holistic clinic, I asked the receptionist if any counsellors practised there. She replied that most of the practitioners at the clinic 'did a bit of counselling along with the treatment'. As a counsellor I instantly felt my role had been rendered defunct. Think about the tables being turned – imagine a counsellor who, within the counselling session, gave neck manipulation as a sideline.

The imagined situation and the casualness of the receptionist's remark led me to wonder how people view counselling. On closer enquiry I found that one practitioner, a reflexologist, had attended a short counselling skills course. She was an empathic, warm person but she had no counselling qualifications. I felt she wasn't a counsellor, or in fact counselling, but she was employing counselling skills, possibly to very good effect. In her capacity as an alternative therapist she was working with the healing model that acknowledged the triad connection of mind, body and spirit. She talked to her clients about their upsets and tensions in relation to their state of health. It is a valid, insightful way to work and forms the basis of holistic medicine and treatment; that is, treating the whole person, each part related to the other, linking cause and effect. If a person holds tension in their stomach, in time they are likely to develop physical problems in that area. This is a simple example but it illustrates the connection between our emotional state and the effect on our bodies.

Insight

Counselling demands versatility and a somewhat chameleon-like ability to work effectively with a wide cross-section of people and a wide range of problems.

The emotional demands and rewards of personal growth

Training as a counsellor requires a willingness to self-examine and to be open about our self. Even on the shortest courses, the trainee will be focusing on personal attitudes, values and feelings in relation to other people and their own lives. How can we have understanding of and empathy for other people if we have little understanding or tolerance of ourselves? In person-centred therapy the counsellor takes a stance of 'unconditional positive regard' towards the client. This is to be non-judgemental, accepting, warm and supportive. If we judge another person negatively we take a superior position to elevate ourselves. To take the role of empathic listener and supporter of another person requires us to drop these attitudes and recognize that we're all in the same position; we're all human. This requires a willingness to self-scrutinize and self-assess.

It's impossible to become a counsellor without entering into personal development, awareness and growth – call it what you will. It has frequently been referred to as a journey taken inwardly and, like most journeys, it has its high and low points, with interesting landscapes to enjoy at times and bumpy rides to endure at others. Be prepared to be challenged, to meet difficulties while you unravel and try to understand yourself before you are let loose on others. The experience can be life changing.

Personal therapy helps us understand ourselves in more depth, how we think, feel and behave. Some of the following issues are likely to present themselves: your expectations of others, personal motivations, problem areas (e.g. conflicts, difficulties, unresolved material), how you relate to another person in intimacy, aspects of your childhood, your values, prejudices and self-esteem.

Insight

Getting involved in counselling can be both exciting and a bit scary as we get in touch with our vulnerabilities and start questioning some aspects of our lives, which can cause temporary disruption or cause us to make major life decisions.

It's not difficult to see why self-exploration is challenging and demanding. It can also at times be frustrating, but sticking with it – what therapists call 'going with **the process**' – does yield rewards. Self-exploration through participating in therapy offers unique opportunities. These include being able to explore our individuality and discovering our potential and inner resources. It's a wonderful opportunity to be open and non-defensive with someone who calls on us to challenge some of our perceptions and a chance to release 'stuck' feelings and reintroduce spontaneity into our lives.

TRAINEES AND FELLOW EXPLORERS

While training you'll be working with others and, when you choose to, sharing intimate details of yourself. This calls for a great deal of honesty and courage. You may well be surprised at aspects of your character that surface when you feel trust for people you are working with in mutual exploration. For example, you might perceive yourself to be a serious person and be shocked to find others perceive you as flippant. Feedback is a valuable source of material for self-enquiry, giving us insight into both positive and negative aspects of our personalities. It lets us know how we react towards others and how they in turn react towards us. Working together in one-to-one practice, triad practice or groupwork demands that we take responsibility for ourselves; this includes looking after ourselves within the group dynamic. People frequently form close bonds when they take part in each other's development, considering it to be an enriching and stimulating experience.

THINGS TO REMEMBER

1 *To become a counsellor a person learns counselling skills, practises the skills and learns psychology theory, but familiarizing yourself with the skills alone will help in all interpersonal situations whether in work or personal life.*

2 *Counselling skills can be learned but certain personal qualities such as warmth and a genuine interest in others can help the counsellor–client relationship.*

3 *Aspects of life experience are an essential element of how well we can relate to other people's problems and while training, and as an ongoing commitment, a counsellor is expected to engage in their own self-development.*

4 *Being non-judgemental doesn't mean quite what the term suggests as we all make judgements about each other all the time. However the counsellor learns to put their judgements aside and separate a person's behaviour from the person.*

5 *Counselling training requires a willingness to self-explore and look at our difficulties, personal attitudes and values. This can be emotionally demanding.*

3

Skills used in counselling

In this chapter you will learn:
- *both the basic and more advanced skills*
- *how to understand specific words used by the client*
- *about the use of empathy*
- *the basics of counsellor–client body language.*

This chapter considers the basic skills of counselling that you
would expect to learn in theory and experience in practice if you
attended any beginners' counselling training.

Sharpening our awareness

Speaking, hearing, seeing, feeling and thinking are all ways we
respond and give attention to each other. At times of emergency we
often have a heightened response to other people in need; both head
and heart go into operative mode. In our concern for the person,
we examine the most effective way to help them find relief from
their predicament and we're highly focused. At other times,
especially when strong emotions are involved, we're often at a loss
about how to be of any help to the distressed person. By identifying
and developing simple skills, we can enhance our ability to be
more fully present for another person when they're distressed or
experiencing difficulties in their lives. Although some readers might

be interested in acquiring skills as would-be helpers rather than counsellors, for the sake of clarity I use the terms 'counsellor' and 'client' to denote the different roles. It would be equally appropriate to use the terms 'helper' and colleague, friend or family member.

The basic skills that counsellors use involve listening, observing, attending and responding. Active listening requires full attention and alertness to every nuance, to what's both implicitly and openly said, thereby helping the client to understand their feelings and thoughts. The ground skills that enable us to respond effectively include reflecting (paraphrasing and summarizing), appropriate questioning and empathy. Responding on an empathic level involves responding to content – to what is being said – and to feelings, by tentatively reflecting back your understanding of what the client is expressing.

Use of questions

Think about how you respond when others come to you for help, advice or general succour. Do you fire a lot of questions at them, questions such as: 'What's wrong?', 'Why are you so upset?', 'Is it something she or he has said to you?' Asking questions might seem the most natural thing to do on these occasions, but questioning can be off-putting if overdone. Questions can be intrusive and too forceful, and could be used to satisfy our own curiosity, rather than help the other person. Yet questions, used tentatively and sensitively, are necessary for the exploration and clarification of facts and feelings.

In counselling, questions tend to be used sparingly because clients are generally encouraged to tackle problems at their own pace. During therapy painful material inevitably surfaces and insensitive questioning from the therapist is likely to be destructive to building trust. One of the tenets of therapy is the belief that people can self-heal, that they possess an innate ability to recognize what they need and, given the right set of circumstances, they can reorientate themselves to what is meaningful in their lives. In other words, most of us don't want other people telling us what to do, nor do we want others delving nosily into our business, but we do appreciate someone being with us in our troubles and listening attentively with sensitivity while we make sense of our situation.

Insight

I am quite an inquisitive, direct person and, in counselling, I have had to learn to gauge the usefulness of a question for either, or both, parties before I go ahead.

CLOSED QUESTIONS

When we ask a closed question, it is usually met with a closed response – a response that doesn't allow any further exploration. Closed questions are useful for information gathering when we need to know specific facts or specific information; for example, in an intake session with a new client when a counsellor notes things like marriage status, medical details, work details and so on; or in the case of a younger person details of school, college and whom an they live with.

The answer to a closed question is often 'yes', 'no' or 'don't know'. The closed question begins: 'Do you', 'Can you', 'Have you', 'Is it', 'Would you say', 'Could it', 'Don't you think' and so on. The problem with questioning that invites a 'yes' or 'no' type of reply is that it can leave both parties facing a blank wall and can lead only to more questioning. While you are bombarding someone with questions, their feelings are subdued. In contrast, open questions allow further exploration of meanings, thoughts and feelings, and encourage clients to say more.

It's a good idea when using questions to ask yourself what the purpose is, and if it's assisting or hindering the helping process. You might be information gathering when it would be more appropriate to wait, giving the client time to get in touch with feelings associated with what they are telling you. The excessive use of questioning (for instance, by an inexperienced counsellor) can be a ploy to distance the counsellor from the client, when the counsellor is uncomfortable with their own feelings or responses to what the client is expressing or with silences during the session. A golden rule when counselling is to use your ears and eyes more than your mouth!

WHY? WHY NOT?

'Why' is best used sparingly. Think of a question like 'Why did you do that?' and how loaded it is. The word 'Why' implies that the answer is instantly accessible. It might involve validation or denial of the client's actions and can result in a defensive response. 'Why' can sound accusatory – it might be taken as disapproval and trigger feelings from the past, of getting things wrong. 'Why' is also difficult to answer in relation to feelings. It can take the client into thinking mode, as part of an intellectual rationalizing exercise, to avoid the world of emotions. Not surprisingly a question like 'Why do you feel this?' or 'Why do you think that?' is more likely than not to be met with a shrug and 'I don't know', and could result in the client losing track of what they are thinking and feeling.

OPEN QUESTIONS

Open questions are valuable because they enable the expression of thoughts, feelings and personal meanings. They invite the other person to talk, communicate and self-explore. They allow time to explore situations. Open questions begin with 'How', 'Where', 'When', 'What', 'In what way' and so forth. The answers given to questions like these allow the counsellor to have a clearer understanding and help the client to be more specific.

An example of an open question is: 'I'm not clear what you mean when you say that you feel easily hurt. Could you give me an example?' Clarifying non-direct questions can be useful; for example, 'Can you say a bit more about that?' could be used to encourage elaboration and reflection. Open questions have no 'right' answer.

MULTIPLE AND FREQUENT QUESTIONS

Don't ask too many questions – be sparing. It's important to respect the client's right to privacy. Some issues could be delicate and too intimate to rush into. Allow time for trust to develop. The client might feel interrogated rather than supported, especially in the first few sessions when it's crucial to establish trust. It could impede the building of a rapport between you. The frequent use of questions doesn't allow time for the exploration of thoughts and feelings as and when they arise; therapy can then be experienced as confusing, as the counsellor's interest appears to be on a superficial level only. Beware of using multiple questions, with one question superseding another in a string of enquiry, as the client could find it annoying, distracting or confusing, thereby undermining their confidence in the counsellor. Ask one question at a time and listen with full attention to the response.

When you come to practise your skills (e.g. in role play), use questions appropriately – try not to bombard the client with one question after another. Questions form a small part of skills use. Skills like paraphrasing and reflecting feelings and content and other methods of attentive responding motivate the client to talk openly.

LEADING QUESTIONS

Leading questions imply answers that the questioner would find acceptable. Leading – or biased – questions can effectively stop clients expressing their thoughts and feelings for fear of ridicule. For example:

> *'You're not thinking of leaving your children, are you?'*

> *'You're not going to cry, are you?'*

These questions consist of an instructive statement: 'You wouldn't give up your job', followed by a question, 'Would you?' The first part indirectly tells the other person what to do, the second part appears to give an option. Empathic sensitive questioning is neither judgemental nor restrictive.

QUESTIONS TO ASK ABOUT YOUR QUESTIONS

- ▶ *Are you trying to clear up a point? (clarifying)*
- ▶ *Are you information gathering?*
- ▶ *Does the question help your client to explore self and situation?*

- *Does the question have any therapeutic value – i.e. helping in some way?*
- *Are you avoiding anything by asking a question? You might be filling a space, trying to put a client (who you might think is uncomfortable with silences) at ease, or perhaps you find it difficult to manage silences.*

Asking too many questions can be an attempt to force change or to control the direction of the sessions; both can cause the client to deflect from issues rather than focus on them. Let the client move at their own pace; the point after all is to lessen distress, not to add to it. There's a time for challenging when an experienced counsellor feels that the client will benefit from it, but a less experienced person would be advised to challenge extremely tentatively, respecting the other person's right to reach new perspectives in their own time.

SOME GENERAL RULES FOR QUESTIONING

- *Use open questions when possible.*
- *Avoid closed questions which invite 'yes' or 'no' replies, except when requiring the client to be more precise or when seeking specific information.*
- *Use indirect questions as a softer approach.*
- *Use questions sparingly.*
- *Be aware that some forms of questioning can suggest disapproval or criticism.*
- *Use one appropriate question at a time.*
- *Check the purpose of your question before you go ahead.*
- *Be aware of the tone of your voice, the speed of the question, how it's generally delivered and the message it might convey.*

To recap, the purpose of a question is:

- *to clarify – to help the client be more concrete and specific*
- *to help identify problems and what has created them*
- *to gain useful information*
- *to help the counsellor get a clear understanding of the client's situation*
- *to help the client get in touch with unexpressed emotions*

> ▶ to check reality – i.e. 'Did I get that right'? – or specific
>   meanings – e.g. 'You said... I wonder what that means for you?'
> ▶ to explore underlying thoughts, feelings and meanings
> ▶ to enable or encourage further insight into what has been
>   expressed, leading to previously unexplored material.

The following are examples of open and closed questions; note
in each pair how (a) invites a yes/no/don't know answer, while
(b) invites expression of feelings.

1 *(a) Closed question: Were you upset when that happened?*
   (b) Open question: How did you feel when that happened?
2 *(a) Closed question: Could you quit smoking if you really*
       wanted to?
   (b) Open question: What sorts of problems do you think you
       might have if you tried to give up smoking?
3 *(a) Closed question: Do you still love your partner?*
   (b) Open question: Tell me how you feel about your partner.
4 *(a) Closed question: Could it be that you start arguments with*
       your wife?
   (b) Open question: What happens when you and your wife
       argue?
5 *(a) Closed question: Were you sad when your grandmother died?*
   (b) Open question: How did you feel when your grandmother
       died?

Number 4 is an example of how a closed question can also be
challenging. Open questions focus on feelings and content.

Unlike the (a) questions, the (b) questions address associated
feelings – inviting the client to talk about feelings such as fear, hurt
or dependency. Number 2(a) could be experienced as a challenge – as
a judgemental remark relating to strength or weakness of character.
In contrast, number 2(b) is a more empathic form of questioning,
acknowledging the possible difficulty of the task.

Notice the language that you use when questioning. The word
'quit' in number 2(a) might be appropriate to use, depending on

the language your client uses, but it could add to the sense of being challenged. The words 'if you really wanted to' could also be loaded with implication if out of context with what your client has been saying. It could seem that you are suggesting that they don't really want to give up and be seen as criticism.

Use of empathy

Insight

For me, empathy is about letting your guard down, letting go of preconceived ideas and tuning into the other person's world.

Empathy has been described in a number of ways: as if walking in another's shoes, entering into another person's frame of reference, or having the ability to experience life as the other person does by temporarily entering into the client's world of thoughts, meanings and feelings. Empathy is an expression of the regard and respect the counsellor holds for the client whose frame of reference (their values, thoughts, meanings, feelings, cultural influences, experiences and perceptions) could be quite different from that of the counsellor. It's crucial that counsellors don't lose themselves in their client's material and that they retain their own sense of self. The client needs to feel 'held' as well as understood. True empathic responding does both. To be held therapeutically means to feel that the counsellor is capable of accepting and supporting us through anything that we, as clients, bring. The counsellor conveys to the client that they are non-judgemental, unshockable and strong enough not to need protecting from what the client might think is their unacceptable or even hateful side. It can be a marvellous relief to admit all and let go of what we fear might be inappropriate thoughts and feelings, and to meet with an accepting, empathic response.

Empathic responding circumnavigates all the other skills. The ability to empathize with the other person is enhanced by an ever-alert attentiveness to facial expressions, **body language**, gestures and so on, and not only to what is being openly conveyed but also to the underlying implications. Intuition or 'hunches' have a part to play in empathic responding.

On the subject of trusting his intuition – the feelings, words, impulses and fantasies that emerged when he was facilitating in groupwork – Rogers, in his book *Carl Rogers on Encounter Groups*, wrote:

> *While a responsible business executive is speaking, I may suddenly have the fantasy of the small boy he is carrying around within himself – the small boy that he was, shy, inadequate, fearful – a child he endeavours to deny; of whom he is ashamed. And I am wishing that he would love and cherish this youngster. So I may voice this fantasy – not as something true, but as a fantasy in me. Often this brings a surprising depth of reaction and profound insights.*

EMPATHY AND SYMPATHY

Empathy is sometimes confused with sympathy. When we feel sympathy for someone we view them with pity: 'Poor Jennifer – she really can't cope now Harry has left her.' Pity is often linked with victimhood. While pity makes a victim of the sufferer, empathy empowers them; it says: 'I have a sense of your world – you're not alone, we'll go through this together.' The other person becomes an important subject of our interest rather than someone whose problems are far removed from our own experiences. We can tell we're objectifying someone when in our minds we slot them into a sociological category or stereotype like 'the abandoned wife', 'the single parent' or the adolescent 'delinquent'. Classifications like these can limit empathic understanding of people as individuals.

Carl Rogers talked about his own initial experiences of being counselled. He relates, in *A Way of Being*, how he felt he was being rescued from the chaos of his feelings:

> *These persons have heard me without judging me, diagnosing me, appraising me, or evaluating me. They have just listened*

and clarified and responded to me at all the levels at which I was
communicating. I can testify that when you are in psychological
distress and someone really hears you without judgement on
you, without trying to take responsibility for you, without trying
to mould you, it feels damn good!

....
Insight
I like to think of empathy as the heart of the body of counselling.
....

Awareness of body language

Our inner emotional state is communicated through our
bodies. We give each other messages through body movement,
the intonation of our voice, facial expressions, posture, gestures
and eye contact. Some of these movements might be slight or
fleeting but in the heightened atmosphere of one-to-one counselling
they are more often than not registered. When we counsel others
we need to be aware of two sets of body language, our own and
that of the client. As a helper our body needs to demonstrate
behaviour that's facilitative. In psychological terminology,
non-facilitative behaviour is called 'adverse stimulus'. We might
inadvertently display an attitude that's off-putting to the client.
We might look bored, yawn, fidget or demonstrate other distractive
behaviour. Another example of adverse stimulus is punitive
attention – when the helper looks stern, perhaps tight-lipped,
raising their eyebrows or staring fixedly at the speaker. It's not
difficult to appreciate how this type of response is off-putting to
the client.

Other mannerisms such as picking at your fingers, shrugging or
sniffing could also be distracting. We might think that we avoid
all these, but it can be a revelation to watch ourselves counselling
on video. It's not uncommon for trainee counsellors to be shocked
to see themselves smiling inanely throughout a session or to see
themselves constantly shifting around in their chairs or nodding
constantly like a nodding-dog!

POSTURE

Our posture reveals the degree of interest we have in the client. When we sit back, away from the other person, we might seem to distance ourselves from them; and when we lean towards them we engage and show interest. Similarly, when we cross our arms and legs we convey the message that we are less open to the other person; that we're in some way protecting ourselves by closing off. In contrast, a relaxed and attentive posture tells the client that we're comfortable with ourselves and with them in the helping process. Although it would be unnatural to sit totally still throughout, too much shifting around can be distracting.

As with everything in life, there are always exceptions to the rule and sometimes what seems like a mistake often proves to be useful. I personally think it's good to learn the skills and also retain as much of ourselves as possible so that we respond in both a spontaneous and an appropriate way. An example is that if we find ourselves crossing our arms and legs during the session, rather than thinking 'Oh no, I shouldn't be doing this', it might be more useful to observe yourself and note, 'I have my legs and arms crossed. I wonder why? Perhaps I'm uncomfortable with what's being expressed, or it might be that, in some way, I'm reflecting what the other person is feeling.'

A person-centred counsellor who finds themselves yawning at times throughout a session, in the spirit of being genuine and congruent, might say to a client something to the effect, 'I'm yawning again and I can see it's off-putting to you. I do feel a bit bored... I don't want to be bored and it makes me uncomfortable that I'm yawning when you're talking to me. I think maybe I am reacting to what you're saying because you have repeated it many times.' Although Carl Rogers is more widely known for his 'unconditional positive regard' (from the Core Conditions Model), in the interest of being 'real' (genuine, congruent) with a client he would be direct and honest about his feelings and reactions towards the client.

THE TONE OF VOICE

The tone of our voice also acts as an indicator of our thoughts and attitudes. If we speak too quietly or hesitantly the other person could find it hard to have confidence in us as a helper. It would be counter-productive to be too forceful or bombastic in the way we interact. If we talk clearly at a fairly steady level rather than sounding rushed or excited, and without mumbling or stumbling over our words, then we're probably getting it right. Sometimes it's appropriate to mirror the tone of the client's voice to help them hear the emotion conveyed.

Although humour can play a part, it's not a good idea to be jocular with your clients. It can inhibit their expression of deeper feelings and they might wonder if you're taking them seriously. It's not the counsellor or the client's role to entertain or cheer the other person up. That said humour will come into counselling quite naturally at times and there's nothing wrong with that.

Insight

I personally find it helpful to spend a few minutes, before a client arrives, sitting quietly, relaxing my body and being aware of my feet planted firmly on the floor – it all helps centre and ground me.

WORDS AND BODY LANGUAGE

Words can be either congruent or incongruent with what our body is demonstrating. For example, we might say 'I understand' while looking perplexed, or say 'No, that doesn't shock me' having raised our eyebrows and crossed our arms and legs. What the body's doing is an indicator of deeper, sometimes unconscious feelings. A common display of incongruence is: when a client says they're angry while smiling, or that they're deeply sad but show little emotion. This can tell us that the client isn't comfortable in expressing their true emotions. What the client and counsellor hear is reinforced or contradicted by what they see demonstrated by the body language or facial expression of the other person.

The client's body language

While we, the counsellor or helper, need to be aware of our body language, it's also our work to decode, understand and interpret the body language of our client. What might their body language tell us? Body and facial expression can inform us about hidden feelings. For example:

▶ *She's angry – her mouth is tensed. Her eyes are narrowed and she's leaning back in her chair and is avoiding eye contact.*
▶ *He's very upset and near to tears – he has placed his hand up to his forehead and his mouth is twitching. He's leaning slightly forward and his head is down.*
▶ *He's eager to be understood – he's leaning towards you, with his feet placed firmly on the floor; he gesticulates freely with his hands, he's talking intently and his eyes are fixed on yours.*

Reflecting skills

Paraphrasing, summarizing and mirroring are ways of reflecting back the client's thoughts and feelings. They're methods of reiterating client expression in order that:

▶ *the client can (re)hear what they've said,*
▶ *the client gets a sense of themselves, i.e. how they're expressing themselves – as if a mirror were being held up to them*
▶ *the counsellor checks what they're understanding (meanings, thoughts and feelings) is correct*
▶ *there's clarification of certain points (without asking intrusive questions)*
▶ *the material is made more 'manageable' for both counsellor and client*
▶ *there's ongoing communication between counsellor and client*
▶ *threads (of what the client has said) can be joined together to make a more coherent whole.*

PARAPHRASING

Paraphrasing involves reflecting back the content and feelings of what the client is saying by drawing out the salient parts. Usually the content is repeated in the counsellor's own words, which gives a slightly different perspective on the material. Paraphrasing is best used at natural intervals or when it seems appropriate to reiterate what is being conveyed. It lets the client know that you are following what they say, that you're attentive to their personal details and understanding of their feelings and meanings.

As individuals, counsellors will paraphrase differently – as with all the skills there is no absolute set formula. Counselling would be wooden and unspontaneous if there was. Counsellors develop their own style. Some talk more than others; some might put emphasis on one or two skills in preference to others.

Examples of paraphrasing

Example 1
The client's statement:
When I was a teenager I used to wish that my dad was dead – because he was cruel to me at times – and when he did die, a few years later, I felt a mixture of relief and sadness but the relief made me feel guilty, and now 15 years on I still feel guilty when I think of some of the things I said and did to him.

The counsellor's response:
For a long time now you have felt guilty about your negative feelings and actions towards your father when he was alive.

(Contd)

He could be very harsh with you at times and when he died you felt a sense of freedom as well as sadness.

Comment: In these examples the responses reflect back, in the counsellor's own language, the content of what the client has related and also the client's feelings.

Feeling words from the counsellor's response: guilty, negative, harsh, freedom, sadness.

Example 2
The client's statement:
My teenage daughter lives with her father in another town and when she comes to stay with me I get irritated with how demanding she seems to be. She's always asking questions in great detail about how I spend my time and who I go out with… and everything else, and she won't entertain herself either and expects me to be a constant source of amusement.

The counsellor's response:
When your daughter comes to stay with you, you feel overwhelmed by her need for your love and attention. You feel irritated by her enquiries into your personal life and you wish she could be more self-sufficient while she is with you.

Feeling words and phrases: overwhelmed, love and attention, irritated, personal life, self-sufficient.

Example 3
The client's statement:
I have broken up with my partner, although it was my doing – because I was feeling claustrophobic, restless, and felt I was losing my own identity. I have found living on my own a difficult experience. It seems like I am caught between the old adage of 'I can't live with them, and I can't live without them.'

The counsellor's response:
You left a relationship because you felt stifled by it and unable to express yourself while you were in it, but you find it hard living alone and sometimes you miss your ex-partner.

Feeling words and phrases: stifled, express yourself, hard living alone, miss.

Example 4
The client's statement:
When it gets dark I feel a sense of hollowness. A void emerges and I don't know how to fill it. Sometimes I end up drinking my way through it, which in a sense seems to keep me occupied, and although I know I have a drink problem I don't feel I have the energy or imagination to fill the void more creatively.

The counsellor's response:
You drink in the evening because you feel an emptiness inside, you're low at the moment and feel unable to tackle the problem in a self-nurturing way.

Feeling words and phrases: emptiness inside, low, unable to tackle, self-nurturing.

To recap, paraphrasing has the following aspects. It:

▶ *gives the client an opportunity to hear what they are saying, in a slightly different format, which can lead to new insight*
▶ *is a way of reflecting the content and feelings of what the client is saying*
▶ *entails content and feelings being reflected back in the counsellor's own words*
▶ *demonstrates the counsellor's attentiveness*
▶ *gives the client an opportunity to clarify anything the counsellor is misunderstanding and the counsellor an opportunity to check that they are getting it right*
▶ *is a way of keeping contact with the client.*

MIRRORING

Mirroring bears a resemblance to parroting and has to be used with sensitivity to be well received by, and useful, to the client. The counsellor mirrors by, for example, repeating a line a client has said or mirroring an expression (take care that this is not straight mimicking – it should be subtle). A client might say, 'I'm enjoying my new job, it's a big challenge but I like challenges most of the time,' with a grimace at the end of the statement. You might have noticed that he seems to have mixed feelings about his new job and is perhaps wondering if he has made the right decision in accepting it or doubting that he is up to it. To check this out you could subtly mirror the grimace and pick up on his words: 'Most of the time...' This could help him get in touch with what's worrying him; it might be another challenge in his life that he hasn't yet mentioned.

SUMMARIZING

Summarizing is similar to paraphrasing, but it means putting together larger chunks of information when a client has talked for a length of time. While paraphrasing is relevant to one statement of whatever length, summarizing puts together a few or many. It's a way of keeping contact with a client, showing that you're following what they're saying and that you have an understanding of their underlying feelings. Another purpose of summarizing is that it brings together different threads of what has been expressed, providing an overview that enables the client to make connections.

There might be an overall theme that can be brought together by summarizing. For example, a client might spend a lot of the session saying how low he feels about different relationships he has with other people and, although the story differs each time, a unifying theme emerges. He's said that his father is undemonstrative and critical of him, no matter how much he tries to please him; his wife is sexually unresponsive to him although he is tender and affectionate with her; and a friend he recently supported through a divorce now seems to have no time for him.

These themes could be joined together to give a summary of the different things that have been said, and by then adding an interpretative summary such as: 'I think what you're saying is that you feel, although you try your best to get close to those who matter to you, you feel that they don't respond to you or appreciate you in the way that you would like.' An underlying theme could be repeated throughout a session or even over a number of sessions. Accurate summarizing can sharpen the client's perception of what lies behind repetitive thoughts, feelings and behaviour.

The point of both paraphrasing and summarizing is to assist in further exploration of troubling issues, to help the client reach new insights into their problems. It's especially important when summarizing a lot of received information to finish with an enquiry about the accuracy of your understanding. You can check this out by saying, 'Is that what you feel?' or 'Does that sum it up?' or simply 'Am I getting this right?' Otherwise you might be going off on an agenda of your own. Use your own language when you summarize and try not to use stock phrases because these can sound stiff and could be experienced by the client as insincere. The idea is to learn skills, not set formulas. When you become familiar with the skills, you can trust yourself to use your positive qualities to respond with what is needed at the time.

To recap the uses of summarizing:

1 *It's useful at intervals in the session to give a sense of connection between threads or themes of what the client has said.*
2 *It gives the client an overview of their situation or experiences and moves the session along.*
3 *It's useful towards the end of a counselling session, to highlight the central concerns.*

MINIMAL RESPONSES

Minimal responses are made to demonstrate the counsellor's attentiveness and understanding of what is said and also to encourage the client to continue. Minimal encouragements convey interest. Minimal responses include:

- ▶ *mm, uh-huh*
- ▶ *nodding*
- ▶ *using one word such as 'so', 'and', 'then'*
- ▶ *repeating one or a few key words the client has used*
- ▶ *restating the exact words of the client's statement apart from placing it in the second person. For example, the client says: 'I feel so stupid'; the counsellor says: 'You feel so stupid.' This is particularly useful when the comment is uttered as a throwaway line that could be covering a deeper hurt*
- ▶ *silence is another form of minimal response that allows the client time to think, feel and find expression.*

Insight

Keep connected with the other person by demonstrating your interest with regular responses however slight – a nod or 'mmm' does just that. I also like to check from time to time how they are feeling and I ask things like 'Is that useful?', 'Does that have any meaning for you?'

WORDS

People use specific words to communicate inner emotions. It's more difficult to say to someone, 'I completely lost control and I was destructive in the way I behaved' than 'I was in a rage.' The word 'rage' says a lot more than 'angry'; the word 'joy' is more revealing than 'happy'; the word 'morose' more specific than 'sad' or 'depressed'; the word 'devastated' more emotionally packed than 'hurt' and so on.

A word of caution – inevitably, it can happen that counsellors have a different understanding of a particular word or phrase from the client, so check that your understanding corresponds with the client's meaning. Clients whose culture or background differs from the counsellor's might use a word in an unfamiliar way. In paraphrasing and summarizing, the counsellor uses their own words to reflect back their understanding; the words that are used need to reflect accurately the client's meaning but they can also put emphasis on a feeling, offering the client more insight. A client might say, 'I am very tired,' and in paraphrasing the counsellor might say, 'You are exhausted.' This could lead the client to say, 'Yes, I am exhausted – I really don't think I can go on like this,' leading to a cathartic release of emotion. Refer to the evocative/feelings word list on the following pages and see what feelings particular words evoke in you.

List of some evocative/feeling words

I feel...
I am...

accepted	carefree	embarrassed	ignored
acknowledged	careless	empowered	interested
affectionate	caught out	empty	irresponsible
aggravated	cautious	enthusiastic	irritated
aggressive	cheerful	evil	
alone	confused	exhausted	jealous
angry	content		jittery
anxious	cosseted	feckless	joyful
appreciated	criticized	free	jumpy
assertive		friendly	
attractive	daring	frightened	keen
attuned	dehumanized	furious	kindly
awful	delighted		
awkward	dependent	great	light-hearted
	depressed	grief-stricken	listless
bashful	devalued	guilty	lonely
belittled	devastated	gutted	loved
best	dirty		loving
betrayed	discontented	happy	
bitter	disgusting	heartbroken	mad
bored	disheartened	heartened	manic
burdened	disloyal	heavy	miserable
	distant	heavy-hearted	moany
	distressed	humiliated	morose
		hurt	mournful

(Contd)

3. Skills used in counselling 53

naughty	petrified	silly	unloved
needy	powerful	strong	unsupported
neglected	powerless	supported	uptight
nervous			useless
	raging	tense	
obliged	rejected	torn	valued
optimistic	respected	troubled	vulnerable
ordinary	respectful	trusting	
outcast	responsible		wanted
overcome		ugly	weak
	sad	unappreciated	weary
passionate	secure	unattractive	willing
pessimistic	shy	uneasy	worn out
			worried

More advanced skills

SILENCES

Managing silence can be difficult for the inexperienced counsellor, yet silences can be very productive. It can take some time to feel comfortable with silences. Ask yourself the following questions:

- ▶ *How comfortable am I with silences?*
- ▶ *How often do I spend time by myself in silence?*
- ▶ *What associations do I have with silence?*

Allowing silences gives the client space to reflect. As a new counsellor you might experience awkwardness at handling a silence but your threshold of silence will increase with experience and you'll be able to discern between different types. Sometimes clients are nervous, especially in the first or second session, and a protracted silence can be excruciatingly uncomfortable for them. If this happens it's advisable to acknowledge the rising discomfort by saying something like, 'I imagine it's difficult for you to be here' or ask, 'Are you feeling uncomfortable?' This will serve two purposes. First, it will break an uncomfortable silence and, second, it's likely to lead to disclosure of feelings. Clients can get lost in their own thoughts and feelings or feel overawed by them, and a silence can then occur. A summary of what you have understood could be useful at such a time. Sometimes a silence begins because the client is hoping for something from the counsellor; this might be reassurance or confirmation that the counsellor has been listening, or has understood what has been said.

Insight

Practising of meditation, visualization and mindful concentration – where we put all out attention into our surroundings, using all the senses – can all be helpful in developing an ease with silence.

Emotions experienced during a silence – for example, feelings of awkwardness or anger – can help the client access material they're avoiding or are unaware of. Transferential material might come to the surface. **Transference** is when the client 'transfers' emotions, rooted in the past or elsewhere, to the counsellor or other person. The counsellor or helper might become a punitive parent whose way of punishing was to emotionally distance themselves from the 'offender' by means of silence. You might then say something like, 'I sense that you are feeling uncomfortable with this silence and I remember you saying that your mother used to get angry then refuse to speak to anyone in the family for days.' The client could make connections, realizing how deeply this has affected them, both in their childhood responses and in their adult reactions towards other people who appear to 'switch off' from them. Silences are more often than not constructive, even if a little awkward. A protracted silence often has an air of expectancy about it. Silences often lead to new ground. It would be a mistake to presume always to know what a particular silence was about.

In *On Learning from the Patient*, psychotherapist Patrick Casement writes: 'The therapist's openness to the unknown in the patient leaves more room for the patient to contribute to any subsequent knowing, and what is thus jointly discovered has a freshness which belongs to both.' Silences can give us an opportunity to be open to the, as yet, unknown.

IMMEDIACY

Immediacy involves working in the 'here and now', within the dynamic of the counsellor–client relationship. The skill of immediacy can be used to:

1 *bring the client's feelings back into the relationship*
2 *enable the relationship to reach greater depths of intimacy*
3 *challenge the client–counsellor relationship by looking at what's going on between them in the 'here and now' (e.g. in the moment)*
4 *help the client to see more clearly and own, both in positive and negative ways, how they relate to others and the effects of this*
5 *help the client to see and deal with their resistance, i.e. being late, missing appointments, etc*
6 *look at how the counsellor–client relationship is developing*
7 *give the client an opportunity to air any anxieties, doubts or dissatisfactions, e.g. relating to their expectations of counselling.*

Appropriate times to use immediacy include:

▶ *when the session is directionless, seeming to be going in circles, yet you feel that something is in the air that needs clearing;*
▶ *when there's tension in the room, e.g. resentment or anger;*
▶ *when transference or* **countertransference** *(transference involves the misplaced transference of emotions and their affects to a person – see Chapter 7 for a fuller explanation) is interfering with the process;*
▶ *when there's attraction in the relationship – e.g. a counsellor might notice that a client has begun to dress more provocatively and is coquettish in their behaviour;*

- *when there's a dependency – the counsellor might like to address the way a client is increasingly seeking approval or advice;*
- *when something new and fresh has developed in the relationship, e.g. a deepening trust.*

Examples of immediacy

Example 1

Immediacy is a skill used by the counsellor to address directly issues that the client is expressing indirectly. For example, a client says, 'I don't like my teacher/boss/partner – they are so critical of everything I do.' The counsellor could see this as an opportunity to help the client access negative thoughts and feelings that they might be harbouring towards the counsellor. The counsellor says, 'I wonder if you are talking about me too? Perhaps you feel criticized by me and would like to tell me that you don't like me.'

Example 2

This example corresponds with the fourth bullet point in the list opposite. A young woman is expressing something indirectly through her dress and behaviour. A male counsellor might bring the subject into the relationship by tentatively saying something like, 'I've noticed you're dressed in a way that shows off your body [she is wearing a very short skirt and low top] and I'm experiencing you as flirty – I wondered what's going on for you.'

This type of situation is not an unusual one. Sometimes when clients feel valued by a counsellor of the opposite sex, they confuse the attentive responding with other forms of intimacy, including sexual. This applies particularly to some clients who have experienced sexual abuse, and their sense of worth has become mixed up with their sexuality. By using immediacy, the counsellor brings to the client's attention their pattern of behaviour and gives them the opportunity to explore and understand the issues.

(Contd)

Example 3

Immediacy can be used at the onset of counselling; e.g. 'I'm aware that this is a strange experience for you' or 'You might be feeling scared/embarrassed coming here and telling me this' or 'I imagine it's very difficult for you to be here in this session. What are you feeling at this moment?'

The counsellor conveys empathic understanding right at the beginning by using immediacy. Its use also demonstrates a willingness to engage in a therapeutic involvement.

Example 4

An example of how immediacy is used to address issues of dependency is a situation when a client wants the counsellor's approval all the time, repeatedly asking what they should do.

The counsellor might respond with, 'I notice how often you ask my opinion. I wonder what this is saying about how our relationship is developing…' Another example is when a client appears upset because a holiday break is coming up when the counsellor won't be available for a few sessions. The counsellor's use of immediacy in this situation could be, 'You've been very quiet since I reminded you of the holidays coming up. Perhaps you're feeling that I'm abandoning you.'

Example 5

Immediacy is at times used to address the client's resistance (towards therapy) as it's happening. The client might have ambivalent feelings towards therapy and part of them doesn't want to assist in the counselling process; instead they offer resistance. Immediacy helps the process by enabling the counsellor and client to look at the ambivalent feelings.

Examples of resistance include lateness or missing sessions, and the use of passivity and silence when the client has previously talked openly. In this situation the counsellor can address what's happening in the 'here and now' by saying, 'I've noticed you're very quiet today; normally you talk quite freely and I'm wondering if there's a reason.'

The main benefits of immediacy are that it gives the client opportunities to experience difficulties in relating to other people in a new way; issues are aired and explored with interest within the client–counsellor context and are seen by the client not only to be non-damaging but to have a positive, constructive outcome.

Insight

The use of skills like immediacy and challenging can be more palatable to the client when the counsellor introduces them as 'hunches' or ideas rather than absolute truths, thereby giving the client the option to take issues on board or reject them (they may not be ready for our astute observations!). It isn't uncommon for a client to deny something at the time and then come back to it when they are ready. It's never a good idea to insist.

CHALLENGING

Challenging is used to help the client explore inconsistencies in their behaviour or how they express themselves. For example, 'You say you feel really angry when he does that, yet you laugh as you tell me.' Another example would be: 'You appear to be withdrawn today and I'm wondering if it's because I was not able to make it here for your session last week.' (Remember, it's the behaviour that's challenged rather than the person.) In **cognitive behavioural therapy** a client's irrational thoughts might be challenged and the client encouraged to replace them with more realistic affirming thoughts. Challenging or confrontation work best when a good working relationship has been established. The client is then less likely to hear the challenge as criticism or feel threatened, and is therefore more likely to be able to make good use of it.

It can be a relief to be challenged in a therapeutic (i.e. helping) situation because it gives an opportunity to look at areas where we've become 'stuck'. Hopefully the client will understand that they're with a person who can see the inconsistencies of their behaviour and the ways they protect themselves, and yet demonstrate interest and be non-judgemental. Being challenged by another person and feeling accepted and not harshly judged can help us accept ourselves. We have a received sense of 'It's OK to be imperfect.' When we're constructively challenged, it invites us to own our behaviour and accept responsibility for it. The counsellor challenges the client to own their thoughts and feelings in the interest of self-awareness and self-acceptance. Instead of using a generalization like, 'Anyone would have felt miserable if that had happened to them,' the client is encouraged to claim (and thereby accept) their thoughts and feelings – for example, 'I feel miserable because...'

Challenging others necessitates honest assessment of our ability to challenge ourselves. For example:

- ▶ *Do you deal effectively with your own problems?*
- ▶ *Are you open to being personally challenged?*
- ▶ *Do you challenge yourself?*
- ▶ *Are you willing to engage deeply with others?*

Challenging helps the client to self-challenge and is best used when there's a possibility of change. It's appropriate to use it in situations where something is being avoided or remains unknown to the client. For example:

- ▶ *The client's non-verbal behaviour is incongruent with what they say.*
- ▶ *The client ignores or fails to recognize self-defeating or self-destructive behaviour.*
- ▶ *The client avoids talking about an issue that's obviously troubling them.*
- ▶ *The client self-contradicts, distorts or uses rationalization or manipulative behaviour.*

▶ *The client fails to recognize the consequences of their behaviour.*
▶ *The client demonstrates signs of resistance – missing sessions, being late or claiming their problems are miraculously solved.*
▶ *The client has little sense of reality.*

Examples of confrontation

Example 1
The following is an example of confronting incongruence between body and verbal language. The client says, 'It didn't really bother me when my dad left' in a flat, depressed tone of voice, sighing while changing position in the chair.

The counsellor's confrontation:
'When you said it didn't really bother you when your dad left I noticed that the tone of your voice was flat and you sighed heavily when you shifted around in your chair.'

Note: The counsellor reflects what they have observed and heard but gives no extra interpretation, allowing the client to offer their own understanding from the feedback.

Example 2
Here is an example of how to confront a client when they're continually avoiding an important issue by changing the subject. The client has briefly referred to the hurtful actions of a friend several times during the session but then deflects from the subject by talking about seemingly unrelated (trivial) material.

The counsellor's confrontation:
'I'm confused – I've noticed that you have begun talking a few times about how hurt you feel about your friend's behaviour, but then you make a joke and change the subject altogether.'

Note: The counsellor began by expressing their feelings by saying, 'I'm confused,' followed by a concrete statement of their
(Contd)

observation without any interpretation. Because there's no judgement implied, a response like this is usually experienced as non-threatening.

Example 3
The following is an example of confronting that addresses repetition in client behaviour, blaming and excuses. The client has come to session after session complaining of a situation that he's in – he blames others, says he's going to do something about the situation, then offers excuses when he doesn't.

The counsellor's confrontation:
'I hear what you are saying. There are difficulties in the situation you are presently in. You've been going through this for some time now and I wonder what concrete steps you are taking towards sorting it out.'

Note: Again this confrontation is factual but not accusatory or rejecting. It challenges the client to reassess his passive attitude.

SELF-DISCLOSURE (SOMETIMES CALLED 'HELPER SELF-SHARING')

The counsellor might, at times, feel that it's appropriate to share some personal experience or detail about themselves with the client. The purpose of self-disclosure, on the part of the counsellor, is to model non-defensive self-disclosure, to enter more fully into a congruent relationship (as in person-centred therapy) and to help the client in some way. It is certainly not to meet the needs of the counsellor.

An example taken from my own work was when a client felt she was 'going mad' after the death of her husband. She felt that he was in the room with her at times. I told her that I had had similar sensations when someone close to me had died. This appeared to help her.

Be clear about why you choose to self-disclose. Self-disclosure on the part of the counsellor can help to 'normalize' the client's experiences or behaviour and make them feel that it's reasonable to feel or behave in the way they do given the circumstances. Obviously it wouldn't be helpful to give this kind of assurance to someone who was suffering from a delusional disorder or was showing signs of mental illness.

Insight

Remember, it's all about the client, not the counsellor, so ideally the motivation behind any counsellor disclosure is to assist the client in some way. Counsellor disclosure needs to be used carefully because it can feed the client's curiosity about the counsellor's life. I usually say something like, 'I don't usually tell clients about myself as the whole point of counselling is to focus solely on the client but I think it may help if I tell you that...' And I keep it brief, just enough to let them know that other people have similar experiences and that I understand what they are saying.

FOCUSING, TIMING AND PACING

It's important that no one is hurried by a counsellor's agenda. If we're new to counselling or are desperate to help someone solve a problem, we might want to see results. Individuals have differing needs and approach their own healing or reach a resolution of their problems, in their own way, and in their own time. It wouldn't be helpful for the client to have information or feelings teased out of them. However, counsellors often work with clients within a time-limited framework that requires focusing on specific problems.

Because it's not uncommon for agencies to offer six to eight sessions to a client, the time needs to be fully utilized, the work highly focused, containing a structure which includes:

▶ *a beginning – where client history and information is gathered and a client–counsellor relationship is established*

- *a middle – the active stage that includes identifying and working through specific problems*
- *an ending – which acknowledges work that has been achieved, issues that still need addressing and the way forward for the client.*

The success of brief counselling work depends to a large extent on the counsellor's ability to keep the work focused and on the client's own motivation.

THINGS TO REMEMBER

1 *Counselling skills employ active listening and considered responding.*

2 *Trainees begin by practising basic skills such as the use of questions, paraphrasing and summarizing then later move on to the more advanced skills such as the use of challenging and immediacy.*

3 *The particular words people use to describe feelings and events can indicate to the counsellor possible sources for further exploration of deeper meanings or emotional affects.*

4 *Counsellors learn how to read clients' body language. Facial expressions, posture, movements, hesitations and other bodily signals communicate deeper thoughts and emotions.*

5 *Counsellor self-disclosure occurs when the counsellor tells the client personal details about themselves or their lives. Although usually counsellor details are considered best put aside so that the client can be the exclusive focus in the therapy, sometimes when counsellors tell the client a little about their own life experiences it can be affirming of the client.*

4

··

The benefits of acquiring counselling skills

In this chapter you will learn:
- *through examples, how the skills used in counselling can enhance your personal life*
- *how counselling skills can be used in the workplace*
- *how a teacher, a doctor and a probation officer benefited from learning counselling skills*
- *how the core conditions can be activated.*

The use of communication skills in personal relationships

Essentially, counselling is concerned with communication, yet clearly it's different from other interpersonal exchanges. Except when we're in exceptional circumstances, we use communication skills or interpersonal skills every day of our lives. In our work and leisure time we listen to each other, notice what others are doing and how they appear to be feeling, and we talk to each other on various levels. The use of counselling skills differs from other relationship skills in that there's emphasis on attention to one person only (the client), who is communicating their life details, their thoughts and feelings both past and present, to the other (the counsellor). The counsellor puts aside their own preoccupations and self-concerns and gives their full attention to the client.

Counselling isn't a reciprocal relationship based on conversation. In ordinary everyday social interaction we expect people to share their thoughts and feelings to varying degrees. People give advice and help each other by relating to and identifying similarities in emotions or events that they've experienced. Their intention is to say: 'I understand where you're coming from, you're not alone.' They aim to comfort and to lessen the other person's pain and feelings of alienation. Although valuable in establishing social bonding and integration, this kind of support is not always enough.

SUBJECTIVE SUPPORT

As unskilled helpers we tend to weigh the suffering of other people by comparing it to our own experiences and how we deal with them. When we're in a close relationship with another person it can be harder to be objective. If we experience someone else's problems from a subjective viewpoint we could hear something they say as a criticism and become defensive. Without extra skills to inform us we might continue to relate to and appeal to the part of their persona we find most acceptable and comfortable for us. Changes in other people often call for changes in ourselves and in the way that we relate to each other.

Insight

Even the most skilled, effective counsellors don't have perfect relationships or always interact positively with others in their personal life. A male colleague recently told me that he frequently isn't very sympathetic to others in his private life, yet he is a very patient, empathic counsellor – which just shows that purposely applying skills works!

How skills can be applied to personal and work situations

▶ *Listen carefully and attentively, without being defensive or attacking.*

- ▶ *Use your powers of observation – notice the person's body language, appearance, gestures, posture, eye contact and tone of voice.*
- ▶ *Don't bombard the person with questions but do invite them to expand on things they say that seem important or if you don't understand something.*
- ▶ *Use questions to open out what the person is trying to convey and to expand your understanding of the other person's thoughts, feelings and meanings.*
- ▶ *Paraphrase (repeating, not verbatim but in your own words) to check and clarify the content of what's been said and the feelings behind it.*
- ▶ *Use minimal responses such as 'Yes', 'mm', 'uh-huh', nodding, etc. to demonstrate attention, to show you are following what's being said and to encourage further exploration.*
- ▶ *Summarize when the person has talked for a while. Keep track of and join together themes, to check you've understood what's been said and to help the person get an overall picture.*
- ▶ *Use immediacy to address 'here and now' issues in the relationship.*
- ▶ *Use challenging and confrontation tentatively – examine your motives, don't use them to accuse or humiliate; examine your own agenda and challenge the behaviour, not the person; your aim is to help the person in some way, perhaps to broaden their awareness of their behaviour and how it affects others.*

An appropriate time to use confrontation skills is when a person has become rude or angry towards others or is repeatedly demonstrating destructive behaviour. At work it might be necessary to confront an employee who is continually late, or at school a pupil who is bullying other children. Remember the aim of the confrontation. Is it intended to achieve a greater understanding of the problems? Be aware of whose needs are being met by the confrontation. Do you need to express your own frustration, irritability or stress? If so, it could be more productive to use immediacy skills to address what's happening between the two of you. Be 'real' yourself. Tell the other person about your feelings if they're conflicting; say, for instance,

'I would like to help but I'm frightened/angry/upset,' but convey this in a way that's not dismissive or rejecting of the other person.

Using the example of Colin from Chapter 1, imagine what the response might be if he told a friend or a member of his family about his feelings of hopelessness. A subjective way of responding might be one of the following.

1 A friend's possible response
Let's suppose that Colin's friend responded to his depression by saying, 'I felt like that when I lost my job but something will turn up, you'll see,' or, 'Come on, it's not as bad as it seems. Have a drink, that'll cheer you up. This isn't like you.'

Colin's friend is trying to do what comes automatically to most people; he tries to cheer Colin up to take his mind off his problems when staying with his feelings could prove more helpful for him. While the friend's responses intend to reassure, they're likely to have the opposite effect. The solutions offered represent his inability and unwillingness to investigate Colin's predicament any further. He thinks that Colin is just 'down in the dumps' and that he's not behaving like the Colin he knows – he'll soon 'snap out of it'. Each time he sees Colin, and it might become less and less frequently, he attempts to bolster him up by being cheerful himself.

2 His wife's possible response
Colin's wife might say: 'Pull yourself together; look at the effect you're having on your family. I don't know what's got into you, you're just feeling sorry for yourself. You have responsibilities to face up to – you're being pathetic. I've got problems too, but I have to get on with things.'

This response is more condemnatory than the last example. Living with Colin, she's more involved on a daily basis than his friend is. She's becoming increasingly critical of him because he appears to be rejecting her and the life they have led and she feels afraid. Her way of dealing with Colin's depression is to withdraw her affection from him, which leaves him feeling more desolate and unlovable in his present emotional state.

Her response suggests that she thinks he is being self-indulgent and that the only way she can accept him is when he is 'strong' and supportive. In her view, he has duties towards his family that he's not fulfilling.

These two responses reveal the individual's requirements of Colin, as a friend and as a husband. In both cases there is a reluctance to face the depth of his anguish. Words spoken in reaction could actually make him feel worse and more alienated from his friends and family.

Neither of these responses addresses the emotional devastation Colin is experiencing. Friends and family might find it hard to be anything but subjective in the help they offer. It can be frightening when someone close to us becomes depressed and they appear to change in character. Colin's anguish seems apparent to his friend and wife, but he's neither permitted nor encouraged to explore it. To ameliorate the distress of people close to him, he is indirectly asked to bury (as he might have been many times before) his deeply felt emotions and to 'just get on with it'.

Insight
People are often at a crossroads in their lives when they decide they need counselling, and it can be encouraging to say to the client (or a friend you're supporting) that, as well as being a time of difficulty, it's also a time full of potential.

Self-indulgence or a developmental stage?

The Scottish psychiatrist Ronald D. Laing suggested that a psychological breakdown is better regarded as a breakthrough. What Colin was experiencing can be regarded as a developmental challenge. Nothing in life is forever or guaranteed. We change, our circumstances change, sometimes cruelly. Within our lifetime we have many adjustments to make, physically, psychologically and spiritually. We're likely to encounter failure, rejection, death of those we love, the breakdown of a relationship, ageing and depression – to name but a few life crises. It is often said that when one door closes another opens. Hopefully it's true, but it has to be acknowledged that sometimes we find ourselves in the middle of a cold, stark place with only the closed door in view. We might, like Colin, feel helpless and shut off from those around us. At difficult times we need someone to have the courage to really hear us and accept this desperate part of us. Many of the responses we get from friends and family, who basically wish us well, focus on how we'll feel in the future. They say things like 'Things will get better, you're just going through a difficult time' and don't deal with how we feel in the present. It's crucial that the present feelings are acknowledged and accepted. When one person adopts the use of counselling skills it allows the other person to focus on their problems. They don't have to worry about how the other person is feeling.

APPLYING THE CORE CONDITIONS OF PERSON-CENTRED THERAPY

The telling question is: Were Colin's friend and wife showing signs of encouraging him to talk and were they really listening to him? (Take note that Colin, his wife and friend are fictitious characters whose responses are exaggerated to give an example of a worst scenario situation, to illustrate a point.) Let's look at how the core conditions of Rogerian person-centred therapy might be applied. (Read about the Rogerian core conditions model, in more depth, in Chapter 7, Section 2.)

Unconditional positive regard

What can unconditional positive regard mean in relation to Colin, his family and friends, and their largely subjective responses to his anguish? Do they respect him? They would probably argue that they both love and respect him. But the key point is whether they are able to demonstrate that they fully accept him when he's in crisis and needs their understanding. Using the short description of their responses as representing their general attitude to Colin's problems, we can appreciate that he needs some help rather than cheering up or being ridiculed. It would help if people close to him could:

▶ *respect his right to express his emotions*
▶ *accept different aspects of his personality – some positive, some negative*

- *respect his right to have different values from theirs*
- *respect his right to self-exploration and self-discovery*
- *accept his right to change.*

They need to be able to be objective, accept what Colin is saying, without blocking out or censoring the painful truth of his situation. Colin's wife and friend might think that what they're saying to him will help but:

- *Are they adopting a non-judgemental stance?*
- *Are they accepting his vulnerability?*
- *Are they able to see beyond their own requirements of him?*

Congruence and genuineness

Being congruent is when a person is fully genuine and not hiding behind a front. They're being honest about their own feelings and being open to the other person. So would you say that Colin's wife and friend are being honest and open with him? For example:

- *Are they sharing their real feelings with him? – perhaps fear, inadequacy, anger or pity.*
- *Are they affirming that they hear what he's saying?*
- *Are they able to admit that they don't have the solutions?*
- *Are they willing to enter the struggle with him – rather than retreating into the safety of 'quick fix' answers?*

Insight

Being genuine is essentially about being yourself, and when using skills to help a family member or friend it's useful to talk about how you feel as well to some degree to let them know how things affect you. However, make it clear that they are the main focus of concern. We are being genuine when we are fully present in the moment with the other person.

Empathy

Would you say that Colin's wife and friend are empathic in their responses? Are they showing him that they are willing to enter into his experience with him as if they were experiencing the same, effectively walking in his shoes? Empathic response would mean that:

- *they really listen to him*
- *they focus on Colin's thoughts and feelings*
- *they're able to put their own requirements and problems aside*
- *they're able to be involved in what he is going through without getting totally lost in the process*
- *they can differentiate between Colin's and their own feelings (fear, pain, loss, etc.).*

By acquiring counselling skills you won't become a counsellor *per se*. However, by learning how to use some of the skills and by familiarizing yourself with core conditions you can enhance the relationships in your life, helping you to acknowledge and understand both other people's feelings and your own.

Had Colin's wife and friend had knowledge of certain skills, they could have responded differently. They could have listened actively and adopted the values of respect, genuineness, empathy and acceptance. They would have been able to own their feelings and avoid projecting their anxieties back on to Colin.

DISENTANGLING THE WEB

Familiarity with the basic skills and core conditions can in time act as useful 'antennae', giving us a keener awareness of what we and other people express in our behaviour. Most of us don't possess the skills to listen actively. We need to learn skills such as summing up, checking that what we have heard is correct, reflecting back the other person's thoughts and feelings and asking open questions.

By adopting valuing qualities like positive regard, acceptance and empathy we can be both closer to, and at the same time more detached from, the person we want to help. Saying to ourselves that the other person deserves our time, respect and warmth allows us to concentrate on them in depth. By adopting the use of the skills we can become more aware of our own reactions, our feelings and how we generally relate to people.

The acquisition of these skills is empowering. It can help us gain insight into other people's behaviour as well as our own. Shakespeare described human relationships as a 'tangled web'. They're not always easy and yet they're the main source of human fulfilment – in marriage, partnership, family life, community life and work. Lack of communication is often cited as the reason why relationships break down. Without the tools of good communication we're apt to respond defensively when, for example, others are angry with us. We feel blamed and rush to our own defence without finding out the associated reasons and feelings of the other person. We take offence at each other's moods and actions if they're at odds with, or in some way exclude, our own. Also we might lose a sense of ourselves in relation to other people.

Insight

Human relationships suffer when we don't listen to each other. That is obvious. Counsellors and mediators know that, when there are problems between people, if those in conflict really start to listen and hear the other person's point of view, breakthroughs are made.

Uses of counselling skills in work settings

Many people benefit from the use of counselling skills in their jobs. Those who work in the caring professions – such as nurses and social workers – might have had relevant skills included in their training. Those in any job that involves interaction with other people could benefit from learning counselling skills, including those working in large corporate companies in personnel departments and managerial roles. With this in mind, let's look briefly at a few examples of how people can and do use skills and adopt core values at work. In the main example I draw on my own experiences of working in groups with young people in a school environment.

TEACHERS AND COUNSELLING SKILLS

It's widely recognized that teachers play an enormously important role in a young person's life. Between the ages of 5 and 16 years or older, children spend more weekday hours in the school environment with teachers than they do with their parents. Any educational system has high requirements of its pupils. The smooth running of schools depends on pupils' collective and individual ability to conform to these requirements. To a large extent individuality is subjugated to the needs of the collective identity of the school as a whole. Both teachers and pupils are required to conform to certain behaviours. This is necessary for the safe and effective management of establishments that sometimes contain 1,000 or more people.

There are pressures on both teachers and pupils to maintain academic performance. Inevitably, some children have difficulties which may relate to their home life, peer group pressures, schoolwork or slotting into the school environment. Counselling skills can help the teacher communicate empathetically and effectively with a child who is in trouble in some way.

A child or young person in trouble

Teachers realize that a happy, well-adjusted child tends to work more productively, both separately and with others. I use 'well-adjusted' here to mean a child who has self-esteem and a strong enough sense of self (what Freud termed 'Ego strength') to engage with others within the school environment. At a counselling agency where I initially trained there was a high proportion of teachers among the trainees. They recognized that at times their pupils needed emotional support that they would try to give but sometimes felt unable to do this satisfactorily. One of these teachers commented that it was a fine balancing act trying to be sympathetic to pupils' problems while also maintaining boundaries. He felt that acquiring some counselling skills would help him cope with testing situations where he was acting as confidant to a child. He realized that his main role was that of a teacher, not a counsellor, and appreciated that he was deficient in the skills he needed to console the child and encourage them to get further help if needed. He recognized that in his role as a middleman, he would benefit from learning additional skills.

Communication problems between teacher and pupil

A child might be quiet, withdrawn or sullen, increasingly miss school, and never get homework or projects in on time. They're likely to feel the wrath of a teacher when clearly they need help. The teacher, too, is likely to be stressed, overworked and exasperated by the individual needs of this troublesome child. The child is **acting out** – their behaviour is saying that there could be something drastically wrong in their life and they're not coping.

In this type of situation communication can break down rapidly. The child is in deep water. Punitive measures serve only to alienate them further. It becomes a pupil versus teacher and school situation, and the problem can escalate. Sometimes the child is eventually excluded from school. The resources needed to educate expelled children can be enormous, and these resources could have been placed within the school setting at the onset of problems. Ideally, schools would have a resident counsellor who would provide troubled pupils with individual support, support that says: 'We appreciate that something is wrong in your world, we want to understand and help you. To do this we'll set time aside to spend with you, to look at your needs one to one – you're worth that attention.' Unfortunately having a counsellor as a member of staff isn't usually regarded as a necessity and lack of funds is often cited as the reason.

Clearly it's in the interests of both pupils and teachers that pupils are able to address their feelings within the school environment. This calls for clear boundaries. It wouldn't be in the interest of the smooth running of a school to have a riot of unleashed emotions. If dissatisfactions and problems are to be held and contained, there needs to be a place to register them before they escalate into something less manageable – this could be the school counsellor or it could be a skilled, empathic teacher who is capable of putting counselling skills to use.

Example

During a group session I facilitated in a school, it became apparent that the pupils, who were between the ages of 13 and 14, were feeling aggrieved. They told me that they hadn't been informed that the timetable had been changed. They had come to school that morning expecting to have a double session of PE that they enjoyed, and found instead that they were to have a double session of science. This meant that they would be carrying their PE kits around all day. They were annoyed because this wasn't the first time this had happened. I asked if there were any procedures in place at the school to air grievances, and they said, 'Nobody would listen.'

I suggested a role play as a way of helping them express what they were feeling. Two boys volunteered, one to act as teacher, the other to represent the pupils. The group then made a list of things they would like to say. The 'teacher' sat in the room in the middle of the group circle, and the 'pupil' went outside the room and knocked on the door. The exchange went like this:

Teacher: Come in.
Pupil [looking hesitant as he comes in]: Please, sir, I'd like to talk to you about what happened today. We're really fed up that you didn't let us know that we would be having science instead of PE. [The teacher looks impatient and keeps checking his watch.]
Teacher: I haven't got time at the moment; see me about it tomorrow.
Pupil: I thought you would say that.
Teacher: You'll have a new timetable by the end of the week.

The teacher continues to look busy and the communication ends. The pupil goes off grumbling to himself.

The brevity of the exchange left me feeling quite frustrated, a feeling that I guessed mirrored the pupils' feelings. We all returned to the group circle and discussed what had happened. Some of their observations were surprisingly empathic:

(Contd)

- *The young people in the group did not feel on the whole that the teachers listened to their grievances.*
- *They acknowledged that the teachers were very busy.*
- *They said that the teachers were often preoccupied.*
- *They realized that the teachers were answerable to other teachers and that they had to check things out.*
- *There were some teachers (no names were ever used) whom they didn't like.*
- *They said that the teachers they didn't like treated them unfairly in some way.*

When I asked the pupils about their feelings in relation to grievances, they made the following comments:

- *They felt upset when teachers ignored them.*
- *They felt angry.*
- *They felt that their views were not respected.*
- *In school they felt disempowered – they had no voice and were treated like 'little kids' and their feelings were disregarded and didn't matter.*

I asked the pupils how they expressed these feelings. In answer there were a lot of shrugs, 'Don't knows' and a 'What's the point? You'd only end up getting detention or something.' It didn't occur to any of them that they could express their dissatisfaction and frustration because they associated strong feelings with not being heard and possible punishment.

When I asked them how frustration and dissatisfaction expressed itself in their behaviour, they suggested the following:

- *They sometimes hated the teachers.*
- *They might sometimes take it out on each other.*
- *They didn't feel like doing any work.*
- *They sometimes felt alienated from teachers and school.*
- *They didn't want to do homework.*
- *They were grumpier at home.*
- *They didn't want to go to school.*

The school given as an example was by no means atypical. It's possible that many schools have communication problems between teachers and pupils as well as between teachers themselves. In fact, some of the teachers I spoke to at this particular school prided themselves on the improved communication they felt they had with the pupils. The example demonstrates the undercurrent of largely unexpressed strong feelings that young people can harbour when they feel no one is listening to them.

Insight

Some people seem to be naturally more gifted with interpersonal skills than others. However, if you're not one of them, have faith – interpersonal skills can be learned and a key element is learning to listen well. We've all heard people say of someone they value, 'S/he is a good listener.'

Skills that could have been used

The teacher in the role play would have responded better if he had applied the basics of counselling skills and the core conditions. He could have stopped, listened and asked interested open questions, taking the opportunity to develop a relationship with the pupil. When he told the pupil that he was too busy, that could have been interpreted as dismissive and uncaring (they and their grievances are not at all important to him – as if they don't exist). The comment about the new timetable has a subtext that could be understood to mean that he considers himself to be beyond mistakes. In both these responses he fails to acknowledge his humanness and seems to regard himself as above criticism from pupils. Because of this he loses a valuable opportunity to make contact with the pupil and repair the damage.

I'm sure that by now you have an idea what core conditions are and how they can be applied. Without wishing to labour the point, we'll briefly look at how the teacher might have put these and listening skills to good use.

EMPATHY

If the teacher had demonstrated that he was able to understand that the pupils were missing something they enjoyed doing, and that they'd been given no prior notice to allow them to adjust to the change, it would have conveyed empathic understanding of their situation. He would have also have appreciated that, to help them let go of the grievance, it was important that they could register a complaint and receive an apology and an explanation.

UNCONDITIONAL POSITIVE REGARD AND RESPECT

It's a well-accepted fact, backed by social learning theories, that a child learns from example – what behavioural psychology calls 'vicarious' means. If we assume this is true, then it follows that, if a teacher consistently treats pupils with respect, then the pupils will reciprocate. He could have demonstrated positive regard by acknowledging the pupils' upset, thanking the pupils for informing him of their grievances and commending the representative for taking on the task of approaching him.

CONGRUENCE AND GENUINENESS

The Rogerian meaning of 'genuineness' applied to teaching would involve engagement with the pupils as individuals. In any profession it is easy to take refuge in a role that distances ourselves from situations that challenge us, especially if our energies and resources are already stretched. The teacher would have been 'real' with his pupils if he had acknowledged (to both himself and them) that people in authority could get things wrong at times. He could have apologized and told the pupil that steps would be taken to rectify the mistakes. When authority figures appear infallible it can engender fear in others about their own imperfections.

ACCEPTANCE

Good teaching or 'facilitation of learning' (a term favoured by Carl Rogers) can instil a sense of self-worth in a child, not only by encouraging academic achievement but also by teaching children to value themselves and other people. To make this possible they need to feel that they're (most of the time at least) accepted and valued by others and that they have a part to play as individuals.

If a teacher is able to use the core conditions and is familiar with various counselling skills, then they can put these to use in various contexts – in a one-to-one relationship with a child or young person who is demonstrating antisocial behaviour and also in relation to the class as a whole, in the understanding and management of group dynamics.

The following account is by a teacher who trained and worked as a volunteer counsellor of young people. He relates how counselling skills continue to enhance his teaching role.

If one considers counselling to be a specialized or more insightful form of communication then it is an essential skill for all teachers. Most young people are not natural subscribers to education within its institutional form, especially when they may be taking ten subjects, a number of which they will believe to be irrelevant. A significant proportion of students are gently coerced into learning by parents, teachers, various societal institutions and the fears that they may have about their futures. This leads to conflict of interests between the students' reluctance and the demands placed upon teachers from school management and national government to get better and better results regardless. This conflict of interest will often lead to potential confrontation (especially given the natural rebelliousness of teenagers struggling with the developmental stages of separation and identity development).

It is in the minimization of conflict and confrontation and the creation of a partnership for learning that counselling skills are so necessary. Counselling skills such as:

- ▶ *being able to hear what is not being said*
- ▶ *hearing the general tone of the communication*
- ▶ *the reading of body language*
- ▶ *the creation of a body language that does not enflame situations*
- ▶ *being able to surmise what emotions may be behind a specific response*
(Contd)

- *being able to ask open questions that broaden discussions rather than narrow them*
- *being able to listen to strong emotions being articulated*
- *hearing and seeing the transference*
- *allowing an individual to feel heard*
- *empathizing with young people.*

The most important factor has been that I can step outside my role as a teacher and see the broader picture. It is the knowledge that any student is a part of a broader picture that enables me to deal in a more empathic way with them.

An uncomfortably high proportion of the students that sit in front of us are damaged in psychological ways. The wound they carry can be from divorce, bereavement, abuse, poor parenting and many that we can't imagine. Some will be the traumas that are associated with development and the teenage years, which can seem unimportant to adults but earth-shattering to them. Because these students are not blank slates and school is not treated in isolation, I can end up with a child who may be sullen, explosive, resentful, depressed or just simply unhappy. It is easier to deal with the angry, resentful and rebellious student; the problem is being made visible. The worrying ones are the unhappy and depressive; it's not visible. Most young people of this age have not learned to be reflective about where the feelings and moods come from. They simply act out.

This is where counselling skills are worth their weight in gold. Firstly, in the recognition that this is acting out and not just a troublesome individual. It will often be that some action on my part will have mirrored a raw spot in their life, and it is safer to react against me than the real source. It is no different from the transference that happens in counselling sessions. Counselling skills allow you to question in a supportive, non-threatening and empathic way that can bring the background issue into focus. They allow you to hold the anger or resentment in a safe way. To confront in a gentle fashion. Most importantly, they can allow you to help a child see where the current emotions are coming from and to build in mechanisms that can allow that child to express them safely and build more productive behaviour patterns.

Roy Radcliffe

DOCTORS AND COUNSELLING SKILLS

A doctor told me that he had undertaken brief counselling training because he was increasingly dissatisfied with his lack of ability to be fully attentive of his patients. He realized that many of his patients needed to feel that they were being listened to and responded to as if they were important. He appreciated that his manner was not conveying his genuine concern.

He considers that the counselling skills he has acquired have helped him to look more deeply at the patient as an individual. Subsequently he's more inclined to suggest that a patient who is suffering from depression has counselling or psychotherapy than to prescribe antidepressants automatically – he now prescribes these less frequently. He told me that he's more likely than before to ask depressed patients, and patients who have persistent symptoms that resist medication, open questions about what's going on in their lives and their relationships with significant others as a means of assessing appropriate treatment.

PROBATION OFFICERS AND COUNSELLING SKILLS

I asked an ex-colleague of mine who had trained and worked as a counsellor how she uses her skills in her new career as a probation officer. She said that the skills she learned are of great value to her. She can engage with her clients (young offenders) on an empathic level, appreciating the whole person. She's more likely to make links between the offender's crimes and their past childhood, which helps her to write pre-sentencing reports. In these she might comment on events in the offender's childhood that she considers to have had a contributing effect, resulting in poor self-esteem and an inability to handle difficulties. She stressed that this in no way makes her a 'soft touch'. The counselling skills help her to challenge effectively, in an unthreatening manner. This might include challenging the offender's attitude towards issues of power and control. Having the skills also helps her to recognize certain patterns of behaviour. She commented:

> *Sometimes a persistent offender enjoys having a problem in the sense that it in some way defines him. He becomes caught up in a cycle of repetition of events. By tentative challenging I can bring issues into the open. In this way he can choose to own his behaviour and make some sense of it.*

The knowledge and practice of listening and responding skills can give us more choice about how to deal with some stresses in the work environment. It's important, when we use counselling skills, that we're aware of our limitations as helpers, recognizing when we're perhaps out of our depth and when it's time to refer a person to someone with appropriate training and experience – otherwise there can be a conflict of roles. The objective isn't to overload ourselves with responsibilities but instead to lighten our load by improving our relationships with those around us.

THINGS TO REMEMBER

1 *Counselling skills can be put to good use in workplace relationships as well as personal relationships.*

2 *By learning basic counselling skills, such as the effective use of questions, summarizing and inviting people to expand on what they say, we can be both more objective and empathic.*

3 *Active listening and adopting core conditions values deepens our understanding of other people's point of view.*

4 *A person's unconscious body language tells us a lot about their emotions and state of mind and gives us insight into the feelings behind the words.*

5 *When challenging someone, it is important to challenge their behaviour rather than them as a person.*

5

Enjoying the exploration

In this chapter you will learn:
- *ways in which you can develop self-awareness and understanding*
- *about the use of visualization and meditation*
- *about stress management and assertiveness training models*
- *how to work with dreams.*

> **Insight**
>
> Generally people don't know themselves as well as they
> think. Consequently we learn a lot about ourselves when we
> participate in self-discovery type workshops or counselling
> courses where we look at what's important to us in life
> and are encouraged to express ourselves emotionally
> and creatively.

Preparing to become a counsellor begins with gaining insight
into ourselves – how we think, what matters to us, our main life
concerns and how we relate to other people in various situations
and levels of intimacy. How can we hope to 'walk inside another's
shoes' when we don't fully walk in our own?

There are many avenues to self-understanding and development.
This chapter introduces techniques and methods that not only
increase our personal awareness but also complement and
enhance the use of counselling skills. They are suggestions only –
some might interest you and others might not.

Attending workshops

Taking part in workshops or training sessions offered by trained and experienced therapists gives us opportunities to focus on various aspects of ourselves and our lives, including:

▶ *how we behave in particular situations and towards others*
▶ *particular life experiences*
▶ *our self-image*
▶ *our fears, our hopes*
▶ *transition periods*
▶ *our value systems*
▶ *our goals*
▶ *how we play – e.g. express spontaneity, exuberance and joy*
▶ *issues of dependency*
▶ *self-reliance – coping mechanisms/strategies.*

A range of workshops offered by counsellors and therapists, or others with appropriate knowledge, is advertised on noticeboards in libraries, holistic clinics, colleges and universities. Take advantage of these as they are usually good fun as well as informative. See advertisements for workshops in periodicals and magazines concerned with mind, body and spirit issues or contact BACP (see Taking it further) to find out what's on offer in your area. Workshops address such diverse subject matter as gender issues, sexuality, 'the inner child', stress and tension reduction, laughter and many more. Some deal with specific emotions such as anger or grief.

Insight

Play is a natural way to de-stress. Children play in any situation – we see this in news coverage when children living in conflict zones act traumatic things out through play. Adults also benefit from play in whatever form they like, be it sport, amateur dramatics or having fun 'mucking about' with a partner. I have noticed in counselling that, when a client makes an effort to reintroduce some fun into their lives, their troubles seem lighter.

Myths, legends and fairy tales are media used by therapists to stimulate imagination and creativity and to access individual inner potential. This might involve role play, visualization or guided imagery using elements of myth, fairy tale or legend.

For example, in a guided imagery you might be taken on a 'magical mystery tour' of your own imagining and imaging, entering into mysterious labyrinths and being asked questions by the therapist guiding you such as:

▶ *What do you find in the labyrinth?*
▶ *Someone or something comes to assist you. Who or what are they? What does it/do they look like?*
▶ *They help you move forward. How?*

The person leading the guided imagery/visualization will ask you to focus on your feelings at particular points (e.g. fear, hope, jubilation, expectation, apprehension, sense of achievement). Exercises like these are designed to help you draw on your inner resources and integrate disparate elements of the self. Personal values and priorities are also explored. The labyrinth could, at some point, reveal a room full of treasure or a transformational character. It's the participant's own imagination, or elements of their unconscious, that supplies the content of the 'story' and therefore what's revealed is specific in meaning to the individual.

Insight

Some exercises may take you out of your comfort zone in which case you have a choice either to accept the challenge and work through your discomfort – which I had to do when I decided to participate anyway and ended up enjoying myself – or give yourself permission to sit one out (which I have also done). Making these kinds of choices in training reflects the bigger choices we make in the outside world, in our everyday lives, and can be as informative as the exercises themselves. For example, it can lead us to question things; for example, 'Do I always play it safe – and if so, am I losing out on something by doing so?'

Visualization

Visualization is also a way of attaining a relaxed or meditative state. The following visualization exercise is based on an exercise from Roberto Assagioli's *Transpersonal Development: The Dimension beyond Psychosynthesis*:

Visualization exercise 1

Let us imagine a closed rosebud. Visualize the stem, the leaves and, at the top, the bud itself. It is green in appearance because the sepals are closed; then at the topmost point there is a pink tip. Try to visualize this as vividly as possible, keeping the image at the centre of your **conscious mind**. As you watch you gradually become aware that movement is taking place: the sepals begin to pull apart as their points turn outwards, enabling you to see the closed pink petals. The sepals move further apart... now see the bud-shaped petals of a beautiful, delicate rose. Then the petals also begin to unfold. The bud continues to expand slowly until the rose is revealed in all its beauty and you are able to admire it with delight.

At this point try to breathe in the scent of the rose and smell its characteristic perfume – delicate, sweet and pleasing to the senses. Take in its scent with pleasure. The symbol of perfume has also been used frequently in religious and mystical language ('the smell of holiness'), as indeed perfumes have been used in rituals (incense, etc.).

Next visualize the whole plant and imagine the force of life rising up from its roots to the flower, producing this development. Pause in awed contemplation of this miracle of nature.

Now identify yourself with the rose or, to be more precise, 'introject' the rose into yourself. Symbolically become a flower, a rose. The same Life that animates the Universe, that has produced the rose, is producing in you that same, if not a greater,

(Contd)

miracle: the development, opening up and irradiation of your spiritual being. And we have the choice of taking an active part in our own inner flowering.

The following is an exercise from *Teach Yourself Visualization* by Pauline Wills (now out of print) and should follow a simple relaxation exercise.

Exercise 2

The sea

Imagine that it is a beautifully warm and sunny day and that you are lying on the beach in a small sandy cove, surrounded by grey cliffs that have small green rock plants growing out of their crevices. You feel the softness of the sand beneath you and its slight movement as some of the small grains trickle through your fingers. Look at the blue sky above and sense the warmth from the sun penetrating your body. Close your eyes and listen to the cry of the seagulls and the roar of the waves as they break on the shore.

Lying and listening to these sounds, you become aware of the waves breaking on the shore and the sea travelling across the beach until it very gently laps over your feet. Initially the water feels cold in comparison with the warmth of the sun. As the water recedes, you feel it draw out and take with it any tension that has accumulated in your feet. Your feet relax and feel heavy. The next wave breaks and gently rolls over the sand, covering your feet and your legs. The coldness of the water feels invigorating. It recedes and takes your tension with it. Your legs relax. Hearing the next wave coming and breaking on the shore, you wait for the water to touch your feet and then move over your legs, hands, lower part of your arms and abdomen. The muscles and organs in your abdomen contract slightly as they experience the coldness of the sea. The water recedes and you allow it to take your tensions with it. Listening, and waiting expectantly, you prepare yourself for the next wave. It comes and covers your body up to your neck.

A slight shiver goes through your body as the water comes into contact with your chest. But this is compensated by the feeling of lightness and relaxation that you experience when the water has drawn out and takes with it all your tension.

You know that the next wave will cover your entire body, but you are not afraid. Your intuition tells you that you will be able to breathe normally under the water. Wait and listen. It is coming. You embrace the water as it covers you and you give to it all your tension, toxins and pain with gratitude and love. The water slowly recedes. It leaves you feeling completely relaxed and renewed, physically, mentally and spiritually. A feeling of joy pervades you as you once more become aware of the warmth of the sun revitalizing and re-energizing the whole of your being.

When coming out of relaxation, gently start to move your feet; then flex the muscles in your legs; gently move your fingers; breathing in, raise your arms up over your head, stretching the whole of your body. Breathing out, bring your arms back down to your sides. Repeat this twice more, then open your eyes and slowly roll over on to your left side and sit up.

Freud recognized that in playing a part we find out more about ourselves. Here's an example of a self-exploratory exercise using a fairy tale.

Exercise 3

1 *Think of a fairy tale most appropriate to your life. Which particular character do you identify with?*
2 *What associations do you have with your chosen character?*
3 *What happens to them?*
4 *What aspects of the story disempower or empower the character you have chosen?*

(Contd)

Counsellors sometimes refer to archetypal fairy tale or mythical figures. Useful parallels can be drawn between the experience of the representing figure and the client. For example, I had a client who had incredibly long hair and was very insecure in her relationship with her boyfriend. She regarded him as a passport to an exciting life that she thought would be closed to her if he finished their relationship. She had mentioned more than once that she would like to cut her hair but her boyfriend loved it (it was waist length and very thick). I commented that what she was saying reminded me of the fairy tale story of Rapunzel – we discussed how perhaps her hair represented a means of escape into the world of her boyfriend. It was food for thought, and opened up exploration of her self-image and self-esteem.

THE JOHARI WINDOW

The Johari window originally devised by Jo Luft and Harry Ingham is presented in *The Johari Window: A Graphic Model for Interpersonal Relations*. This model challenges our self-awareness, our ability to share ourselves with others and our willingness to explore the unknown. The Johari window offers a four-part representation of ourselves (see Figure 5.1).

1 *Known to all: The view from this is open and seen by everyone. This represents what we freely express for others to see, including our behaviour and attitudes. The view can be extended by self-disclosure.*

2 *Blind area: We can't see this area of ourselves; it's unknown to us, but others are aware of it through aspects of our behaviour and body language. Our self-awareness can be extended by feedback from others.*

3 Hidden area: *This area represents the private part of ourselves: our secrets, shame, guilt feelings and so on. We are aware of it and choose not to share this part with others. We can choose to self-disclose, allowing others a view into our private world.*

4 Unknown to all: *This view of the individual is closed to everyone. It represents part of us that we, and others, are unaware of. It holds unconscious needs, impulses and anxieties, and our untapped potential; we can gain insight into this part of ourselves through the counselling process.*

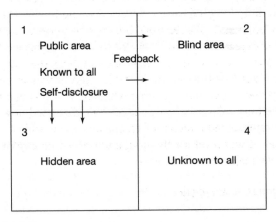

Figure 5.1 The Johari window.

Source: Jo Luft and Harry Inham, The Johari Window: A Graphic Model for Interpersonal Relations.

Use the Johari window to assess yourself, as follows:

▶ *What do you express freely – what are you comfortable with about yourself that you share with others?*
▶ *How do you feel about the blind areas – the aspects of you that other people can see but you are unaware of?*
▶ *What feedback might upset you?*
▶ *What feedback might help you?*
▶ *What constitutes the private part of you?*
▶ *If the fourth part of the Johari window represents the unconscious part of you – closed to everyone, including yourself – how do you imagine you will access it?*

Assertiveness training

Learning assertive behaviour has value for the would-be counsellor or helper because assertiveness – contrary to widely held beliefs – is not about bulldozing the wishes of others or, indeed, linked to any other form of aggression. Assertive behaviour is neither aggressive nor passive, but is concerned with clear, honest, direct communication.

Assertive skills encompass:

▶ *taking responsibility for our own thoughts, emotions and behaviour*
▶ *paying attention to human body language (sometimes called non-verbal communication)*
▶ *addressing the defensive behaviour of self and others*
▶ *learning how to deal with criticism – giving and receiving*
▶ *learning how to deal with compliments – giving and receiving*
▶ *challenging and confronting – giving and receiving*
▶ *specific techniques – e.g. being clear and concrete*
▶ *prioritizing areas of our lives – asking clearly for what we want and examining values*
▶ *self-esteem – valuing ourselves*
▶ *decision making – choice awareness*
▶ *accepting refusals, disappointments, rebukes – and surviving*
▶ *'unlearning' particular non-effective behaviour – e.g. covert manipulative interactions with others.*

The **assertiveness training** model highlights four styles of behaviour commonly adopted by individuals in relation to others:

▶ *assertive*
▶ *passive*

- *aggressive*
- *passive/aggressive.*

For example, the passive/aggressive person is covertly manipulative and 'others blaming' and, although they aim to dominate or win, they present themselves as non-competitive and passive.

We can learn assertive behaviour by reading relevant books or attending assertiveness training classes. Assertiveness training teaches awareness of our fears and blocks, and teaches us how to relate to other people in a more direct and non-aggressive way. We find out, for example, about how many of us live in fear of what other people might think of us and how our internalized 'shoulds', 'musts' and 'oughts' govern us. Assertiveness training addresses our irrational thoughts and beliefs, and shows us how we can replace these with alternative rational beliefs. A knowledge of assertiveness techniques is useful to a counsellor in helping clients look at their behaviour. Irrational thoughts and beliefs are a focus of cognitive behavioural approaches and in transactional analysis 'shoulds' and 'oughts' are examined within the framework of 'drivers' – such as 'be perfect', 'hurry up' and 'be strong' (often these are parental rules that we've taken on board and self-impose).

EXAMPLES OF IRRATIONAL AND RATIONAL BELIEFS

Note how the irrational beliefs are hard to maintain and the rational beliefs are easier on us.

Irrational beliefs	Rational beliefs
I must always please others	It's unrealistic to expect that I can always please others
I must never be angry	It's OK to feel angry at times
My happiness depends on other people's behaviour and attitudes	The source of my happiness is within me and isn't dependent on other people

Assertiveness skills help you to get in touch with and deal with areas of weakness in communication with other people; for example, many people find it difficult to challenge or confront others without becoming defensive, giving up, or becoming aggressive. Assertiveness helps us to be concrete, with no hidden agendas. We can learn to say what we mean.

Insight

Overall, counselling encourages us to be easy on ourselves and its ultimate goal is one of personal empowerment.

Stress management

Counselling involves holding and containing the stress of other people. Empathic responding requires an awareness of what the other person is feeling and attempting to convey on various levels. As a counsellor you're aware of other people's stress, but what about your own? Stress management involves identifying the signs of stress:

1 *Physical effects*
   Palpitations, sweating, tenseness in muscles, loss of appetite, shaking, sleeplessness, 'butterflies' in the stomach. When we are stressed adrenaline is released, causing a raised level of tension in our muscles; we sweat to cool the body and our blood pressure goes up, preparing us for a 'flight or fight' response.

2 *Emotional effects*
   Depression, anger, resentment, distress, panic, fear, unhappiness, unrest, guilt, despair, impatience.

3 *Effects on logical thinking*
   Inability to 'think straight' – analyse, make decisions, obsessional thoughts, forgetfulness, misjudgements, with flashes of intuition and of clear thought.

4 Effects on behaviour
Increased dependence/reliance on others; withdrawal from others, from responsibilities, work, etc.; agitation, low concentration levels, loss of temper, shouting, crying, aggressive drinking, 'road rage', no enthusiasm for life generally.

Through stress management we can also identify:

▶ *personal triggers, i.e. what brings stress on*
▶ *coping strategies/escape mechanisms, i.e. how we deal with stress, how to build on stress reduction*
▶ *support systems – personal support network, e.g. family, work, friends, church, organizations, community.*

Methods of dealing with stress include:

▶ *changing behaviour/cognitions, i.e. what we tell ourselves ('I can't cope'), catastrophizing*
▶ *becoming more assertive*
▶ *using problem-solving models, goals, targets*
▶ *learning relaxation techniques: meditation, visualization and other ways of unwinding and enjoying ourselves (e.g. dancing, singing, yoga – which combines exercise and relaxation, painting).*

Relaxation

Try a simple relaxation technique that you might like to pass on to clients who suffer from high anxiety or stress levels. Edmund Jacobson introduced the following relaxation technique in the late 1930s. It was later (1961) adopted by Joseph Wolpe in his Systematic Desensitisation Treatment.

The exercise involves tensing and relaxing in turn various groups of muscles throughout the body until a deep state of relaxation is reached. The exercise would initially be therapist-led. Once it has been learned by the client it can be practised independently when needed.

A simple relaxation exercise that works as a deep muscle relaxant

The instructor begins:
'Lie on the floor on a thick large towel or mat with your legs straight and arms by your side. Let yourself get comfortable. Close your eyes and relax. Notice the sensations within your body and surrender yourself to the experience. Breathe naturally and easily.'

Notes for the instructor: The person leading the relaxation speaks in a slow, quiet, monotonous tone of voice. The instructions may vary slightly. Some individuals may feel too exposed lying down and may prefer to sit in a comfortable but upright chair while practising the exercise. The usual sequence is to work through the body, first tensing, then relaxing the various parts of the body. Begin with the toes and feet and work gradually upwards, finishing with the top of the head.

The instructor continues:
'Breathe in deeply, tensing the muscles in your feet. Hold your breath for a few moments while you tense the muscles in this area... Breathe out heavily, letting the tension go until your feet are completely relaxed. Tell yourself to relax on the out breath.'

Notes for the instructor: In this manner the instructor leads the client up through the body, addressing the main muscle groups: feet to calves, calves to thighs, thighs to buttocks, buttocks to abdomen, abdomen to chest and back, chest and back to fists, fists to arms, arms to shoulder and neck, shoulder and neck to muscles of the face, muscles of the face to scalp and top of head. Each instruction (e.g. tense the muscles in your abdomen as you breathe deeply) is followed by the instruction to hold the intake breath for a few seconds while the muscles are tense, then to relax and breathe normally. A sense of the travel of relaxation up through the body is given by summing up at certain points, when the instructor might say, 'Breathing normally, notice a feeling of relaxation and well-being flowing up from your feet through to your calves,' and so on. The exercise is completed by focusing on the whole-body state of relaxation.

The instructor concludes:
'Breathe naturally and place your awareness in the relaxed flow of energy freely moving around your body. Notice your breathing; on each exhalation feel yourself becoming more and more relaxed… In a few minutes you will come back into your surroundings feeling relaxed and refreshed. Allow yourself to enjoy the feeling of well-being that permeates your body and mind… When you are ready, open your eyes, roll over on your side and support yourself with your arm in a half-sitting position. Stay in this position until you are fully ready to sit up.'

Notes for the instructor: Allow the participants or individual client some moments to relish the state of relaxation. This type of exercise may make people very relaxed and some even fall asleep. Yawning is common as tension is released from the body. It is therefore necessary to bring people back slowly into the surroundings.

Meditation

Insight

Meditation slows breathing and heart rate, giving the body a rest from everyday strain. Many counsellors practise meditation as a way of shedding the problems of others they carry in their minds.

The **object relations** psychoanalyst Donald W. Winnicott talked about the therapist's position of 'not knowing' – an open, receptive way of being, devoid of expectations and preconceptions, an emptying out. In *Playing and Reality*, he writes, 'If only we can wait, the patient arrives at understanding creatively and with immense joy, and I now enjoy this joy, more than I used to enjoy the sense of having been clever.'

Counselling work is stimulating, interesting and, at times, emotionally demanding. Counsellors are likely to spend quite a few hours a week with people who are troubled, unhappy or stressed out. You'll hear sad, cruel and touching personal stories. You'll be with people when they express strong emotions such as anger, fear, disappointment and grief. In the counsellor–client relationship you're likely, at times, to represent the client's mother or prime carer from the past. Although you'll learn to work with this, rather than hook on to it, you'll be aware of the neediness of some clients and of the hopes and expectations they have of counselling.

Simple meditation techniques are invaluable to a therapist as a means of unwinding, resting and recharging energy supplies and of developing non-attachment skills. If it attracts you, join a meditation class or learn a few simple meditation techniques that you can use in a spare moment. Begin with a simple ten-minute meditation exercise.

Meditation exercise 1

Sit in a position you find comfortable that allows you to breathe freely. It's important that you wear loose comfortable clothes. Close your eyes and let everything drop away. Relax your body. Focus on your breath entering and leaving your body. Try not to interfere with the process – let it be. Calmly direct any wandering thoughts back to your breathing.

Naomi Ozaniec writes in *Beat Stress with Meditation* (Hodder Education, 2010):

> *Meditation enables us to develop a watching consciousness, it enables us to give birth to the watcher within. Buddhism names six root delusions and 20 secondary delusions. Looking at these takes us straight back to ourselves for there is no other place to be. The path to the Western mysteries is traditionally opened with the injunction, 'Know Thyself'. When you are ready to seek yourself, you are ready to begin meditation in earnest. But do not be*

mistaken – though your quest may undoubtedly take an outward form, the journey really takes place within. Perhaps it is time for a new injunction, the path may be opened in a thousand different ways. The phrase 'I am that I am' might serve as a new starting point for, in truth, you do not have to journey to find yourself, you merely have to open your eyes to who you, as you, are. This new injunction does not prevent change or growth, it merely affirms that you can own all that you are in each and every moment. Try meditating with the phrase and see if it brings you meaning.

The six root delusions are:

1 *Attachment – our attachment to objects exaggerates and distorts.*
2 *Anger – anger destroys peace of mind and is harmful to the body.*
3 *Pride – through pride we exaggerate our own status.*
4 *Ignorance – this is considered to be the root of all delusions.*
5 *Negative doubt – this refers to aspects of the negative results of doubting the validity of Buddhist teaching.*
6 *Mistaken views – this refers to the way in which the philosophical views we take direct behaviour and action.*

Meditation exercise 2

This exercise is taken from *Beat Stress with Meditation*. Choose one of the root delusions as subjects for daily meditation. Try to see how this quality functions in your life. Become aware of the feelings and circumstances associated with it. Are you going to loosen the grip of this quality in your life? Stay with your chosen subject until you feel you have gained in understanding. You can always return to the same subject at a later date. When you are ready, choose another subject and examine it in the same way.

Psychosynthesis is a transpersonal or spiritual model of psychotherapy that incorporates many techniques embracing art, music, guided fantasy (visualization – note the visualization exercises earlier in this chapter) and meditation. The Italian founder of psychosynthesis, Roberto Assagioli, was familiar with numerous fields of study, including the psychodynamic movement, anthropology and spiritual teachings. He believed meditation gave rise to a contemplative inner silence, leading to a receptive and pure consciousness of being.

Even short meditation sessions can create a sense of peace, improve concentration, attention and focusing, and act as a battery recharger. Some therapists say that through the regular practice of meditation they have increased their sense of intuition. Meditation instils an inner calm. It creates a familiarity with contemplative silence, with 'listening to the echo'.

Dreams

Insight

We explore our daily concerns in our dreams and by paying attention to our dreams we can learn not only more about the problem but also how it can be tackled creatively. Clients often report that their dreams become more vivid when they are having counselling – as if layers of experience are being unravelled.

Dreams are focused on in the analytic, psychodynamic, Jungian and transpersonal approaches, all of which consider dreams to be a direct line to the unconscious mind. Freud regarded dreams to be the royal road (*via regia*) to the unconscious, and Jung believed dreams to contain messages from the pool of the collective unconscious (see Chapter 7).

In **Gestalt therapy**, founded by Fritz Perls, the 'empty chair' process helps the client to examine dream material – characters, symbols or objects from a dream are focused on and communicated within the therapy room. The client (dreamer) can actively imagine the dream or symbol, or person, into the chair and ask questions, or else sit in the chair and personify or become the character, symbol or motif. In this way fragments of dreams are reconstructed to form a deeper understanding as elements of the unconscious work with the conscious in the 'here and now'.

Anthropologist Arnold van Gennep and religious historian Mircea Eliade wrote about the respectful attention paid to dreams in primitive cultures; in ceremonies and rites of passage a dreamy, trancelike state facilitated creative exploration and learning. The ancient Egyptians built dream temples, and the Christian Bible refers to dreams as a source of instructive wisdom. Biblical stories, in both the Old and New Testaments, refer to dreams as a medium through which God communicates with people. In Numbers 12:6 we find 'Hear my words: If there is a prophet among you, I the Lord make myself known to him in a vision, I speak with him in a dream.' The future is revealed in a dream in Genesis 20:3–7: 'But God came to Abimelech in a dream.' Mary's revelatory dream in Matthew 2:12 gives instruction: 'And being warned in a dream not to return to Herod, they departed to their own country by another way.'

Dreams have been traditionally regarded as practical, instructive and transformative, and to contain messages from the spiritual or transpersonal element of the human **psyche**. The dream world is a magical realm where time and space are transcended along with the limitations of the linear, logical mind. During dreams we experience a heightened awareness, an amazing capacity for detail, and we're alive to our creative self and our individual inner world of meaning. Dreams are rich in diverse imagery and symbolism, and, although there are many books that aim to tell us the meanings of specific symbols, they don't take into account the idiosyncratic content of dream imagery.

ACTIVE IMAGINATION

Carl Jung introduced a technique he named **active imagination** to facilitate interaction between Ego and the unconscious; he used 'active' to differentiate between the usual passive meaning of 'imagination'. Active imagination is a conscious activity entered into to engage the unconscious and Ego in dialogue.

There are variations on this technique; one of these is designed to assist dream analysis. The dream is re-entered by a process of relaxation so that exploration of dream symbols, motifs and characters can take place. The dreamer becomes an actual participant in the dream scenario, entering into a dialogue with dream characters. Questions can be asked and changes can be consciously made as a way of gaining illuminating insights into problems and dilemmas.

How to begin

Begin the inner journey and make contact with your unconscious mind by paying attention to your dreams. Keep a notebook and pencil by the side of your bed and write down as much as you can remember of the content of your dreams on awakening. Spend some time thinking about your dreams, and about what they mean to you.

If you have written an account of the dream you can prepare yourself before re-entering it. Ask yourself what you would like to address:

1 *Begin by identifying key characters.*
2 *What questions do you have for them?*
3 *What are you feeling, seeing, sensing at specific points in the dream?*
4 *What remains hidden from you?*
5 *What changes would you like to make? – e.g. conclude an unfinished task or journey.*

When you've finished the exercise, make notes on any new information, understanding and personal insights. The idea is that, by giving attention to the inner dream world, you'll become familiar with unconscious processes and begin to interact with them consciously. You might like to try to apply the technique of active imagination as a precursor to working in this way with clients in the future.

Dream exercise

Make yourself comfortable by sitting or lying down in a position that you feel relaxed in. Close your eyes and breathe slowly and deeply. By 'letting go' and relaxing, relocate yourself back into your dream. You can ask for information by focusing on particular characters. Listen to the inner voice and let new insights unfold without asserting any conscious will on the proceedings.

Try out alternative courses of action or outcomes.

Try out a new way of responding to situations; for example, facing a fearful image or confronting a task.

THINGS TO REMEMBER

1 *Counselling training starts with getting to know ourselves –
   our strengths and weaknesses, our blocks and blind spots.*

2 *Counsellors and other therapists run workshops or classes
   that encourage 'self-growth', which basically means getting to
   know and accepting disparate sides of ourselves.*

3 *If we don't look after ourselves as counsellors, we can
   become stressed and burnt out. De-stressing methods such as
   meditation and visualization give the counsellor relaxation
   and switch-off time.*

4 *The learning of assertiveness skills is useful for clients and
   counsellors alike as they teach us to communicate in a
   straightforward, non-threatening way.*

5 *Attention to dreams is a (often revelatory) means of
   understanding ourselves and what's going on at a deeper
   (unconscious) level.*

Part two

A deeper understanding – training to a professional level

6

....

Course components

In this chapter you will learn:
- *about the origins of counselling*
- *what counselling training courses involve, including the role of personal therapy*
- *the basics of groupwork and supervision*
- *about the professional adherence to codes of ethics and practice.*

_____

Background

Counselling started becoming professionalized in countries like Australia, New Zealand and Great Britain in the late 1960s and early 1970s, when training courses in counselling were offered for the first time. This followed a precedent set in the USA in the 1950s by the work of Carl Rogers and his contemporaries. Originally a person training to become a psychoanalyst would undergo personal analysis for a considerable time. Receiving analysis from senior analysts was at the time the only method of becoming familiar with the workings of psychoanalysis. It was the responsibility of the training analyst to decide whether or not the candidate was suitable material to become an analyst. Fritz Perls, the founder of the Gestalt approach to therapy, was analysed by Wilhelm Reich, an associate of Freud. Gradually other methods of teaching and learning were added as the canon of analytical literature grew; case discussions were opened out to include analysts in training and theoretical seminars were introduced. It was the humanistic therapists, with their emphasis on the experiential, who introduced innovative ideas about therapy and, with these, new training methods evolved. In the 1940s and 1950s Carl Rogers and his associates experimented with different training techniques in client-centred therapy, and some are still in use – notably students watching and commenting on films of counselling sessions, students as co-therapists in sessions, personal growth groups, and peer and self-assessments. Skills training as a structured approach came later with the writings of the likes of Richard Carkhuff in *The Art of Helping* and Gerard Egan in *The Skilled Helper*, who recognized the potential of counselling-based skills in terms of 'human resources' and 'helping skills' respectively. Counselling training has become highly structured and systematized, especially in an academic setting. Training courses are thriving and are today available in a variety of forms in universities, colleges, training institutes and agencies in many parts of the world.

Insight

When I was choosing a Diploma in Counselling course, the first steps I took included asking other counsellors about their courses, looking on the internet and collecting prospectuses from colleges and universities and other counselling training venues. I also read about different counselling approaches to help me decide which seemed to suit me best.

Choosing a course

Professional associations offer accreditation to courses that meet their standards and this is worth keeping in mind when you select your course. Courses on offer range from non-certificated starter courses at basic skills level to diplomas, Masters degrees and PhDs. Counselling has become highly professionalized, especially in the USA. People do practise without professional credentials, considering themselves to be counsellors, but this is generally frowned upon by qualified practitioners and professional organizations alike because the ethical standards and the integrity of the unqualified practitioner go unmonitored.

Courses can be very expensive, and the cost of the personal therapy, usually a condition of the professional course, adds to the expense. Over a period of usually two or three years the total can seem extortionate and a criticism of counsellor training systems is that it's only the financially solvent – and that usually means middle-class people – who can afford to undertake training. However, financially disadvantaged people are usually eligible for help with fees/books. Some universities and colleges offer reduced fees for those on state benefits and candidates can apply to charities and organizations that offer funding.

A diploma course in counselling, geared to a professional standard, usually comprises of a foundation year, which might be certificated as a first stage, followed by a further two years. The complete training is likely to take three years part-time – possibly one day per week, although some courses entail weekend and week blocks of training. To find a course that suits you, look at various prospectuses which tell you things like: the conditions of entry, the format and content of the course, and the facilities of universities, colleges and training institutions. Before being accepted on a reputable course that leads to a professional qualification, you'll be required to have training and/or experience relevant to the level you are hoping to enter. For example, a Diploma in Counselling course might require a candidate to have completed a certain number of hours' training through previous courses and/or to have had relevant experience working in a counselling capacity with an agency.

The candidate's work experience might be taken into consideration if it has involved understanding of and working with social or cultural diversity, or the use of counselling skills. You could find out about agencies offering counselling in your area, which will include work relating to specific groups and problems (i.e. family and couple relationships; sexual orientation; one-to-one counselling; telephone counselling; crisis counselling; drugs or alcohol abuse; physical, sexual or mental abuse; health-related counselling; counselling aimed at older or young people). The *Yellow Pages* contain details of many agencies, which are usually very keen to have new recruits and will gladly send details of their training programmes, policies and practices.

Joining an agency that offers counselling is probably the best way to begin because of the training they offer, the availability of clients to work with and the back-up of close supervision. Established agencies or organizations usually work to ethical standards specified by a professional (overseeing) association, and they therefore have professional accountability through membership. At least some of the staff members will be accredited by a professional organization.

Key course components

- ▶ *Theory*
- ▶ *Counselling skills*
- ▶ *Work on self-awareness*
- ▶ *Supervision of practice and 'outside' client work*
- ▶ *Written assignments*
- ▶ *Written exams or vivas*
- ▶ *Ongoing assessment (by tutor, peer and self)*
- ▶ *Research work (in some cases) – this is usually at Masters degree or PhD level.*

AIMS OF TRAINING COURSES

- ▶ *To develop an understanding of particular theoretical approaches – e.g. that of psychodynamic, person-centred, Gestalt, **developmental psychology**, interpersonal development, groupwork and dynamics.*
- ▶ *To further develop and acquire ease in the use of counselling skills, enabling discreet use.*
- ▶ *To deepen understanding of self in all areas – personal values, coping mechanisms, defences, expectations, prejudices, belief systems, etc.*
- ▶ *To give insight, guidance and support and to check that the trainee is working ethically with clients.*
- ▶ *As a method of testing, deepening knowledge and understanding.*
- ▶ *To test summation of learning, knowledge and understanding of theory, integration and application, skills competency, professional issues, personal awareness, supervision and self-assessment.*

- To monitor progress, checking and encouraging development of weak spots, allowing movement to another stage of learning.
- To explore the contributions made by research, gain awareness of research methods, train in compiling and producing an original piece of work.

Acquiring skills

Insight

Practising the skills in groups can be nerve-wracking – but remember that other people are nervous too and the tutors/observers aren't expecting you to be perfect.

Skills practice forms an important part of the majority of counselling training courses. A basic skills course would contain mainly skills learning and practice, including a familiarization with Rogerian core conditions. The psychodynamic approaches are rich in theory and techniques that form the main skills (e.g. managing resistance, understanding defences, working with the transference and other unconscious processes). Integrative approaches that utilize the concepts, theories, techniques and applications of one or more approaches usually include a skills component, with Rogerian core conditions forming the baseline of skills use (as proposed by Carkhuff in *The Art of Helping*). The human resources development model later added 'action skills' such as immediacy and confrontation. The three-stage model of self-exploration, understanding and action, developed in Egan's *The Skilled Helper*, is another model that is widely used. Note the move from the specialist arena of 'therapist' to the layperson terminology of 'helper'. Literature became directed towards other workers who would benefit from helping skills; that is, doctors, nurses, business people and those in pastoral care. The micro-skills training approach, introduced by Ivey and Galvin, sets out a programme of skills for therapists, business and medical interviews. Skills models tend to be adapted to suit the course; for example, a course might not include the 'influencing skills' or 'structuring a session' of the micro-counselling model in the repertoire of skills adopted, although structuring 'brief counselling' might be included in a skills programme. What's included largely depends on the orientation of the course. Skills can be adapted to fit into a particular cultural or social context.

METHODS COMMONLY USED IN THE TEACHING/LEARNING OF SKILLS

- ▶ *Video demonstrations of 'expertise' in skill*
- ▶ *Practice in triads of 'counsellor', 'client' and 'observer'*
- ▶ *Brainstorming*
- ▶ *Class handout examples of 'positive' and 'negative' use of skills*
- ▶ *Video recordings, taken while practising the skills in triads, using role play or personal material*
- ▶ *Performance feedback given by tutors and others.*

The aim of familiarizing the trainee counsellor with these skills is to widen their repertoire of responses to client material and help them to discriminate between effective and ineffective ways of communicating or intervening. The minimum requirements for a competent counsellor are that they have a workable knowledge of theoretical models, a range of skills, and have developed self-awareness.

PRACTISING WITH OTHERS

> **Insight**
> While some trainees will bring very personal issues to practice, others choose to protect themselves by using less potentially upsetting material. While training, I tried both and would recommend the latter approach, especially in the early stages of the course when we don't know the other participatants so well.

During the training you'll be practising the skills with other trainees – with a partner or others, using role play or personal material. Role play is what happens when the person acting the part of the client adopts a role and set of problematic circumstances to present to the person acting as the counsellor. The client has the script of the role they adopt to work from. The person playing the role can develop the character, improvising details that will enhance understanding of the 'story'.

The words 'acting', 'improvising' and 'script' may suggest something akin to amateur dramatics, which might seem daunting to the person who is the client. Don't worry; good acting ability is not necessary. Role play is more a matter of entering into the set of circumstances – rather like the practice of empathy. The brief script you will read prior to taking on a persona is a guideline or baseline story and you'll inevitably bring parts of your own life experience to the part. The counsellor's knowledge is limited to a few brief facts, enough to give them the bones, to which the client adds meat with the help of the counsellor's interventions. This triad formation, when one person acts as counsellor, another as the client and the third person as the observer, is an ideal format for skills practice. Individual skills can be practised by focusing on one area at a time, such as: empathy, paraphrasing, questions, summarizing and so on.

A typical structure for skills practice is as follows:

The client talks for 20 minutes, giving the counsellor an opportunity to use a particular skill. At the end of the 20 minutes the client gives feedback to the counsellor (a few minutes), at the end of which the counsellor talks about their experience in their role (a few minutes). Finally the observer gives feedback to both the client and counsellor in relation to the encounter, but mainly to the counsellor in relation to their adeptness in using the skills (a few minutes). Roles are swapped so that each person has the opportunity to be in each.

The role of observer

Insight

It's easy for the person in the observer role to appear like a 'clever Dick' when giving feedback. Although they are trying to demonstrate how they could have done things better, it's hard for the one who is practising the skill not to become defensive. It's best not to take it too seriously – practice is practice after all.

The role of the observer is to watch over the interaction between counsellor and client, either writing notes or making mental notes with regard to the exchange. The observer notes the whole content of the session: the process, what happens, how, why, when, silences, awkwardness and so on, and the body language of the two participants.

When an exercise is finished the observer comments – that is, gives feedback – on the ways the counsellor helped (or didn't help) the client to explore issues generally, and also on how they met the criteria of specific tasks set by the exercise; for example, did they paraphrase effectively and summarize at the end of the session? Were they able to reflect back feelings to the other person (client)?

The observer also gives feedback to the person who's in the position of the client, commenting on anything that they think could be helpful; for example (observer addressing the client), 'I noticed when Jack [the person in the counsellor's role] asked you to tell him more about what happened, you looked hesitant, as if there was a moment when you were deciding if you wanted to, and then you went ahead and explained and explored your feelings more, and it was as if a light had come on and you looked relieved.'

When the observer gives the client or counsellor feedback, they listen without interruption until the end; then they can comment on the accuracy of the observations.

Another role of the observer is as timekeeper, checking that the others keep within the time limits of the exercise: for example, 20 minutes each for a particular role. The observer's presence is discreet and they quietly remind the others that their part of the exercise is coming to an end.

The observer usually maintains a low profile while the other two are engaged in the exercise, sitting in an unobtrusive position in the room, out of direct eye contact with the others.

FEEDBACK

The benefit of working with other trainees is that you can give and receive feedback. Feedback is information given to us by other people about our counselling skills practice. It's potentially a valuable learning tool. The use of feedback requires a specific approach if it's not to become open to abuse or sycophantic appraisal. It requires honesty, self-scrutiny and humility. It's not easy for any of us to have weaknesses pointed out and feedback needs to be given sensitively. Feedback can also be affirming when our strengths are highlighted. It's invaluable in helping us identify our strengths and weaknesses in the way we apply the various skills. Giving and receiving feedback can be difficult. It's not an opportunity to 'get at' someone. In order that receiving feedback can be helpful to an individual, the person needs to be able to do the following:

▶ *understand the information being offered to them;*
▶ *consider the information;*
▶ *act on the information.*

Try to take feedback as impersonally as you can, remembering that it's one person's view of your work. If you receive critical feedback on the same subject matter from three or more people, then it's probably worth taking their comments on board, even if you don't like them. Giving feedback requires us to be candid in our opinion without being offensive; for example, it would be totally inappropriate to say. 'That was useless, I could do better than that,' but appropriate to say, 'It seemed when you did… it had this effect… Perhaps you could have…' Be respectful and sensitive without pussyfooting; remember that feedback has a constructive purpose. Your intention is purely to help the other person in improving their application of skills.

Giving feedback
Here are ten useful points to bear in mind:

1 *Be clear in what you are trying to say.*
2 *Be non-judgemental. You're entitled to have your view of the other person or of their 'performance', but keep it in mind that your views are not facts but are coloured by your own perspective. The one receiving the feedback and other observers might have different views.*

3 *Address the person you are talking about directly as 'you' and use 'I' statements to own your thoughts, feelings and opinions. For example: 'I think that it was helpful when you summarized at that point' or 'I feel that it might have been more helpful to your client if you had stayed with the silence.' Using terms like 'most people' (e.g. 'Most people think that you asked too many direct questions') makes it difficult to decide if you are just repeating what you have heard from others.*

4 *Use neutral and objective words. Describe what you have observed or experienced rather than evaluating or interpreting. To say 'I noticed that you interrupted quite often when she was talking' is more helpful and acceptable to receive than 'Your ego gets in the way – you seem incapable of listening to material with an emotional content.'*

5 *Feedback is concerned with specific behaviour or effects, not the character of the recipient.*

6 *Try to be specific by identifying the words or behaviour that you are basing your feedback on.*

7 *Verbal and non-verbal messages need to be congruent. If they're at odds with each other, then you will be sending conflicting messages resulting in confusion. For example, if you say, 'I think this information will help you,' with a tight-lipped expression and avoiding eye contact, that will confuse the listener.*

8 *Feedback is concerned with specific behaviour that's under the individual's control to change. It would be ludicrous to tell someone, 'You haven't got an empathic face,' but it would be appropriate to say, 'As a counsellor, you look stern at times during your practice session.'*

9 *If the recipient of the feedback becomes defensive or emotional, it's advisable for the giver of the feedback to accept and deal with it rather than trying to reason with or convince the recipient.*

10 *The recipient deserves respect as a person and as a learner of new skills.*

Both 'negative' and 'positive' feedback are useful – don't forget to comment on what was done well. Giving positive feedback before negative feedback is considered a more acceptable approach.

An alternative is a feedback 'sandwich', consisting of first positive, then negative, then positive feedback.

Receiving feedback
Try to consider these points when receiving feedback:

▸ *Listen attentively, without commenting, until the person who is giving the feedback has finished.*
▸ *Try not to be defensive or to overreact to feedback. It's an opinion and is worth considering, but it's not gospel.*
▸ *Resist any temptation to defend, deny, apologize and so on.*
▸ *Check out anything you have heard that you're unsure of, repeat the comments and ask questions if you're unclear of the meaning.*
▸ *Evaluate the accuracy and potential value of what you've been offered.*
▸ *Decide yourself what's relevant and useful to your progress.*
▸ *Obtain additional information from as many other sources as are available to you, noting your own thoughts and feelings and how other people react to you.*

Giving and receiving feedback is part of working with other trainees and is integral to the personal growth element of acquiring counselling abilities.

Developing self-awareness

GROUPWORK

....

Insight

Groupwork can feel pretty unsafe at times as strong feelings are evoked. I recommend reading about group dynamics and processes before embarking on a course. It helps to be forewarned.

....

Working in groups is commonly used as a method of developing self-awareness and interpersonal skills. As we have seen, the small group is used in the development of supervision skills, offering feedback and insight relating to each other's work with clients. Other groupwork is concerned with personal development and group processes. The key word to sum up the purpose of groupwork is 'insight'. Experiencing oneself with and separate from others in a group is a learning process *par excellence*, likely to stir up complex, ambivalent, primary feelings such as rivalry between members, a need to merge with others, a need to assert one's own individuality, projections on to others (what can't be personally owned) and fantasies about self and other group members.

The facilitator or conductor offers interpretations of content and feelings of the group, addressing the following aspects:

- ▶ *Group regressions – infantile expression, e.g. sibling rivalry.*
- ▶ *Repetitive conflict situations – often between two or three members of the group who 'act out' for others.*
- ▶ *Sub-grouping – forming smaller groups to make the environment safer.*
- ▶ *Scapegoating – one or two people represent 'bad' elements of the group (dangers) that cannot be individually acknowledged or divulged.*
- ▶ *Long silences – withholding, withdrawing mechanisms, unwillingness to take risks.*
- ▶ *Defence and coping mechanisms – e.g. shutting off, playing safe, intellectualizing.*
- ▶ *Fantasies – about self and others related to early experiences; e.g. 'If I say what I think/feel then I'll be destroyed', 'I'm the leader of the group', 'The facilitator is attracted to me/disapproves of me.'*

The facilitators might intervene with an interpretation if they feel that anxiety levels are becoming destructive, that participants are missing the point or the process is in a 'stuck' mode, saying, 'I wonder if what's happening here is…' or 'Perhaps it's too painful for the group to acknowledge…'

Groupwork might be an integration of humanistic, psychoanalytic and cognitive behaviour modes of relating and reflecting social/political patterns. For example, when the directive, given by the facilitator, is that the group is not therapeutic and is focusing in the 'here and now', strong **defence mechanisms** will come into play and might be interpreted by the facilitator in terms of Oedipal conflicts, rivalry, projections, denial, or an impulse to symbolically 'kill off', integrate, or oppress another in the group. Generally, interpretative comments are addressed to the group as a whole but they're addressed to individuals when the facilitator feels it would serve a positive purpose – perhaps in order to take the heat out of a situation or to challenge the person's behaviour or attitudes.

Positive experiences from groupwork

- *Participants feel valued by others.*
- *Participants feel supported by others. They give and receive mirroring.*
- *Members engage in a process of identification and empathy to help them resolve their own conflicts.*
- *Deeper levels of communication are reached – in a therapeutic context, things that couldn't be communicated previously can not be shared.*
- *Builds trust, confidence, affirmation of self.*
- *Helps individuals to re-own 'split off' parts of themselves.*
- *Stronger understanding of self in relation to others.*
- *Understanding of unconscious processes of groups and social situations.*

The group matrix

The concept of the group matrix has evolved as a symbol of the way individual mental processes form a communication and interactional network with others.

In the 1950s and 1960s Siegfried H. Foulkes was a consultant in psychiatry, psychoanalysis and group analysis in Great Britain and the USA. In *Therapeutic Group Analysis*, he describes the group matrix as: 'The hypothetical web of communication and relationship in a given group... the common shared ground which ultimately determines the meaning and significance of all events, and upon which all communications and interpretations, verbal and non-verbal, rest.'

The matrix has also been described as an interpersonal, intrapsychical and transpersonal web – invisible channels of communication that hold both positive and negative potential for the group.

In *Practical Use of Dream Analysis*, Carl Jung described the matrix as a symbol of the mother: 'the mother as matrix, the hollow form, the vessel that carries and nourishes, and thus stands psychologically for the foundation of consciousness.'

The 'hypothetical web of communication and relationship' corresponds to the beliefs of ancient religions and traditions that what an individual thinks or feels affects others as individuals of the group and the group dynamic as a whole (see Figure 6.1).

Each matrix pattern is unique to the particular group, fed by each individual's experiencing and what they bring to the group from their past. The foundation matrix is what we bring from our own social network, including our belief systems, culture and ways of interacting.

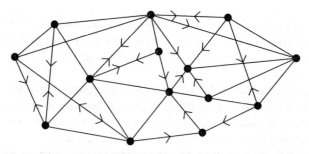

Figure 6.1 The matrix represents a web of transpersonal, interpersonal and intrapsychical relationships.

The individual can be seen as a nodal point (represented by dots) in the group. The lines and arrows represent the interaction between all individual members of the group.

Insight

Basically, groupwork demonstrates how we are connected in subtle ways that we are usually unaware of and how the energy or psyche of individuals affects the group as a whole, from moment to moment. It's perhaps more positive to think of the dynamic being like an Elizabethan-type dance (with its, coming together, seperating, circling, and intertwining movement) as opposed to the chaotic interface of insecure egos.

Supervision

During training the trainee is given supervision by either a course tutor or an outside supervisor (i.e. someone who comes in to carry out the task). Peer supervision is often a feature of diploma-level courses, where the trainees learn the skills of supervision by observing the tutor at work and by practising under the watchful eye and listening ear of the tutor/supervisor.

Supervision always plays an important, supportive part of a counsellor's work. It's a 'sounding board', a safety net and a method of learning from a therapist who usually has more training and experience than the counsellors they're supervising.

THE ROLE OF THE SUPERVISOR

Proficient supervision gives the trainee counsellor room to 'move around' the client, helping them to understand the client from different angles. The following are ways the supervisor assists:

▶ *As a safety net for the counsellor they offer support and protection.*
▶ *As a third party they offer another perspective – a new insight, the 'aha' factor. The supervisor might, for example, use symbolism or imagery to extend understanding.*
▶ *To help the counsellor explore transference and countertransference.*
▶ *To monitor the counsellor's work – e.g. check that they're working in an appropriate way with the client (that is, within*

ethical standards), including an exploration of theory and techniques being used.

▶ *As 'outside' observers they can see blind spots and help the counsellor to explore 'stuckness'.*

▶ *To explore the client-counsellor relationship – 'the working alliance'.*

▶ *To help with planning and structuring – questions such as 'Where are you going with this?' assist in clarification.*

Insight

Supervision is another area where trainees can feel not good enough. Above all, focus on it as an opportunity to explore your work and learn from others, just as they will from you.

Safety net

The supervisor bears a lot of responsibility. They can be contacted by the counsellor if there are any major problems with a client that can't wait until the next supervision session; for example, in the case of a disclosure concerning abuse, which either directly affects the client or poses a danger to another person, or if a client talks about suicidal intention. A supervisor needs to be au fait with the legal obligations and requirements of certain situations and the policies and procedures of the agencies or institutions they work within. They're in a position to give advice and information to the counsellor if or when it's required. Supervision is highly skilled and those in supervisory roles are usually required to have specialist training to be accredited by a professional association. Supervisors have usually had many years' experience as practising therapists.

As a third party the supervisor gets to know the client via the counsellor – through the information that the client has given the counsellor, the content of the session and the counsellor's sense of the client's inner world. The supervisor doesn't usually come into direct contact with the client. Primarily the supervisor's work is to help the counsellor to focus, explore and reflect on client–counsellor issues. In order to do this the supervisor needs information about:

▶ *The setting – where the counsellor works, contracts, number of sessions offered, frequency of sessions.*

- *The client – background details, history to help build a picture, e.g. medical problems, family details.*
- *Presenting problems – the client's reasons for coming to counselling.*
- *Issues – what needs dealing with, what is happening, what is the most important issue at the moment.*
- *Process – how is it moving forward, any changes, new focus.*
- *Theory – what theories/theoretical models are being referred to.*
- *Issues for supervision – what does the counsellor want from supervision.*

It's a requirement of professional associations that to qualify for accreditation, a counsellor must have regular supervision from an appropriately qualified supervisor. (Supervisors check that counsellors work within a code of ethics and code of practice.) The association will stipulate the ratio of hours of counselling to hours spent with a supervisor (e.g. four hours or four 50-minute sessions of counselling require one hour of supervision). Professional associations are very helpful with enquiries and are often an excellent source of information and resources.

GROUP SUPERVISION

Group supervision is sometimes a practical option for small agencies and is a common component of training courses. Peer supervision means a small group of counsellor trainees acting as supervisors for each other, usually with a tutor as the main supervisor and overseer of proceedings. Client casework is presented in the session and the trainee counsellor who's presenting client material in supervision gives the other members of the group written relevant details, including: agency setting, contract, client details (the client's real identity is protected by using their initials only or a pseudonym), history, family relationships, presenting problems, current issues, what's happening in the counselling process and theory referred to. A genealogical chart is sometimes included in the notes for easy reference. The trainee also gives an informal oral presentation of the client's case. When they've finished talking through the case history of the client to the others, the other members then give their contribution, taking a supervisory role. This includes asking questions to help clarify details, challenging and offering observations with regard to relational elements, transference issues or incongruences in the presentation.

TRANSFERENCE AND COUNTERTRANSFERENCE IN SUPERVISION

The feelings of both client and counsellor are exposed through transferential material. The supervisor might say something like, 'It sounds as if he is looking for mothering in you. How does that make you feel?' or might home in on the countertransference, using imagery to describe the counsellor: 'I see you flapping about like a mother hen, anxious about her little chick.' The purpose of making these sorts of observations is to offer the counsellor new insights; for example, into how the client is experiencing the counsellor in the transference, the client's feelings and behaviour and meanings, and the effects the client is having on the counsellor and the work. (See Chapter 7, section 1 for more details.)

Parallel process
An interesting dimension of transference is the parallel process – what's happening in the client–counsellor relationship is likely at times to be echoed in the counsellor–supervisor relationship. For example, using the simple illustration above, the counsellor might feel exasperated, frustrated or angry with the supervisor and the supervisor, observing this development, might point this out and say: 'I sense that you're getting frustrated and angry with me as if I'm not giving you something. Maybe you would like reassurance and nurturing from me... a bit like your client?' The supervisor might withhold the words 'like your client', seeing if the counsellor makes the connection, or might be more explicit: 'You would like me to mother you.' (A supervisor of either sex could say this since 'mothering' in therapeutic terms means 'nurturing and caring for'). The parallel process is an 'acting out' of the client or counsellor material and is a very useful tool for understanding what is happening in the 'here and now' of a client session in relation to the 'here and now' of the counsellor–supervisor session.

There's likely to be counsellor–supervisor transference and countertransference. For example, the counsellor could experience the supervisor as a critical parent (negative transference) or 'nurturing mother' (positive transference). The supervisor will be aware of the likelihood of corresponding countertransference reactions. Projection could also become an issue to work through. The counsellor who doubts their abilities as a counsellor might project dubious attributes of an 'authority figure' on to the supervisor, seeing the supervisor as tyrannical or a 'know it all'; or in the positive (but equally unreal) see the supervisor as a 'guru', 'seer' or omnipotent.

It may be helpful at this point to recap on the difference between projection and transference:

▶ **Projection** *involves thoughts and feelings that can't be acknowledged as the person's own, and are therefore attributed 'safely' to someone else. The threatening aspect of the self could be an 'authority figure' or the one who likes to think they 'know-it-all' (as illustrated earlier, projected on to the supervisor).*
▶ **Transference** *is when a person displaces or 'transfers' an emotion or affective attitude that belongs to a person and relationship from the past (usually a parent), or near present, on to a person in the present (e.g. the therapist in the here-and-now relationship).*

Theory and practice

Insight

The study and application of theory can feel quite daunting (as counselling courses have become more academic), but, I believe, if we have a genuine interest in a subject then we assimilate the information without a lot of effort. Think of all those young lads who have never excelled academically yet can tell you the names and clubs of every footballer on the planet. I rest my case.

Part of the training will concentrate on the theoretical underpinnings, concepts, beliefs and aims of various approaches concerned with counselling. Developmental psychology, group theory and dynamics, mental health issues, ethics in counselling, bereavement, child abuse, aspects of sociology (class, race and cultural issues and gender issues) are all probable additional topics. Lengthy booklists are given out. The student needs to know and understand theory as well as how to apply it.

With this in mind, theory periods usually involve lectures given by tutors, followed by questions and forms of practice, such as small group discussion, brainstorming or exchanges of ideas and experiences (at times writing these down on flipchart paper). For instance, following a lecture on gender issues a large group of 20 or more trainees might be asked by a tutor to form smaller groups containing four people in each, providing a 'safer', more intimate environment to address questions for discussion; for example: 'Think back to when you first became aware of gender roles. Was it a positive or negative experience? What happened? How did you feel? How has that experience influenced your feelings and attitudes towards the opposite sex?' The members of the group talk to each other about their experiences and the effects for a period of time (possibly 20 minutes). At the end of the discussion, the large group reforms and a representative from each small group in turn relates the salient points of what has been said. The tutor might write some of these on a flipchart for further discussion.

This kind of exercise develops self-awareness, crucial to counselling other people. Knowledge of theory and how the trainee is applying it is also explored within supervision sessions and in assignments.

Personal therapy

> **Insight**
> Personal therapy can be costly but some experienced practitioners will reduce their fees for trainees. Don't forget to add personal therapy costs to your overall training costs.

Personal therapy is also commonly a compulsory element of the training of a professional counsellor. Personal therapy enhances understanding by:

▶ *Developing an ability to separate own material from that of the client – i.e. dealing with unresolved personal conflicts.*
▶ *Learning from the counsellor/therapist subliminally, taking in how they are working/relating.*
▶ *Being a client, building an understanding of what it feels like to be a client – e.g. vulnerable, apprehensive, dependent, trusting.*
▶ *Giving experience of the processes and the stages of counselling – e.g. beginnings, endings, transference, resistance.*
▶ *Deepening self-understanding of own personal issues, making links with childhood experiences and 'stuck' patterns of relating to others, through transference, exploring personal defences, resistances.*

Exams and ongoing assessment

It's worth considering what methods are used to assess learning on a course that interests you. Some people find exams a terrible pressure, while others prefer them to extensive ongoing assessments. Written theory-based exams may be set at the end of each year. Some courses are more academic than others; some require the implementation of research methods, for example. Most commonly, testing procedures involve skills observation, written assignments, peer, tutor and self-assessments, and written exams or vivas.

VIVAS

A viva usually combines oral and written elements, an audio or video recording accompanied by a verbatim transcript of a section of the recorded session. Typically a viva will take the form of questions and discussion around the presented case material. Usually the counsellor in training makes, with the permission of the client – and, when working with an agency, the agency's approval – a few recordings of a counselling session and one recording is chosen for the viva presentation. The recording doesn't have to be technically perfect but is chosen to reflect use of theory, skills, awareness of the counselling process and so on. The following criteria are taken from a university professional diploma course in counselling.

Viva case study presentation example

To complete this assignment you must:

1 *Provide a tape recording (audio or video) of one counselling session with a client.*
2 *Provide a verbatim transcript of a five-minute section of the same counselling interview.*
3 *Complete the attached case study pro forma making reference where possible to the transcript provided.*
4 *Submit two copies of each of the above for assessment by the date stated. These three elements will then form the basis of a discussion between yourself and two assessors. Each case discussion will last approximately 45 minutes and will take place in the supervision group slot.*

Levels to explore:

1 *An overview of the whole work with client to date.*
2 *The work of the presented session.*
3 *What is happening during the five-minute transcribe.*
4 *General reflection on your own practice.*

Criteria for assessment:

1 *Competency/skills – evidence that the student has acted in a caring and skilled way in all dealings with clients. This will include indicators of core process skills (genuineness, warmth, empathy), ability to manage boundaries of time and space, and evidence of maintaining a sound working alliance with the client.*
2 *Professional issues – evidence that the student has maintained personal boundaries and professional standards. Demonstration*

of a clear awareness and practice in relation to ethical issues, including confidentiality.

3 *Use of theory* – evidence that the student understands the relationship between theory and practice in their work.

4 *Integration* – where differing approaches have been used, evidence that this integration (or eclecticism) has been thought through.

5 *Personal awareness* – evidence that students are aware of and able to cope with their own process within the counselling relationship. Evidence that students make appropriate use of personal therapy where personal issues are raised in the counselling relationship.

6 *Supervision* – evidence that students have made appropriate use of supervision to help them work more effectively with clients.

7 *Self-assessment* – evidence that the student has a realistic appraisal of their own involvement and effectiveness within the counselling relationship.

OTHER METHODS OF ASSESSMENT

Insight

Ongoing assessment, assignments and dissertations can be every bit as stressful as exams, so it is wise to try and pace yourself by planning and sticking to a timetable of work and not trying to cram everything at the last minute as some of us (myself included) tend to do.

An educational institution uses assessment to gauge if an individual has reached the necessary standard in the work, either to move on to the next stage or for the attainment of an award. Assessments are both summative, to assess the point a student has reached, and formative, helping in the development of an allotted task or goal. Assessment is an ongoing process where tutors, in a teaching role or as facilitators, are continually observing and noting the trainee's work in various learning situations; for example, via role play or using personal issues in skills practice, in supervision groups, personal development groups or interpersonal groups, and in the contributions made in theory, learning and discussions. It's common practice to use a combination of tutor, peer and self-assessment at a culmination point of learning skills or theory. For example, the first year of a counselling training course might concentrate on skills practice, and at the end of the year students are assessed on their level of competence in using the skills. Feedback is usually given both orally and in written form. Peer assessments of an individual's ability to use various skills will be based on observation of the person counselling others and the personal experience of being counselled by the candidate in the triad format of skills practice. The individual student might also be asked to assess their own abilities, highlighting strong and weaker aspects of what they have learned.

Written assignments are another method used by tutors/trainers to assess the learning of skills and theoretical perspectives. In academic settings and in training institutes alike, students are usually asked to produce a minimum of two or three essays per year, of 2,000–3,000 words, and a dissertation or project at the end of the last year of the course. The student is most likely to be asked to choose a topic for the dissertation that reflects the learning accumulated from the course and that has relevance for their client group. For people who haven't studied for quite some time and aren't used to planning and compiling a critical piece of written work, there are many self-help study books on the market that contain study tips, including various methods of structuring and planning essay assignments, and also exam strategies. Many colleges, universities and training institutes produce study starter packs or booklets to help the rusty student, with guidelines on how to organize study time, use libraries, plan workload, make lecture notes, read effectively, find relevant information, take notes from literature, write essays and reports and compile a bibliography.

Integrationism

Rather than describe themselves as counsellors who follow a single approach – humanistic, psychodynamic and so on – many practitioners describe the way they work as 'eclectic' or 'integrationist', meaning that they work with a combination of approaches. The term **eclecticism** is used to describe the selection of what the counsellor considers to be the most appropriate ideas and techniques from an array of theories or models, particular to the client's needs at the time. In **integrationism** a new model emerges by bringing elements of different theories and models together in a complementary fusion. In the 1950s, when humanistic views were coming to the fore, comparisons were made with other approaches, looking for meeting points and divergences. John McLeod concedes in *An Introduction to Counselling* that it would be difficult to define a 'pure theory': 'All theorists are influenced by what has gone before. Freudian ideas can be seen as representing a creative integration of concepts from philosophy, medicine, biology and literature.'

Many counsellors who initially trained in one approach extend their therapeutic repertoire by incorporating ideas and skills from other approaches. Let me clarify this with an illustration from my own work.

Example of integrationism

My own initial training (a certificated one-year foundational course) followed the psychodynamic model of working with unconscious processes: resistance, denial and transference. The 'blank screen' approach was encouraged, whereby we allowed the client to project their fantasies, projections and anxieties, also allowing an 'optimal frustration' (see Chapter 8) – all to help the client recall, re-experience and finally expunge disturbance through (cathartic) emotional release. This was all very well in theory, but it led to a constant source of discussion between counsellors, allowing the airing of opposing opinions.

I was among the counsellors who felt that, since the client group we were working with was 14 to 25-year-olds and many of them had experienced problems with institutionalized systems (e.g. education, the law) and abusive relationships with adults,

(Contd)

to present counsellors as detached and clinical people was counterproductive in many cases. For example, one of the bones of contention was how to greet the client. The 'blank screen', abstinent approach dictates that the counsellor waits for the client to proceed with what is uppermost in their mind – that they are released from having to begin with distracting social niceties or following the counsellor's agenda. It was very apparent that, at times, the young people experienced the lack of welcome as coldness, 'expert' aloofness or even hostility, reinforcing the client's negative view of themselves in relation to others. The general consensus was that while an abstinent approach can be useful for the client, it's unlikely to be so at the onset of therapy when the client is unsure of the surroundings, is embarking on a new psychological relationship with the counsellor, and is troubled and feeling vulnerable. For this reason person-centred skills and values were introduced.

In the early stages it's important to establish a working alliance, with counsellor–client rapport, and if a counsellor is able to convey empathic understanding, warmth and acceptance then the client is more likely to relax and place trust in both the counsellor and the counselling process.

Insight

The majority of clients are nervous in the first one or two sessions and I believe that some extended warmth from the counsellor is crucial at this point and may mean the difference between the client staying with the counselling or deciding they can't hack it and not coming back. This is possibly most true of people with anger problems or low self-esteem and those who are feeling particularly vulnerable.

Person-centred core values are integrated into many approaches as a way of addressing these initial difficulties and establishing trust. Many counsellors working primarily with other approaches concentrate on these at certain times in the therapy; for example, at the beginning and end. While systematic training in integrative therapy has been established and is commonly adopted in both academic settings and training institutes, some practitioners oppose the appropriation of parts of approaches (i.e. eclecticism), regarding it as a chaotic hotchpotch of ideas and theories with no clear, consistent rationale. Practitioners who use an eclectic approach sometimes say that they use their intuition to inform them about what would benefit the client at any given time; for example, suggesting visualization at one time and goals as strategies at another. The ability to be flexible and to use elements of different approaches spontaneously and effectively depends on a counsellor's broad-based knowledge of a range of theories and skills and the ability to use these with competence. Arguably it's an almost impossible standard to achieve.

Eclecticism can be problematic in relation to supervision and training because the individual's methods of working can be highly idiosyncratic and difficult to match. The process of training or supervising another therapist's work depends on a mutuality of terminology, meaning and understanding. A psychoanalytic or psychodynamic supervisor or therapist therefore best understands a counsellor working in the psychodynamic approach. The risk a counsellor takes in following an eclectic pattern of relating to a client's needs is that they become a 'Jack of all trades and master/mistress of none'. Many therapists argue in favour of 'theoretical purity', believing that working in depth with one approach is the most effective method. In contrast, therapists like Michael Khan (in *Between Therapists and Client: The New Relationship*) have shown how two fundamentally different approaches, such as humanistic psychology and contemporary psychoanalysis, can be synthesized to enhance the client–therapist relationship.

MODALITIES OF RELATIONSHIP

Another method of integrating different ideas, techniques and theories is working with an understanding of relationship modalities, as proposed by the psychotherapist and writer Petruska Clarkson. In *The Therapeutic Relationship* she identifies five relationship modalities that are useful in the psychotherapeutic client–therapist relationship. These are: the Working Alliance; the Transferential/Counter Transferential Relationship; the

Reparative/Developmentally Needed Relationship; the I–You Relationship; and the Transpersonal Relationship. Clarkson believes that these relationship modalities, as a way of relating across the different approaches, are always potentially present in the exchange.

Professional considerations

Towards the end of your course, as you focus on the professional work you might undertake, your attention could be drawn once more to ethical issues and practice. National professional organizations publish copies of their code of ethics and practice for counsellors, which provide a guideline for professional use. A code of ethics is likely to encompass values, responsibility, anti-discriminatory practice, confidentiality, contracts, boundaries and competence. Members of professional associations are required to abide by existing codes that provide a common frame of reference; they clarify counsellor's responsibilities towards clients, colleagues and the community at large.

A code of ethics is translated into a code of practice that applies guideline principles to the counselling situation. The code of practice is likely to be concerned with issues including: client safety, counsellor responsibility and accountability, clear contracting and counsellor competence. Professional indemnity insurance, recommended by professional associations, is another safeguard to be considered. It's worth noting that while counselling for an agency the counsellor is offered protection under the agency's insurance cover. Working to ethical standards, acquiring insurance and having adequate supervision become fully the responsibility of the counsellor when they practise privately.

Another consideration, at the conclusion of a course, is further follow-up training; for example, in a specialist area such as family therapy, or in supervision and training, or in attaining a higher level of qualification such as a Masters degree or PhD.

THINGS TO REMEMBER

1 *Counselling came to prominence in the Western world in the 1960s. In the 1950s many psychoanalysts and their contemporaries experimented with new, more relaxed ways of working with their patients.*

2 *Courses in counselling vary greatly in length and depth and you will need to do some research. The internet, personal recommendation, reading around the subject and collecting prospectuses from training agencies and educational establishments are ways to help you choose a course suited to your requirements.*

3 *Some counselling courses, especially at diploma level and upwards, have become highly academic. While some of us enjoy academia, others don't, so it's wise to look at the academic level of courses and their assessment criteria before you choose your course.*

4 *During training you will work with other trainees practising skills, participating in supervision and other personal development type groups and you are likely to be required to have personal therapy for the duration.*

5 *Courses are matched to the level of involvement in counselling trainees choose. For example, training at diploma level is usually geared to a professional level of counselling work. Some courses are accredited by counselling associations such as BACP because they meet their standards, code of ethics and practice for training.*

7

....

The three major approaches

In this chapter you will learn:
- *about the psychodynamic approach to counselling*
- *about the person-centred approach to counselling*
- *about the cognitive behavioural approach to counselling*
- *about the therapeutic relationship and the aims of therapy in these three main approaches.*

The psychoanalytic, humanistic and behavioural models of therapy form the foundations of all other orientations of psychotherapy. In counselling, the psychoanalytical approach is represented by the psychodynamic models. Humanistic approaches include person-centred therapy, Gestalt therapy and transactional analysis. The behavioural approaches include cognitive behavioural therapy and rational emotive therapy (RET). Although the core approaches are fundamentally different – the psychodynamic places emphasis on unconscious processes and transference; the humanistic on the congruent relationship between client and counsellor and the concept of self-actualization; and the behavioural focuses on monitoring and changing the individual's thoughts and behaviour – they have proved that they can be complementary to each other. Many counselling training courses integrate elements of all three.

The aim of this chapter is to give you a sense rather than an in-depth exploration of the three main approaches by outlining the theories, concepts and techniques particular to each.

Section 1:
The psychoanalytic/psychodynamic approach

Origins

The psychodynamic approach has direct links with Freudian psychoanalysis. Sigmund Freud's theories (see Ruth Snowden's *Freud–The Key Ideas*) have been developed, modified and adapted by different strands of psychodynamic theorists. Many of Freud's original concepts remain central to this approach: for example, his theories of the unconscious, transference and countertransference; the importance of formative childhood experiences and relationships; and the use of dreams and metaphor as means of understanding the human psyche. These are among the tools used in the work of the psychodynamic counsellor. We can understand the term 'psychodynamic' by dividing it into its two parts. The first part derives from the Greek root word *psyche* and, in relation to therapy, refers to the tripart combination of the mind, emotions and spirit or soul. The word 'dynamic' refers to the constant interaction and movement between these three forces both internally (within ourselves) and externally in relation to other people and our environment.

Insight

Psychodynamic counselling concentrates on unearthing deep-rooted experiences (often relating to childhood) that have led to the client armouring themselves with *defences* which continue to affect them negatively in the present. Sometimes I think that psychodynamic work is akin to detective work, working with clues (the defences), evidence (the way, for example, the client transfers feelings from other significant people from their past on to the counsellor) and hunches (the psychodynamic counsellor does a lot of interpreting of client issues).

The unconscious

Freud was fascinated by material that he believed lay hidden in the human psyche. He identified three categories of mental process:

1 *The conscious – material (facts, feelings and thoughts) that the patient is aware of in the present.*
2 *The preconscious – material (ideas and memories) that are not conscious but are easily accessed.*
3 *The unconscious – material (desires or impulses) that lie hidden, buried from the conscious mind.*

Freud later identified three driving forces of the mind.

THE ID (IT)

The **Id** is the part of the unconscious mind that contains the instinctual drives and impulses that motivate our behaviour. The primitive impulses driven by our instinctual needs are at odds with the Ego and the Superego. Both of these parts of the unconscious temper the basic drives of the Id. We might, for example, take a strong dislike towards someone; the Id would tell us to harm them or get rid of them in some way while the other parts of our unconscious mind would apply reasoning to the situation. The Id can be thought of as the child part of the unconscious. Becuase it forms the underlying motivations and drives of our actions, it's our spontaneous 'dangerous' side that wishes to follow the 'pleasure principle'. The Id might say: 'This is what I want, what I really really want.'

The Id has two main driving forces:

▶ *Eros – the life-affirming drive of love and sexuality.*
▶ *Thanatos – the drive towards death and destruction.*

THE EGO (I)

The **Ego** is the rational, partly conscious part of the mind that makes decisions and copes with the external world.

The Ego says: 'I am, I can and I will.' The Ego can be related to the more grown-up side of our mind; it takes care of us, telling us we are doing OK. The Ego facilitates mediation with others and adaptation to our environment.

THE SUPEREGO (HIGHER I)

The **Superego** is the 'conscientious' side of our mind. It contains internalized societal and parental rules and taboos. As we take these into our unconscious mind the taboos are translated into 'I should', 'I ought' and 'I must'. The Superego is the source of guilt and ideals. Both the Superego and the Id are largely unconscious.

The role of the analyst was to assist the patient (as they were then termed) in translating unconscious material into conscious understanding. Using hypnosis in treatment, Freud's attention was drawn to the workings of the unconscious mind. An aim was to give the patient insight into areas of their psyche where they had 'stored' an experience that had been too painful or threatening for them to acknowledge fully at the time. These remained in the unconscious mind as repressed memories, causing disturbance in the patient's vital functioning. Freud believed that when patients were freed of these experiences, and the accompanying emotions that debilitated them, they would be more in control of their emotions and be happier.

Freud considered that the source of neuroses could always be traced back to early childhood, although the symptoms of the neurotic conflict could manifest at a later stage. 'Neurosis' (or disturbance), lying dormant in the unconscious mind, could cause strong irrational reactions in later life. An example of this is demonstrated in our anxious responses towards other people. Let's look at an example by briefly sketching a case history.

Case study 3

A young man, in his late twenties, has come to counselling because he's feeling depressed and unable to cope with work. It began when

(Contd)

CASE STUDY

a woman joined his team at work as his manager. He took an instant dislike to her. She continued to trigger very strong feelings in him and he's at a loss to understand why. He's aware that his reactions to the woman are ruining his work life and the strong discontent that he's experiencing is permeating other areas of his life. Eventually, through therapy, he can locate the source of his prejudice towards his female boss. He's been talking about his hostile feelings towards his colleague over a number of sessions and some of the themes the counsellor has put together relate to different expressions of fear – for example, loss of control, sudden anger and feeling threatened by an unspecified source. He's also mentioned that he finds it difficult to form words coherently in her presence. The counsellor notes the 'infantizing' effect this woman appears to have on him and asks him if his colleague reminds him of anyone. He smiles and says that she physically resembles a woman who looked after him when he was a child, when his mother went out to work. When he spent time with her in her home, he experienced the woman as mainly indifferent but sometimes hostile towards him. She forced him to eat foods he disliked to the point of vomiting and made him sleep during the day, which his mother seldom did. He felt frightened and humiliated by her. He also reveals that he associated the woman with separation from his mother and feeling helpless and abandoned. This insight proves to be useful to the client, enabling him to see his colleague separately from the 'bad woman' image he had been unconsciously holding.

Freud noted that people repeatedly replay difficult or troubling relationships and situations that were originally experienced in the early years of life. The individual will have the 'compulsion to repeat' the unresolved material, until the unconscious element is brought into consciousness.

Insight

Although many of Freud's theories have been modified and developed over the years, his work still informs modern psychology. For example, I am likely to consider his ideas on transference and client defences in my everyday work, as are most counsellors I know.

Developmental psychology

Psychodynamic theories regard the child's early environment as important and for this reason a psychodynamic training involves the study of developmental psychology. Psychoanalysts, beginning with Freud himself, have formed theories of human developmental stages.

THE DEVELOPMENTAL STAGES DELINEATED BY SIGMUND FREUD

The early writings of Freud divide the human developmental stages into three: oral, anal and sexual.

1 *Oral, 0–2 years: At this stage the infant experiences pleasure through the mouth, mainly through gratification from sucking, so toys and other objects are put into the mouth and 'felt' by the mouth.*
2 *Anal, 2–4 years: At this stage of development the child takes a sensual interest in their own faeces, experiencing a gratification in a substance that they produce. This can result in the child experimenting with smearing or eating or withholding faeces as a means of control.*
3 *Phallic, 4–7 years: The Superego develops within this age range as the focus of interest moves from the anus to the genitals as a focus of gratification. The parents become models for role identification. The Oedipus complex occurs during the phallic stage.*

The Oedipus complex
The term **Oedipus complex** derives its name from the mythical (Greek) figure of Oedipus, who unwittingly killed his father and married his mother. The Oedipus complex is a collection of unconscious desires to 'possess' the parent of the opposite sex and 'eliminate' the parent of the same sex. The Oedipal stage occurs between the ages of three and six and, according to traditional Freudian views, is a universal component of development.

Freud said, 'A child's first choice of an object is an incestuous one' and 'Incestuous wishes are a primordial human heritage. The Oedipal complex (phallic stage) is the central phenomenon of the sexual period of early childhood.' With its dissolution, it submits to repression and is followed by what Freud called the **latency period**. Disintegration occurs for a number of reasons, due to disappointments growing out of the hopeless longing for the parent who is fixated upon, or to a castration anxiety. Castration enters the boy child's imagination when he first views the genital region of the female child, noting the absence of a penis. The boy then believes that all women, including his mother, have been castrated.

The child's Ego turns from the Oedipus complex, replacing object cathexes (i.e. the investing of his libidinal sexual energy in the parent) with other identifications. The father's authority is at this time introjected into the Ego and forms the centre of the Superego. The position appropriates the prohibition against incest and rescues the Ego from the libidinal object cathexes. The Oedipus complex is thereby 'desexualised and sublimated', and the latency period begins.

The Electra complex

The girl child also develops an Oedipus complex, which Freud initially termed the **Electra complex**. The girl's clitoris acts as a penis until she becomes aware that she has no penis and considers herself inferior, which results in 'penis envy'. At first she understands the lack as temporary, consoling herself with the belief that as she grows older she will acquire a penis; later, instead of making the connection between her lack of penis and sexual completion, she presumes castration has occurred. Freud wrote, 'The essential difference thus comes about that the girl accepts castration as an accomplished fact whereas the boy fears the possibility of its occurrence.'

The girl's Oedipus complex is a modified version of that of the boy, basically consisting of the girl's wish to take her mother's position in her father's affection and adopt a feminine attitude towards him. She attempts to compensate for the loss of a penis by desiring 'the gift' of bearing her father's child. The resolution of the Oedipus complex occurs because the wish remains unfulfilled. However, according to

Freud, the two desires – to have a penis and a child – remain in the unconscious, preparing the female for her later sexual role.

Latency stage

The latency stage is from six to puberty. The process that led to the dissolution of the Oedipus complex has saved the penis, but because its function has been compromised the latency period begins, interrupting the child's sexual development. Freud believed that if the Ego has repressed the complex, then the complex will persist in the unconscious within the Id and is likely, at some time, to result in 'pathogenic effect' (disturbance or disease). The genital stage, from puberty to adulthood, follows the latency stage.

ERIK ERIKSON'S EIGHT AGES OF MAN – STAGES OF PSYCHOSOCIAL DEVELOPMENT

Erik Erikson's personality theory places emphasis on the workings of the Ego, rather than concentrating on the unconscious drives of the Id as Freud had. Erikson was a Freudian psychoanalyst whose work extended Freud's stages of development, placing psychological development in a social and historical context. He suggested that, while the foundations of the individual's personality take form in the first two years of life, the personality is constantly developing, characterized by different stages (illustrated by Figure 7.1). Successful development from one stage to the next depends on the resolution of the central task or conflict particular to the stage. These tasks are culturally determined and therefore universal. In *Childhood and Society*, Erikson wrote: 'Each successful stage and crisis has a special relation to one of the basic elements of society, and this for the simple reason that the human life cycle and man's institutions have evolved together.'

The healthy personality combines individual happiness with social responsibility. Erikson believed that the quality of interpersonal relationships was all important, beginning with the infant–maternal relationship. He delineates eight stages of psychosocial continual development in his 'whole life' personality theory. (These are well worth reading in their full form and are offered here in a much abbreviated outline.)

Approximate Age	Stage	Conflict	Potential virtue gained	Societal manifestation
0–1	Infancy	Basic trust v. basic mistrust	Hope	Religion
2–3	Early childhood	Autonomy v. Shame and doubt	Will	Law and order
4–5	Play age	Initiative v. guilt	Purpose	Economics
6–11	School age	Inidustry v. inferiority	Competence	Technology
12–18	Adolescence	Identity v. role confusion	Fidelity	Ideology
20–35	Young adulthood	Intimacy v. isolation	Love	Ethics
35–50	Middle adulthood	Generativity v. stagnation	Care	Education, art and science
50 +	Maturity to old age	Ego integrity v. despair and disgust	Wisdom	All major cultural institutions

Figure 7.1 Erik Erikson's eight stages of psychosocial development.

Source: Erik Erikson, Childhood and Society.

Stage 1 – Basic trust v. basic mistrust

The early stage of infancy (0–1 years of age) is when trust patterns form, the relationship between infant and mother being the prototype. The first social achievement is when the infant is able to let the mother go out of sight without experiencing undue anxiety and rage. Bowel movements and teething are part of the infant's internal (bodily) experiencing and a dynamic is set into action between internal and external frames of reference, involving discomfort and loss. Basic trust wins over basic mistrust when the infant experiences the mother's consistency of provision. Erikson's sensory stage corresponds with Freud's oral stage. Religion is the social construct representing the infantile stage of basic trust. Absence of basic trust results in a continued stage of 'infantile schizophrenia' – a schizoid-depressive position. The basic requirement for therapy is working towards a re-establishment of a stage of trust. If the task to attain basic trust is successful, then hope is established.

Stage 2 – Autonomy v. shame and doubt

According to Erikson, at this stage (approximately 2–3 years old), muscular maturation allows experimentation with 'holding on' and 'letting go'. This muscular maturation stage corresponds to Freud's anal stage. A gradual learning is taking place; the young child has a growing sense of autonomy, experimenting with controlling and directing their behaviour. It's the immergence of the will. Alongside this is the potential to self-doubt since the child is aware of their own limitations. The child needs protecting with firm reassurance from the 'potential anarchy of his as yet untrained sense of discrimination'; otherwise the outcome is feelings of shame and doubt. This stage corresponds to the social constraints of law and order that, Erikson says, reflect 'the lasting need of the individual to have his will re-affirmed and delineated within an adult order of things.' Within these restrictions the child develops their sense of autonomy.

Stage 3 – Initiative v. guilt

The child (4–5 years of age) is developing new locomotor and mental powers, and the growing ability to both initiate and carry out actions can give rise to guilty feelings. This stage of increased locomotor power corresponds with Freud's genital stage, which contains the phallic and Oedipal conflicts. It's the 'play age'. Erikson trained in the Montessori method and he focused on child's play as a means of understanding child development. Increasingly the child, who is developing socially as well as physically, is faced with more responsibilities that bring the opportunity to develop a sense of initiative through decision making and action. The increasing responsibilities incurred by the new-found sense of purpose can bring about, Erikson suggests, 'a sense of guilt over the goals contemplated and the acts initiated in one's exuberant enjoyment of new locomotor and mental power'. The social expression of this is economics.

Stage 4 – Industry v. inferiority

The child is of school age (6–11 years old) when the task becomes one of industrious focusing and the trying out of new skills. The possibility of failure to do so could result in the child feeling a sense of inferiority in relation to the achievements of others. It's a time when the early stage of play becomes more technically focused and therefore the corresponding element is technology. The child is industrious, enjoying the tasks of learning when challenges can be met and a sense of competence achieved. However, failure to carry them out or avoidance of challenges can lead to a sense of inferiority, leading to further avoidances.

Stage 5 – Identity v. role confusion

Integration of a self-identity, that is the Ego identity, is the task of the young adolescent (12–18 years old). The developing youth's prime concern is how they appear to others in relation to their own self-concept. It's a time of emotional flux; a great physiological revolution takes place within and a new sexual identity is also developing. Adolescence produces many challenges, including asserting oneself within peer groups, making the transition from childhood to adulthood and making the transition from school to university or the workplace. It's also a time of idealism and the corresponding manifestation represented in society is ideology. The adolescent experiments in different ways in the quest of self-understanding. Although treated like adults, they're not as yet considered to be full members of society. Role confusion is the underside of successful development of identity. Questions like 'Who am I?' 'What have I to offer?' reflect existential angst. The alienation confusion about who they are can cause depression. A sense of identity or a consistent self-concept needs to be established. Fidelity is the potential virtue gained.

Stage 6 – Intimacy v. isolation

The young adult (20–35 years of age) is ready to fuse their identity with others. They're ready to meet the challenges of commitment to partnerships and 'concrete affiliations' by the development of an ethical strength. They're willing to make significant sacrifices and compromises in the quest for intimacy with others. The successful progression to achieving intimacy with others necessitates the fulfilling of the previous task of establishing self-identity or Ego strength. If the tasks of this stage remain unfulfilled and the conflicts unresolved, the result is a continuing sense of isolation and alienation from others. The societal manifestation of the conflicts presented in the intimacy versus isolation stage of development is the construction of ethics.

Stage 7 – Generativity v. stagnation

In middle adulthood (35–50) a person has (potentially) built a strong sense of identity and an ability to form intimate relationships with others, and the challenge of this stage involves engagement with productive activities – putting accumulated knowledge and life experiences to good use. This could take the form of encouraging the young in their endeavours, or the fruition and enjoyment of the individual's occupation and achievements. The conflicting danger is that the person becomes stuck in their ways and stagnates. The societal manifestation is education, art and science.

Stage 8 – Ego integrity v. despair and disgust

The final stage is maturity to old age (50+). The older person has wisdom to offer from a lifetime's experience. The early phase of this stage is preparation for old age, a gradual summing up of life's achievements and meanings. Declining health and vitality makes old age a reality. Retirement from work could bring on a sense of uselessness, despair and self-disgust, fear they no longer have anything to offer society or personal relationships. Approaching death, the individual can either feel at peace with their life experiences, appreciating the contributions they have made – knowing that they have done what they could (Ego integrity) – or view their lives as having been futile. The corresponding representation in society is major cultural institutions as a part of historical heritage.

Others who have contributed to developmental psychology and personality theories are Gordon Lowe, who also constructed a 'whole life' theory in *The Growth of Personality – from Infancy to Old Age*; Jean Piaget, whose concern was with a child's cognitive development; and the psychologist John Bowlby, who wrote studies of 'attachment behaviour' in relation to human psychological development.

JEAN PIAGET'S COGNITIVE DEVELOPMENTAL STAGES

The Swiss developmental psychologist Jean Piaget was one of the first to study cognitive development in children, focusing on the importance of sensorimotor (sensory and motor mechanisms) and ideomotor (putting ideas into action) learning – the young child's developing ability to translate their perceptions into actions, organizing their thoughts into a series of actions. Within the sensorimotor (0–2 years) stage the infant develops an ability to interact with their environment through the senses. In Piagetian theory the preoperatory stage of cognitive development (2–7 years) follows the sensorimotor stage. The preoperatory stage is offset by the child's 'object concept' of 'object permanence', when the child becomes aware that physical objects are permanent and exist as a separate entity without their involvement in interaction. It's also the time when the child learns the use of a 'system of symbols' – words and language to relate to the world around – but at this stage the child's thought is intuitive rather than logical. The concrete operatory stage or level (7–12 years) represents a leap in cognitive abilities involving the use of logic to solve problems. By now the child can differentiate between ways of communicating and can cope with concrete situations.

Abstract reasoning comes into play in the formal operator level of cognition development (12 years to adulthood). Piaget called it 'the metaphysical age *par excellence*'. In the preadolescent to adolescent stage of development the young person gradually exercises their 'autonomous reasoning' to test the rules of society with a view to finding personal meaning. Piaget identified a first morality as 'heteronomous' to describe rules that are sacred, external and unchangeable. A second 'autonomous' reality, which develops at preadolescent stage, wrestles with the heteronomous morality before replacing it.

JOHN BOWLBY'S ATTACHMENT THEORY

The psychoanalyst John Bowlby, whose work has its roots in Melanie Klein's child development theory, wrote extensively on the theme of attachment with regard to loss, sadness and depression. Bowlby wrote *Attachment and Loss*, a three-volume exploration of attachment behaviour from an object relations perspective, identifying the early human need to maintain close contact with a parent or another significant person. A healthy 'secure attachment' develops when the individual, as an infant and young child, has consistency of care and feels confident and secure in parental availability (mainly that of the mother), having experienced her for the main part to be responsive, loving and safe. An 'anxious attachment' forms when a child has inconsistent 'mothering' or the loss of maternal, parental figures or significant other (a carer). Bowlby wrote that one of the typical patterns of pathogenic parenting was 'discontinuities of parenting'. The early unsatisfactory prototypal attachment relationship can affect the ability to form healthy attachments to others in later life. In *The Making and Breaking of Affectional Bonds*, Bowlby wrote, 'There is a strong causal relationship between an individual's experiences with his parents and his later capacity to make affectional bonds.' He noted that insecure experiencing resulting from inconsistent or poor parenting, involving abandonment or loss, can lead a child or an adolescent to live in a constant state of anxiety, in the fear that they might lose their attachment figure. Anxious attachment can express itself in diverse ways, including anger, sadness and depression, and in difficulties in forming and maintaining relationships with other people.

Insight

I first came across the work of Erikson and Bowlby, and other developmental theorists, 15 years ago when I embarked on counselling training. As a practising counsellor I continue to refer to their work. Bowlby's attachment theory is informative in understanding people's insecurities in relationships and low-esteem issues and I also find Erikson's stages of psychosocial development useful when I'm working with people where age and life stage seem relevant to their problems.

OBJECT RELATIONS

The **object relations** theorists – Donald W. Winnicott, Ronald Fairbairn, Melanie Klein and others – also saw great significance in the child's first impression of the world. The object relations school moved away from the classical Freudian libidinal theories of instinctual pleasure-seeking drives, placing emphasis on human contact and relationships. The term 'object relations' refers to the central theme of the theory, which is that the baby's emotional well-being and development depends on certain relational needs being met. Melanie Klein, who's sometimes described as having bridged the gap between the object relations school and classic Freudian analysis, retained the idea of infantile instincts and drives as basic to the psyche, while introducing the concept of the infant as 'object seeking' as opposed to 'satisfaction seeking'. The infant's instinctive drive is both to survive and to satisfy their needs in relation to a loving, nurturing 'object' or person, usually the mother or a central figure.

The object relation theorists suggested that the mother's breast is an object of satisfaction and comfort that is not always available; therefore a 'transitional object' such as a dummy or a teddy bear is used as a temporary replacement. The 'good breast' and the 'bad breast' are terms used to describe the infant's impression of the breast as **part object** – as a potentially endless source of nourishment and pleasure it is a 'good object', and the frustrating breast that is taken away is a 'bad object'. Winnicott suggested that the child needs 'good enough mothering' – by which he meant a good enough facilitative environment to assist emotional and psychological development.

Klein, who regarded herself as a Freudian, believed that the first few weeks of a baby's life were significant. As a child analyst she used 'play analysis', using drawing and simple play materials and toys to help her understand the psychological world of the child. Winnicott also recommended that the counsellor let the client 'play' as a means of unravelling their story or rediscovering parts of themselves. Problems arise for the baby when the relating to the 'object' as mother or significant carer becomes fraught. This could be through environmental factors, or because of the mother's problems or any other circumstance that upsets the symbiotic relationship. When the relating is incomplete, elements will arise within therapy, through the transference relationship between therapist and client, where issues can be explored in a new and 'holding' environment.

Transference and countertransference

Transference was a term coined by Freud to describe a phenomenon he observed occurring between Josef Breuer, a colleague of Freud, and his patient Anna O., who became increasingly dependent on Breuer and fantasized that she was pregnant with his child. Freud was of the opinion that Anna (her real name was Bertha Pappenheim) had fallen in love with or become infatuated by her doctor, but that the manifest feelings really belonged to a relationship from her past and a resolution of the original disturbance would effect a 'cure'. In a paper entitled 'General Theory of the Neuroses' (1916–17) Freud wrote of transference as 'a newly created and transformed neurosis' that, within treatment, came to replace the original disturbance. He believed that the 'mastering' of the 'artificial neurosis', the transferred emotions, led to the elimination of the illness. However, Freud noticed that his colleague had also become rather involved with his patient, which led him to ponder whether Breuer's overt concern for Anna represented an unresolved conflict of his own. The reaction to client material by the therapist is the **countertransference**, and transference is appreciated as a complex interactional dynamic between the therapist and client and as an invaluable therapeutic tool. Working with the transference encourages unconscious thoughts, feelings and associations from the past to be brought into consciousness in the presence of the therapist. Transference occurs, most commonly, when the therapist becomes (represents) a significant other from the client's past, particularly a parental figure. Freud worked with his patient's recall of the primary repressed material.

Transference happens to an extent in all relationships. All of us transfer unresolved 'stuck' ways of relating, which have their roots in our childhood experiences, to others around us, and especially those we're in close relationships with. If, for example, a person had a domineering, critical father, then as an adult they might view people in authority as having these characteristics and they might regress in how they respond to the other person in a way that echoes the childhood relationship with their father, in an anxious, resentful or deferential manner. Yet the other person in reality might be nothing like the father in personality or attitudes. Transference can manifest inappropriate ineffectual reaction behaviour that interferes with healthy relating. In the therapeutic setting it can bring old conflicts alive and these can be worked out with the assistance of the counsellor, breaking the old patterns of relating.

The 're-experiencing therapist' Merton Gill challenged Freud's belief that therapeutic change came about when the person remembered the conflict. Gill said that remembering alone was not enough and that the client also needed to re-experience conflicts, emotional trauma and impulses in the presence of the therapist. Since the difficulties are acquired experientially, attitudes and meanings can be changed experientially. With the therapist the old conflicts can be emotionally relived under new conditions. When the client experiences and expresses the impulses and anxieties in the presence of the therapist where they are now directed in the transference, the therapist must be willing to discuss them with interest and non-defensively. Finally the therapist helps the client to learn the source of the re-experienced conflicts. The transference offers the client a unique opportunity, in the therapeutic setting, to experience a different response to the original cause of conflict. Whereas in the original encounter the client might have experienced pain, humiliation or rejection, the therapist's response is one of acceptance.

The countertransference is the feelings and attitudes that the counsellor has in relation to the client. Although, as with transference, feelings are initially unconscious, the counsellor gradually notices shifts in their inner responses to the client. If a person had a domineering and critical father they might, in the transference, feel dominated or in awe of a male counsellor. A countertransferential response might be if the counsellor began to feel omnipotent or critical towards the client. Another effect might be that they feel they *should* have the qualities that the client expects, and then feel incapacitated by the transference. Although originally countertransference was thought to be a hindrance to effective therapy, it's now regarded as very useful. Because countertransference is noted rather than acted upon (the counsellor is always vigilant regarding their own feelings and reactions), it provides the counsellor with insight into the problems of the client that perhaps would otherwise go unrecognized. The counsellor might think, 'Why do I feel disapproving?' and make the link with what has been said about the client's father, and this would give the opportunity to explore these feelings further. Countertransference feelings are often brought to life in supervision and are frequently a source of discussion in relation to the counsellor's own unresolved emotional difficulties.

MALAN'S TRIANGLE OF CONFLICT MODEL

The triangle of conflict model (Figure 7.2) helps the counsellor look at the anxieties behind the client's defensive behaviour and thereby understand the underlying hidden feeling or impulse that causes disturbance. Expressing painful or conflicting feelings directly can be frightening – the fear might be that others will find the strong feelings unacceptable, hateful, ridiculous or shameful, or that the person might become overpowered by their emotions. The fear of the consequences of expressing such emotions causes anxiety, and in turn causes the person to defend themselves against both the unwanted feelings and the resulting anxiety. In Malan's model, the apices of the triangle symbolically represent the three parts of the process. The attempt to defend oneself against powerful feelings creates psychological distress, yet the person might not be consciously aware of the feelings at all. Malan's model proposes that psychological distress is brought on by a 'triggering experience' that's congruent with the original damaging experience. The person then attempts to defend themselves against the (repressed) hidden feeling or impulse and the distress it creates.

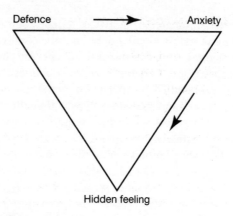

Figure 7.2 Triangle of conflict.

Source: D.H. Malan, Individual Psychotherapy and the Science of Psychodynamics.

Within therapy it's the defence that the counsellor first picks up.
Malan describes the defence and the anxiety as symptoms that
indicate both 'expression' and 'denial'. The goal of the therapy
is to explore with the client the defence and the anxiety that lies
behind the defence, and to help the client confront and contain
the hidden feeling. When the hidden material is held in the
preconsciousness – that part of the psyche the person is (in part)
aware of but is unwilling to acknowledge – then the exploration of
the defence and anxiety can be uncomplicated and the confronting
of the hidden problem much simpler. Unconscious defence
mechanisms, constructed to avoid mental pain or to control
unacceptable impulses, can take a long time to unravel.

It's important that the counsellor is tentative in the interventions
and interpretations they offer, asking questions (inwardly) such
as: 'What are the hidden feelings? Are these feelings accessible?
How painful or anxiety-ridden are the feelings of past experiences?
Can the client express these with me at this time?' Psychodynamic
therapy is concerned with helping the client get in touch with their
deepest feelings and the success of this depends on the building of
trust and therapeutic rapport. Changes and shifts in perception are
monitored by sensitive attention to client responses.

THE TRIANGLE OF INSIGHT MODEL

Karl Menninger first introduced the triangle of insight (Figure 7.3) in his book *The Theory of Psychoanalytic Technique* (1958). While the triangle of conflict forms a model for reaching and understanding the hidden feelings that are a source of conflict and unhappiness in a person's life, the triangle of insight represents a relational model of the source and effect of the destructive feelings. It's a useful tool in understanding the workings of transference.

Often the client alludes to what's going on in the therapy by talking about situations 'outside' in their daily lives – so the client who feels that the counsellor doesn't understand them says that their husband or wife doesn't understand them; the client who feels criticized by the counsellor says that their boss is always criticizing their work. The client might also allude to the therapeutic situation by talking about the distant past; for example, when a break in therapy is pending and the client fears that they won't be able to manage alone, they might talk about how their parents sent them to boarding school when they were very young and how lost and frightened they felt.

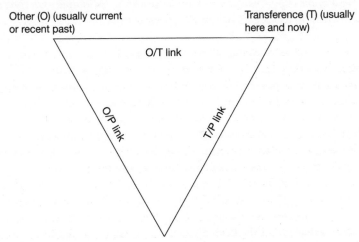

Figure 7.3 Triangle of insight.

Source: D.H. Malan, Individual Psychotherapy and the Science of Psychodynamics.

The psychodynamic counsellor tentatively decodes these messages, making the connection for the client: 'I understand that you felt lost and frightened when you were sent off to boarding school at such a young age. I'm aware that we're about to have a break in the therapy and I wonder if another meaning of what you say is that you are frightened that you won't be able to cope when I go?' Here the counsellor refers to himself or herself as the transferential parent figure (potentially abandoning) because the client is already unconsciously making this connection.

The triangle of insight model represents three categories of persons and sources of relationship experience from the client's life situations:

▶ *Others (O) – are people recently or currently in their everyday life and are connected with the problems they bring to counselling; the person could be a husband or wife, boyfriend or girlfriend, colleague at work or some other person who is strongly impacting on their life at the time.*
▶ *Transference (T) – relates to the counsellor in the 'here and now', when the counsellor represents either an 'out there' other person, or a parental figure from the past.*
▶ *Parent (P) – this apex represents primary, formative experiences relating to parents or parental figures from the past.*

The model illustrates that all are interlinked; for example, as we have already explored, in the transference the client will at some point in therapy experience the counsellor as a parent and 'transfer' feelings that belong to the past into the here and now and to the therapist. In a similar manner the client is likely to bring problems from the past (e.g. with their parents) into their other close relationships. Current or recent experiences with other people in everyday life could also be transferred to the counsellor to be worked out in the session.

Resistances and defences

A major part of the psychodynamic technique is analysing the resistances that put up a smoke screen to protect the defences.

Clients demonstrate resistance in various ways: for example, by being late for sessions; by wanting to finish the therapy in a 'flight to health' (a claim that all their problems are miraculously solved); by missing sessions; and by denial when a counsellor makes accurate observations or interpretations. The resistance betrays a reluctance to discover more, to let down a barrier or open up a protected part of themselves. There are ambivalent feelings: the person wants on the conscious level to have insight into the problems that brought them into counselling in the first place and to deal with life in a more productive self-fulfilling way, but on an unconscious or preconscious level they value and automatically want to hold on to their defences. Defences are a mental armouring that protect the individual from threatening or punitive feelings and were useful (perhaps even life saving) at the time they were acquired. The client needs reasons to let their defences down; they need to feel safe, accepted and understood, and to be able to trust the counsellor to explore painful issues with them. Confronting a defence head on is more likely than not to reinforce it. A skilled, sensitive counsellor respects a client's defence mechanisms and tries to understand the underlying reasons, interpreting them tentatively and gently exploring possibilities in step with the client, who gains self-insight by making subtle shifts in perception.

An analytic tool of **free association** was introduced by Freud to access the unconscious and interpret defences and resistances. Freud encouraged his patients to talk freely about every thought, feeling, image, memory and association that came into their head, however irrelevant, trivial or disagreeable it seemed. In doing so the patient was likely to let out slips of the tongue (hence the term 'Freudian slip'), making associations that could then be interpreted to bring repressed material into consciousness.

Dreams

The interpretation of dreams is another technique employed in bringing unconscious material into consciousness. Freud saw dreams as 'wish fulfilment'; but in dreams too there is a certain amount of repression that forms the latent dream content. The latent dream thoughts are transformed into the manifest dream content by self-censoring functions of the individual's mental activity. The psychodynamic counsellor also uses dreams to, as Freud put it, 'unravel what the dream-work has woven'.

In psychotherapy the psychodynamic approach is differentiated into specific classifications of Freudian, Kleinian, Jungian, etc., but in psychodynamic counselling the psychodynamic model is likely to be taught, learned and practised as an assimilation of aspects of many orientations with a stronger emphasis on Freudian theory. For example, elements of object relations will be included as well as Kleinian theories and concepts regarding 'unconscious phantasies', 'splitting' and 'projective identification' (see Chapter 8); aspects of Jungian psychology would include Carl Jung's views on the relationship between unconscious and conscious processes and of human growth and creativity.

In *Psychodynamic Counselling in Action*, Michael Jacobs draws attention to the point that:

> *Much of the literature upon which psychodynamic counselling draws is written for psychoanalysts or psychotherapists. This does not, however, make it irrelevant for the counsellor, especially where there are case histories to illustrate both technique and the way in which theories of personality development are used in practice.'*

The therapeutic relationship

Insight

Counsellors adhering to traditional psychodynamic methods have been accused of being aloof 'expert' figures. The counsellor may not be feeling that way in the counselling session but the neutral stance the counsellor adopts – so that client material comes to the fore – can be off-putting to some. Like all models of counselling, the psychodynamic approach has its strengths and weaknesses and many counsellors choose to work with two or more models and select the best out of each.

The psychodynamic counsellor adopts a neutral stance based on the 'blank screen' of traditional Freudian psychoanalysis, adopting what's referred to as 'the rule of neutrality', involving a respect for the client's autonomy and an attitude of caring commitment on the part of the counsellor. The 'rule of abstinence' employed by the counsellor is sometimes misunderstood by clients as an attempt by the counsellor to maintain a superior professional distance. The psychodynamic counsellor does not self-disclose, viewing this kind of interaction as detracting from client material. The more a client gets to know the therapist (in the usual sense), the less likely they're able to project and transfer feelings from the past on to them. It's a kind of withholding on the part of the counsellor, but not without reason and therapeutic value; the counsellor holds back rather than engaging in conversation, allowing the client to go on talking and revealing their thoughts and accompanying feelings. The counsellor mightn't answer a question directly; for example, they might instead explore the meaning behind the question. The frustration that the client experiences (sometimes referred to as optimal frustration) is regarded as useful to the confronting of conflicts and hidden impulses. The neutral or abstinent role of the counsellor is also helpful to the containing and holding of client material. As the counsellor's own personality takes a back seat, the client is able to feel therapeutically held by them.

Maintaining boundaries is an important aspect of this approach, involving clear contracting regarding, for instance, frequency and length of sessions and duration of therapy, and creating a confidential and private environment. Assessments and history taking form a baseline of information about the client's early family relationships and experiences. The ending of therapy also has a special significance in this approach – it's likely to stir up past feelings of abandonment and loss that can resurface in last-minute transference feelings. As we've already seen, a central focus of the work is the interpretation of defences and resistances that are brought to the client's attention and confronted with the counsellor. Links are made between past and present and special attention is paid to the client's perceptual world, not only to real experiences but also to how reality is perceived. Increasingly, the psychodynamic counsellor has adopted person-centred values of warmth, acceptance and empathic responding and an interest in presenting themselves as a 'whole' person. The counsellor's own self-development and understanding is a crucial component of the approach. Because personal therapy is encouraged, the psychodynamic counsellor, of course, will have experience of being on the receiving end of therapy as a client, working with transference, exploring childhood material and confronting defences.

Aim of therapy

The psychodynamic counsellor's view of the 'disturbed' person is someone whose everyday functioning is governed by inner conflicts. The psychoanalytic viewpoint understands everyone to have inner conflicts – the point being that normally they're satisfactorily suppressed and therefore manageable. The person experiencing unmanageable difficulties in their life might know something is wrong but not *what* is wrong, whereas the person who functions in a psychologically satisfied way is untroubled by inner conflict in as much as it's manageable and doesn't dominate their life. A central aim is to help the client to become more self-aware and to bring what's unconscious into consciousness. The counsellor's role is to help the client to gain insight and understanding into aspects of the self that were previously unknown. This is achieved by working with unconscious processes, transference, defences, resistances and dreams, to bring conflicts, impulses and feelings to the surface. Emphasis is placed on self-knowledge and insight rather than on attempting to eliminate problems. As Jacobs points out: 'The psychodynamic approach, which the counsellor also shows in action in her or his work with the client, is also often adopted by the client in self-analysis.'

C. G. Jung

Insight

Jung was an incredibly knowledgeable and spiritual man and one of the great luminaries of psychoanalysis whose work continues to inform and influence modern psychology and counselling. Like many other counsellors, I think about his theories in my work all the time, although I am not a Jungian counsellor *per se*.

The work of the analytical psychologist Carl Gustav Jung needs to be mentioned since his contribution to the analytic, psychodynamic and transpersonal approaches has been immense (see also Ruth Snowden's *Jung–The Key Ideas*). Like Freud, Jung was a medical doctor (specializing in psychiatry) who became a pioneering figure in psychoanalysis. Freud, who was Jung's senior by 20 years, was impressed by Jung's pioneering work on schizophrenia. He saw the younger man as a protégé and for a period of six years or so they worked in close association, but in time Jung came to regard Freud's theories on the human sexual drive as limited and restrictive to his own work and they parted ways. Jung's work reflected his diverse interests; from a young age he read extensively, gaining knowledge of philosophy, alchemy, astrology, theology and ancient religions. His main interest was the study of psychotic tendencies in individuals who otherwise functioned normally and he looked for answers in the primitive elements of the psyche. The inspiration that he found in the ancient religions influenced his work – for example, his theories of the individual and the **collective unconscious** which manifest as archetypes in dreams and visions.

He admired Hinduism for the way it integrates concepts of good and evil in the attributes of gods such as Shiva – the creator and the destroyer – because he believed that it's important for our mental health that we acknowledge the negative, largely unexpressed side of the human condition, which he termed '**the shadow**'. For Jung mental stability was a matter of balance, balance between the conscious and unconscious aspects of the personality, including feminine and masculine aspects and intellect and emotion.

DREAMS

Jung considered dreams to be a manifestation of the unconscious mind – a bridge between the conscious and the unconscious elements of the human psyche. He regarded dreams as imbued with meaningful information that guided individuals towards what could fulfil and nourish them. Dreams served as a compensatory or self-regulating form of communication from the unconscious mind that gave expression to neglected or unrealized areas of the individual's true self, or gave warnings when an individual strayed from their 'proper path'. The study of alchemy led Jung to understand dreams as a medium for transforming and purifying psychic energy. He believed that, when information relevant and significant to the whole of humankind is imparted, the result is growth and development for individuals as well as at a collective level.

PSYCHOLOGICAL TYPES

Jung began his work on psychological types through observing the personality traits and temperamental differences between Alfred Adler and Freud and the differences between himself and the other two. His first classifications of the extrovert and the introvert types can be best understood as a frame of reference. The individual adopts attitudes towards life that affects their experience. The extrovert character inclines towards the external world of other people and environment, while the introverted character is oriented to the inner world. In his later work Jung added four functions that operated the psyche: thinking, feeling, sensation and intuition. Just as extrovert and introvert are opposites, thinking is opposite to feeling, and sensation is opposite to intuition. (Jung thought that the intellect was too highly valued in the Western world, at cost to the emotional world of humankind.) In the same way as a person was inclined towards either an extroverted or an introverted expression of personality, the individual tends towards being a predominantly thinking rather than a feeling person or is oriented towards sensation rather than to intuition. In drawing a distinction between sensation and intuition as tools of perception, Jung used the term 'sensation' to mean information that's received through the sense organs (i.e. sight, hearing, taste, smell and touch) and 'intuition' to mean information from the unconscious that is independent of sensation.

INDIVIDUATION

What Jung called 'the process of individuation' is essentially an inner journey embarked on in the second part of life. The first part of life is concerned with being under, then freeing oneself from, parental influence and then establishing oneself as an adult in various roles including useful work, partnering and parenting. Having fulfilled this potential (ostensibly by functioning in the external world), the second part of life is when an individual can achieve a synthesis between their conscious and unconscious self by looking inward. Jung believed the self to be the God within – a 'hypothetical point between conscious and unconscious'. Jung regarded individuation to be a natural psychological process. He wrote: 'The natural process of individuation brings a consciousness of human community precisely because it makes us aware of the unconscious, which unites and is common to all mankind' (*The Collected Works of C. G. Jung*).

THE SHADOW

So that counsellors can facilitate the client's recognition and acceptance of (what they see as) the more unacceptable parts of themselves, counsellors also need to accept (what Jung called) our 'shadow side'. The shadow is to be found in the unconscious part of ourselves and it's often hidden from us. Our shadow represents all the things that we do not or cannot allow ourselves to do or think. It has been likened to the Mr Hyde part of Dr Jekyll. Jung saw the shadow as the primitive, uncontrolled part of ourselves. It's been called the inferior side of ourselves, but perhaps this encourages us to deny it. It's part of us but it's a side that's regarded as uncivilized and antisocial. Jung also used the term to describe characteristics we originally expressed as children but then learned were unacceptable to our parents or society. An example would be: a girl who shows great ability at something that's regarded as traditionally male territory, such as building or engineering, might (through pressure from parents or society) revert to a more widely stereotypically acceptable female domain, such as playing with dolls and nursing. However, the dormant 'antisocial' part of her will remain within her psyche as a source of ill content in her unfulfilled shadow side.

ARCHETYPES

Jung looked at history and the mythology of ancient civilizations for clues to unravel the human psyche. While working with patients with schizophrenia he noted that the visions that they had were strikingly similar to those in mythology, yet the details of these were known to only a few scholars. There was no explanation how the imagery matched so accurately. Jung was to write that archetypes were 'motifs analogous to or identical with those of mythology', and that they were 'found everywhere and at all times in Greek, Egyptian and ancient Mexican myths and in dreams of modern individuals ignorant of such traditions'. He believed this to be more than coincidental. The concept of synchronicity recognizes that there are acausal connections between people, places and occurrences in the world.

THE COLLECTIVE UNCONSCIOUS

Jung coined the term 'collective unconscious' to describe what he considered the true basis of the human psyche. He said that the collective unconscious was 'not individual but common to all humans as the ancestral heritage of possibilities of representation'. Archetypes, he thought, manifest in dreams and visions to help us with human dilemmas. The collective unconscious is like a pool of human situations and experiences that the human psyche can draw on.

ANIMA AND ANIMUS

Jung used the word *anima*, the Latin for 'soul', to mean the feminine aspect of the male unconscious; likewise, the word *animus*, mind or spirit, is the masculine aspect of the female unconscious. Jung introduced the idea of the sexes having qualities of each other – a man having feminine qualities and vice versa. To be whole a person needs to accept and integrate both aspects. He came to these conclusions from studying mythology, fairy tales and dreams where men experienced their souls as feminine and women experienced their souls as masculine. Interestingly, Jung noted that the anima and animus figures tended to come into play in the unconscious when the shadow elements have become accepted and integrated into the opposite sex and further issues come to the fore. In dreams and as outer world projections, figures of the opposite sex represent a collective archetype of relationship that exists between and beyond individual constraints. Jung viewed the anima/animus as functional to our relationship with the collective unconscious.

Characteristics of the psychoanalytic/ psychodynamic approach

THE PSYCHOANALYTIC/PSYCHODYNAMIC APPROACH...

- ▶ *works with unconscious processes – dreams, free association and transference*
- ▶ *focuses on defences as a route to understanding underlying anxieties and hidden feelings*
- ▶ *makes connections between the client's past and present*
- ▶ *insists on a 'rule of neutrality' – an abstinent approach where the therapist doesn't self-disclose and is the expert*
- ▶ *makes interpretations for the client*
- ▶ *relies on knowledge of the client's history*
- ▶ *promotes personal understanding.*

Section 2:
The humanistic/person-centred approach

Origins

Abraham Maslow is usually accredited with the title of 'father of humanistic psychology', which reached prominence in America in the 1950s and 1960s. Maslow is perhaps best known for his 'hierarchy of needs' model (see Figure 7.4).

The model identifies five basic human needs, here listed in the order of importance:

1 *The physiological needs – these are the basic needs for continuing life; for example, water, oxygen, foodstuffs, a need for activity, sleep, bodily elimination, avoidance of pain, sexual expression.*
2 *Safety and security – these are secondary to the absolute necessities; when the physiological needs are met, then a*

Figure 7.4 Maslow's hierarchy of needs model.

Source: Maslow's hierarchy of needs model, A Theory of Human Motivation (1943).

second layer of needs becomes prominent (e.g. safety, stability, structure, boundaries).

3 Love and belonging – the third layer in Maslow's hierarchy concerns close relationships with others (e.g. bonding, having a place in community). A negative response is a movement towards social anxieties and alienation/loneliness.

4 Self-esteem – Maslow identified two 'esteem needs'. Lower esteem refers to a need for respect from others, for status, attention, appreciation and at times dominance. Higher esteem needs are self-generated (e.g. self-respect, sense of achievement, self-sufficiency, independence).

5 To self-actualize – Maslow equates self-actualization with 'growth motivation' – a continuing desire to 'be all that you can be', which involves a need to fulfil personal potential. However, self-actualization is unlikely to be possible until the lower needs have been met. The self-actualized person is someone who is 'reality centred' – able to differentiate between what's real or genuine and what's 'phoney' or dishonest; 'problem-centred' – essentially problem solving and solution oriented; and resistant to 'enculturation' – unyielding to social pressure. Other qualities that distinguish the self-actualized person are spontaneity, creativity and an acceptance of self and others. Living with a 'freshness of appreciation', they have 'peak experiences' more frequently than others. Maslow used the term 'peak experience' to describe mystical experiences; a feeling of awe, exhilaration and appreciation, of being at one with nature or God – similar to what Rudolf Otto called the 'numinous'. Motivating factors of self-actualizers include a drive towards truth, aliveness, playfulness, meaningfulness, unity and self-sufficiency.

The humanistic approach to therapy was named the 'third force'. Maslow is also credited with introducing the 'fourth force', transpersonal psychology. Maslow regarded psychology, in the form of psychoanalysis, to be overly concerned with the neurotic and disturbed, and preferred to work with healthy, creative individuals. He also considered the reductionist, mechanistic theory of behaviouralism to be limited in its view of human functioning. What interested him was 'higher human motivation'. Maslow, along with other humanistic psychologists such as Fritz Perls and

Eric Berne, was heavily influenced by the philosophy of European existentialists and phenomenologists such as Sartre, Kierkegaard, Husserl and Binswanger. Existentialism rejects the idea of a person as a product of heredity or environment, believing instead that individuals are responsible for their own destiny.

The person-centred approach

Insight

Counsellors practising the person-centred approach can be misconstrued as doing very little, as I have heard it reported by some disgruntled ex-clients of person-centred counsellors. I think that they probably expected the counsellor to be proactive in solving their problems and the client-led supporting methods of the approach sometimes don't match with the client's expectations.

The person-centred approach is the main representation of the humanistic approach presented here because its core conditions model, and many of its ideas, have been widely integrated into other approaches. The views of Carl Rogers and his contemporaries have highly influenced people's attitudes towards therapy. Unlike the cognitive behavioural approaches, the person-centred model is non-directive and focuses on the quality of therapy, especially the therapist's attitude towards the client. Rogers and his associates shifted clinical models in psychology away from the medically oriented model. He developed 'client-centred therapy' in the USA in the 1940s and 1950s, working in educational and pastoral settings, but it was in the liberal 'flower power' climate of the 1960s that it really came to the fore. Experimental encounter groups became popular at this time and well into the 1970s as a method of working in the 'here and now'. He carried out extensive research in counselling methods and used interviews, recorded in the early 1940s on phonograph records, as a way of studying and improving psychotherapeutic techniques and supervision. Video recordings are available of Rogers at work both in one-to-one counselling and as a facilitator of large groupwork (see Taking it further).

The Rogerian core conditions model

In a paper entitled 'The Necessary and Sufficient Conditions of Therapeutic Personality Change', Rogers set out a set of six conditions that he regarded as necessary and sufficient to initiate 'constructive personality change':

1 *Two persons are in psychological contact.*
2 *The first, whom we shall term the client, is in a state of incongruence, being vulnerable or anxious.*
3 *The second person, whom we shall term the therapist, is congruent or integrated in the relationship.*
4 *The therapist experiences unconditional positive regard for the client.*
5 *The therapist experiences an empathic understanding of the client's internal frame of reference and endeavours to communicate this experience to the client.*
6 *The communication to the client of the therapist's empathic understanding and unconditional positive regard is to a minimal degree achieved.*

Rogers goes on to conclude: 'No other conditions are necessary. If these six conditions exist, and continue over a period of time, this is sufficient. The process of constructive personality change will follow.' Rogers acknowledged that his six conditions theory was based on the hypothesis that positive personality change occurs in a relationship (condition 1); the other conditions define the necessary characteristics of the persons in the relationship.

In Rogerian theory, and to person-centred therapists generally, the relationship between the counsellor and client in the 'here and now' is all important. With this in mind, let's look briefly at how Rogers himself defined what has been narrowed down to the three core values or conditions from his original model; that is, congruence, unconditional positive regard and empathy.

CONGRUENCE

Rogers equated congruence with genuineness – the therapist's ability to be genuine with the client in the relationship. He wrote that the therapist should be 'a congruent, genuine, integrated person'. By 'integrated' he meant 'whole'; that the counsellor or therapist requires self-awareness and is comfortable with their own experiencing, both positive and negative. The therapist doesn't hide behind a professional façade but is 'freely and deeply himself'. To put it in another way, using another Rogerian term, the counsellor is in touch with and able to be their 'authentic self'. This requires the therapist to be open about their feelings in relation to the client and the relationship. As a guideline on the subject, he wrote: 'Certainly the aim is not for the therapist to express or talk out his own feelings, but primarily that he should not be deceiving the client as to himself.'

The counsellor is not required to relate all their thoughts and feelings back to the client – this would be confusing and unhelpful – but rather the counsellor relates back thoughts or feelings when it becomes apparent that they're in some way either interfering with the therapeutic process or can play a positive role. At other times, Rogers concluded, it might be more appropriate for the counsellor to take the thoughts and feelings that they're experiencing with the client to a colleague or supervisor.

UNCONDITIONAL POSITIVE REGARD

This term was used by Rogers to describe a thorough, caring acceptance of the client. He wrote: 'To the extent that the therapist finds himself experiencing a warm acceptance of each aspect of the client's experience as being a part of that client, he is experiencing unconditional positive regard.' Rogers spoke of 'prizing' the person and of accepting the client as a worthwhile human being. To have unconditional positive regard towards another person means there are no conditions of acceptance, which calls for a non-judgemental attitude rather than a selective, evaluating attitude of accepting some aspects of the client while rejecting others. This stance requires the counsellor to be as accepting of the client's negative expression of 'bad' feelings (e.g. fearfulness, hurt, defensiveness, anger) as of 'good' feelings (e.g. competency, confidence, positive social feelings) and to accept inconsistency of behaviour.

Rogers also defined unconditional positive regard as a non-possessive, non-conditional 'caring', separate from the therapist's own needs, and in terms of valuing the client as a separate person whose feelings and experiencing are facilitated and validated by the therapist. By accepting the client as they are in the present, and extending positive regard without conditions, the person-centred counsellor encourages optimum self-expression in the client.

EMPATHY

'To sense the client's private world as if it were your own, but without ever losing the "as if" quality' is how Rogers described empathic understanding. Empathizing with a person involved, 'sensing' the client's subjective, perceptual world – fears, anger, and confusion – as if they were the counsellor's own, but without 'getting bound up in it'. He wrote of the empathic therapist being able to move around freely in the client's world, helping the client to clarify thoughts, feelings and meanings; and also voicing 'meanings in the client's experience of which the client is scarcely aware'. He concluded that the important elements of empathy were:

- ▶ *that the therapist understands the client's feelings*
- ▶ *that the therapist understands the client's meanings*
- ▶ *that the therapist's comments 'fit in' or reflect the client's mood and the content of what has been said*
- ▶ *that the therapist's tone of voice conveys the ability to share the client's feelings.*

Insight
I, and the majority of counsellors I know, use the person-centred core condition as an underpinning of our work.

Rogers had an optimistic view of humankind; he believed natural human characteristics to be positive, forward-moving, constructive, realistic and trustworthy, and that every organism instinctively moves towards the fulfilment of its inherent potential. Unlike the psychoanalysts who considered the individual to be a mass of antisocial aggressive impulses that needs to be repressed, Rogers regarded the human as having a deep need for 'affiliation and communication with others'. To become fully socialized, he believed that a person needs first to be fully themselves. Each person is considered to be unique. Person-centred practitioners regard the human personality to be complex and diverse, resisting diagnostic labelling or prescriptive interpretation.

SELF-CONCEPT

So, you may ask, what goes wrong? Although the person-centred approach doesn't focus specifically on childhood experiences as a source of unearthing repressed material, as in the psychodynamic approach, it does acknowledge that many aspects of a false self are formed by the individual's need to fit into family and society. Through the process of socialization and what Rogers termed 'conditions of worth' (the self-concept of the child formed by parental and societal values), the potential to become a 'fully functioning' unique person is quashed. In an attempt to satisfy the need for positive regard, the child learns to please others, understanding primarily what aspects of character and self-expression are acceptable to their parents and those around them. Alterations are made and those 'sides' of the self that are unapproved or rejected outright are gradually replaced by behaviour (as expressions of personality) that elicits approval.

INCONGRUENCE

Problems arise when the self – accepted and valued by significant others, first parents, then other social groups, friends or a partner – is incongruent with the 'authentic self'. A state of incongruence has established itself within the individual's self-concept when feelings of inner experiencing are at odds with the self that's presented to the external world. A common example of this is the sensitive boy child who, from a very early age, internalizes parental disapproval of any display of emotion. He experiences parental disapproval and rejection when he cries or shows affection or dependency, and yet he senses that he is met with enthusiastic approval when he is 'being brave', keeping emotions in, being independent and self-contained. He might crave closeness with others all his life but be unable to show emotion or dependence on another person. At the primary stage of his functioning, when he required unconditional love from his parents, he was given acceptance and love only if he met their requirements.

LOCUS OF EVALUATION

The self-concept is how we learn to define ourselves to meet the criteria required for us to be loved and valued. A 'fully functioning' person would demonstrate congruence between their inner world of feelings and sensations and outer expression, evident in emotions and behaviour. The congruent person has a strong self-concept, is able to be open, honest with themselves and others, and to live spontaneously. Rogers identified two ways we make judgements or evaluations: from our inner 'locus of evaluation' – the 'centre of responsibility' which lies within us – and through external evaluations – the attitudes or belief systems of others (parents, society, etc.). When a person acts on their own internal evaluations, those that come from feelings and intuition (gut feelings), they are in touch with the 'organismic valuing process', an authentic part of the self, not governed by the values of other people or by institutionalized values. The individual who loses touch with their internal locus of evaluation lives their life by people pleasing, continually focusing on externally defined beliefs and attitudes. A central aim of the person-centred therapist is to help the client reconnect with their inner valuing processes, to understand what they really feel, what changes they would like to make. The person is ideally then freed from introjected values and self-concepts, and begins to appreciate their individuality.

The fully functioning or 'actualized' person is in this way in touch with their inner world – the personal self-concept is extended not only to 'this is what I am' but also to 'this is what I can become'. Rogers talked of the individual becoming everything they 'can be', meaning having fulfilment, integration and acceptance of all the parts of their character, being able to find expression in love and work – to reach their full potential. It can be seen as impossible to reach this utopian state of personhood, but it is a striving, an ideal and a continuum. Rogers called it 'the good life' – the world of the fully functioning person whose capacity for interpersonal communication is enhanced through positive self-concept and creative interaction with others. The main aim of 'becoming a person', in the Rogerian sense, is to be in a state of full experiencing; being congruent, able to act on our own feelings, guided by our own organismic valuing processes, and living in the 'here and now'. The concept of 'person in process' is central to the approach.

The therapeutic relationship

Insight

It seems to me that humanistic therapy has brought a warmth and humaneness to therapy – breaking away, as it did, from stuffy analytical theories and methods, and regarding counsellors and clients as equals.

While the psychoanalyst endeavours to be a 'blank screen' on to which the patient's transferential material can be projected, humanists regard the willingness of the therapist to engage warmly with the client to be a necessity for therapeutic change. The quality of the interpersonal relationship – supportive, warm, empathic, accepting – provides a safe, validating environment for the client to explore, examine and accept the whole of their self. So that the client feels safe enough to express themselves freely within the therapy, they need to feel equal to and valued by the therapist. Rogers argued that the neutral stance of the psychoanalyst could be interpreted by the client as hostility or rejection, confirming the client's negative self-concept, particularly with regard to their relationships with others.

In 1958 Rogers wrote *The Characteristics of a Helping Relationship*, in which he presented questions that came from his own studies and clinical experiences. The questions reflect the qualitative aspirations he had for himself as a therapist and also for those who would practise person-centred therapy. He asks how he can be with the other person in a way that he is experienced by them as deeply trustworthy, dependable and consistent. Questions relate to the central tenets of person-centred counselling: that the counsellor demonstrates attitudes of warmth and caring, that they treat the client with respect, and that boundaries are important – the counsellor needs to remain separate from the other person, while remaining empathic, caring and acceptant of all the facets of self the client may present in therapy.

The questions that he posed himself relate to the qualities of the counsellor and the philosophy underpinning the therapy. The counsellor is transparently 'real' with the client, open, receptive and aware that the person is in 'a process of becoming'. Rogers considered the therapist's role to be that of a liberator of the client's real potentialities.

The counsellor, too, is in a perpetual state of 'becoming'. Rogers encouraged counsellors to fully be themselves, so that they live life dynamically and are therefore able to communicate from the centre of their being. He recognized that to facilitate the personal growth of others he too must grow as an individual. In order that the therapist can fully receive the client they also must accept all aspects of themselves, including their own reactions to client material.

He believed that all types of evaluative procedures objectify others and that the professional aloof stance of some therapists creates an impersonal environment. He aimed not to judge or evaluate a client's personal world but instead to create a facilitative environment, wherein the counsellor responds sensitively to the other person and makes therapy unthreatening.

Qualities of the counsellor

The person-centred view is that, unless a client perceives the therapist as trustworthy and dependable, the therapeutic engagement will not take place. To be able to convey a trustworthiness the therapist must trust in themselves, in their own ability to experience fully in the 'here and now'; full acceptance of the other person requires the counsellor's acceptance of themselves. Unlike other approaches, the person-centred perspective doesn't rely on complex theories of human personality, nor does the therapist hide behind the professional mask of 'expert'. They engage wholeheartedly in an egalitarian relationship with the client.

The therapist is sensitive and accepts the client as they are in the present, not what they might become. This doesn't mean that the therapist necessarily shares the client's values or beliefs, but means they respect where the person is in their lives at the time. Rogers understood that a person's defences have at least at one time played a useful part in their life and should be respected.

If the counsellor has deep self-awareness, then they are less likely to be overwhelmed by or get lost in client material and therefore are likely to be able to maintain boundaries, while also warmly engaging with the client, encouraging them to experience freely in the 'here and now'. The humanistic therapist has a sense of continuing development as a person in the quest of 'self-actualization', and sees this as an integral part of person-centred work. The person-centred counsellor's genuineness or congruence is at odds with an over-reliance on skills that can lead to formulaic 'professional' behaviour; the main skills of the approach are the adherence to the core conditions and the employment of a reflective, facilitative attitude.

Lastly, the person-centred counsellor is spontaneous and lets the client guide the therapy. Rogers believed in the client's innate intelligence and wrote in *On Becoming a Person*: 'It is the client who knows what hurts, what direction to go, what problems are crucial, what experiences have been deeply buried.'

Aim of therapy

Problems, conflicts, confusions and other presenting issues brought to therapy are seen as a manifestation of incongruence in the client's behaviour and experiencing. The authentic self lies buried beneath introjected (parental, other significant figures and institutionalized) 'conditions of worth'. The 'real' or 'authentic' self has kowtowed to outside 'loci of evaluation' to the extent it has been lost, and the unhappiness and frustrations experienced in living under this mantle are indicative of a need to reclaim the loss. A central aim is to help the client make contact with the organismic centre of their being, to help them re-experience a sense of self-worth and make movement towards changes in their lives. Signs of movement are:

▶ *The client begins to be less concerned with other people's attitudes and judgements and begins to trust in and value their own.*
▶ *They increasingly enjoy living in the present and appreciate the process of personal growth and expression rather than being governed by impersonal objectives.*
▶ *They demonstrate greater respect for others and self, showing a deep understanding of others and self.*
▶ *A valuing of intimacy and close relationships with others.*
▶ *A valuing of honesty and 'realness' in self and others.*
▶ *Accepting responsibility for their own life.*
▶ *A capacity to make considered choices with regard to the direction taken, and to live with a new spontaneity and enjoyment of life, 'towards a valuing of all forms of experience and a willingness to risk being open to all inner and outer experiences however uncongenial or unexpected'. (W. G. Frick,*

Humanistic Psychology: Interviews with Maslow, Murphy and Rogers.)

PROCESS OF CHANGE

> ### Insight
>
> I see the person-centred approach as an optimistic, loving form of therapy, emerging from the progressive mentality of the 1960s – a period of free expression. But it's not simple idealism – person-centred counselling, with its emphasis on respecting clients, has contributed greatly to the establishing of client's rights in therapy.

Change takes place in the psychological environment of the therapy. Negative self-concepts can, person-centred therapists believe, be changed by the valuing and respect given by the counsellor and experienced by the client. Through the non-possessive warmth and acceptance demonstrated by the counsellor the client experiences their own 'essential worth'. At the onset of therapy the client typically finds expression in self-destructive or self-denying behaviours that reinforce a negative self-concept. The counsellor provides a facilitative, supportive environment that is safe for the client to explore behaviours, attitudes, thoughts and feelings. Movement towards a healthy expression of the 'organismic self' – the true inner core of the person's being – takes place because the counsellor is willing to engage wholeheartedly with the client in their experiencing as it happens in the session. The counsellor, too, is human, willing at times, when appropriate, to self-disclose if it will benefit the client or the client–counsellor relationship.

When the facilitative attitudes (core conditions) are steadily present in the relationship, the client begins to gather that they're worth attentive care and valuing – a case of 'if someone else is willing to take the time to listen attentively to what is happening to me in my life, then maybe I will too', 'if someone else is willing to risk an emotional intimacy with me, then perhaps it is safe to reciprocate' and 'if someone else can accept all the disparate sides of me, then perhaps I can too.' Change is made possible by the counsellor's acceptance of the client in their entirety, thereby encouraging the client to explore and accept different aspects of themselves. All aspects, both negative and positive, can then be owned and integrated in a more realistic, healthier self-concept.

Characteristics of the humanistic person-centred approach

THE HUMANISTIC PERSON-CENTRED APPROACH...

▶ *works with conscious processes*
▶ *allows interpretations come from the client's changing perceptions*
▶ *focuses on the quality of the client–counsellor relationship*
▶ *allows the focus to move where the client wishes, to past, present or future*
▶ *is rooted in warm engagement, congruence of the therapist – the therapist is willing to self-disclose*
▶ *is respectful and acceptant of the client as they are presently*
▶ *is non-diagnostic – the client is considered to know best*
▶ *believes people are motivated towards self-actualization and are basically social beings.*

Section 3:
The behavioural/cognitive behavioural approach

Origins

Cognitive behavioural therapy (widely known as CBT) is commonly placed under the umbrella of the behavioural school of therapy. CBT is considered a branch of behaviour therapy but its origins are also in cognitive therapy. CBT is a product of cognitive theories and techniques and behavioural experimentation. Cognitive therapy originated in the 1960s and two therapists, Aaron Beck and Albert Ellis, are recognized as the main innovators of the cognitive school of therapy and their theories and techniques remain central to cognitive behavioural therapy. Behavioural therapy is a strong influence of CBT and it would be useful to look at a potted history of the behavioural approach to therapy (before we move on to look at CBT) as behavioural and cognitive ideas are integrated in contemporary CBT.

BEHAVIOURAL THERAPY

Behavioural therapy, in its various forms, originated from the scientific discipline of psychology. At the turn of the century, and in the early 1900s psychologists like John B. Watson and Edward L. Thorndike conducted experiments on animals to observe their behaviour. They considered the methods of psychoanalysis and introspection, which prevailed at the time, to be unreliable, based as they were on the subjective, inner thought processes of the patient – an area that was neither measurable nor observable and therefore considered unscientific. Thorndike was influenced by Charles Darwin's theory of evolution and the laws of 'the survival of the fittest' and believed that parallels could be drawn between animal and human behaviour. He went on to systematize a theory of human behaviour, based on the observation of animal behaviour, in laboratory experiments. Watson, accredited with coining the term 'behavioural psychology', also believed that research and a body of empirical evidence would lead to psychology being regarded as a scientific practice.

Watson, who termed himself a behaviourist in 1919, was the forerunner of Burrhus F. Skinner (well known for his development of operant conditioning). The main concern of Watson and his contemporaries was the process of learning; they surmised that the basic principle of learning applied to all organisms, including human beings. They believed that, just as behaviour is learned, it can also be unlearned. Traditional behaviourism understands all human behaviour to be determined by learning through classical and operant conditioning. 'Inappropriate', 'dysfunctional' and 'maladaptive' are all terms used to describe behaviour that can be changed through a process of unlearning.

It wasn't until the end of the Second World War, when psychiatric services were stretched to their limits, that behavioural psychology moved from its scientific research base to practical use as a form of therapy. At this time, B. F. Skinner refined Thorndike's theory of operant conditioning, and it was his version that was widely adopted by behaviourists. Behavioural theory is based on two experimental paradigms: Skinner's operant conditioning and Pavlov's dogs, used to demonstrate classical conditioning.

Operant and classical conditioning

BURRHUS F. SKINNER AND EDWARD L. THORNDIKE – OPERANT CONDITIONING

Thorndike used the term **operant conditioning** to describe behaviour that is largely determined by its consequences. He noted that animals learned responses because they affected their environment. Following a particular behaviour led to a reward of some kind – for example, touching a latch resulted in food becoming available. The learning of a task was strengthened when an action resulted in reward. Thorndike termed this the 'law of effect' and understood it in terms of trial and error on the part of animals rather than an innate intelligence, linking his observations with Darwin's theory of evolutionary selection; that is, species that adapt to their surroundings adapt their behaviour and therefore stand a greater chance of survival.

Skinner built on the work of Thorndike and it was his method of studying operant conditioning that was eventually widely adopted. Skinner's theory was based on the idea of reinforcements playing a motivational role in the learning of new tasks. Positive reinforcement describes the strengthening of a response by the incentive of a stimulus as reward. Negative reinforcement describes the strengthening of a response by removing an unpleasant stimulus (e.g. a loud noise). Reinforcements can be food, stroking, praise or encouragement. Gradually the animal would recognize that certain behaviour ended in favourable results, which led to a mastering of the task. In contrast, an operantly conditioned response is based on the premise that if something isn't reinforced it will gradually die out – this is referred to as 'extinction' in behavioural terminology.

CLASSICAL CONDITIONING – PAVLOV'S DOGS

A definition of **classical conditioning** is: 'One particular event follows another.'

In the early 1900s a Russian psychologist called Ivan Pavlov held experiments to observe the associative learning of animals. A famous experiment involving dogs, a meat dispenser and a light demonstrated different responses to stimuli. Unconditional responses were replaced by conditional responses to stimulus through a process of association. Over a period of time a neutral stimulus (e.g. the light) is associated with a reflexive stimulus (food) – even when food is no longer dispensed – resulting in a conditional response (e.g. salivation) to the neutral stimulus alone.

Applications and techniques

Experiments carried out on animals – such as these that formed the basis of behaviourist theories – might seem to have little relevance to human behaviour. Behavioural psychology has been criticized as presenting a picture of human beings as malleable and passive victims of external stimuli. Perhaps the greatest contributions behavioural models have made to human psychology are their observations on motivations and learned behaviour: for example, how young children look to their parents, or other significant figures in their lives, to 'model' behaviour. Cognitive theories went a step further in linking thought processes – how individuals view themselves and their environment – with emotions and behaviour.

Insight

When people talk to me about their serious, anger-related problems, the first thing I wonder is 'Where have they learned that it's appropriate to let out frustrations and anger in uncontrolled ways?' More often than not a significant figure

in their childhood has modelled unhealthy angry behaviour.
It's then a matter of clients re-educating themselves, learning
techniques and coping strategies, or more productive ways of
expressing anger.

CHILD DEVELOPMENT

Albert Bandura's **social learning theory** stressed the prominence of
vicarious, symbolic and self-regulatory processes in psychological
functioning. Social learning theory views human behaviour in
terms of a reciprocal interaction between cognitive, behavioural
and environmental determinants. The child learns vicariously from
their parents, acquiring behaviour modelled by significant others.
Bandura proposed that individuals didn't simply react to external
influences, but rather they select, organize and transform stimuli
around them. From a behavioural point of view a child who has
repeated temper tantrums or is aggressive to others has learned
that this behaviour elicits attention from their parents and others
in contact with them – in other words, it pays off. The attention
is the reinforcer that tells the child that their behaviour is having
an effect. If steps are taken to demonstrate to the child that their
behaviour is not working, they'll gradually drop it (extinction).
If they found, for example, that when they had a tantrum their
behaviour was ignored or that they were given time out alone
in their room (or on the 'naughty step') for an interval as a
consequence of that behaviour, and if this was further reinforced
by receiving attention through other means (e.g. through socially
approved of behaviour), then the original inappropriate behaviour
would cease. Reinforcers of the new behaviour could be praise,
encouragement, privileges or treats. The behaviour of others in
the family might also have to be readjusted. A child can learn
inappropriate behaviour through vicarious factors; from observing
antisocial or maladaptive behaviour in their parents.

Through laboratory experiments (using animals) psychologists
found that immediate reinforcement is the most beneficial form.
There is a temporal (time-related) relation between a response and
its reinforcer. An operant response is weakened when the reinforcer

is delayed. In human terms, it's more effective to praise (reinforce) appropriate social behaviour immediately; for example, when a child shares toys with a friend or attempts a task with care. It follows that it's best to discipline a child for bad behaviour when it happens rather than later, when the child might find it hard to associate behaviour with consequences.

Behavioural therapy follows the basic assumption that some psychological problems are acquired through learning experiences and are subsequently maintained by the pattern of events. Its method of treatment focuses on the challenge and reversal of the negative or ineffective learnt experiences. Traditionally behaviourists are less concerned with the abstract (such as feelings) and there has been little emphasis on the therapist–client relationship. Unlike psychoanalysts, behaviourists regard the symptom as the problem, not the underlying causes.

PROBLEMS TACKLED BY BEHAVIOURAL THERAPY

> ▶ *Antisocial behaviour – social learning – development of new behaviours (social skills deficit – unlearning inappropriate behaviour).*
> ▶ *Anxiety-associated behaviour – including obsessional and compulsive behaviour, phobias, sexual dysfunctions.*
> ▶ *Appetitive behaviour – including anorexia nervosa and sexual deviance.*

Widely used in the treatment of anxiety, phobic and obsessive compulsive disorders and sexual dysfunctions, behavioural therapy also lends itself to social learning programmes in child development and to helping to extend social and communication skills in adults who exhibit inappropriate, dysfunctional behaviour. The criteria for client suitability include:

> ▶ *the problem can be defined in terms of observable behaviour;*
> ▶ *the problem is ongoing and to some extent predictable;*
> ▶ *the situations or objects triggering the response are identifiable;*

▶ *the client is motivated – willing to co-operate with the therapist – and wants to change their behaviour and to take an active role in the process.*

TREATMENT PLAN

Behavioural treatment incorporates a variety of techniques that aim to solve problems by bringing measurable and observable change to the client's behaviour, altering behaviour patterns in specific currently dysfunctional areas. The treatment is modified to suit each individual's needs. In the case of panic attacks or phobias, the exposure principle is followed where the client is gradually exposed to the disturbing object or situation (gradual emersion) in a process called **systematic desensitization**. This technique has been widely used to treat phobic and obsessional compulsive disorders and is used in CBT. There are two types of exposure:

1 *Vivo exposure – when the actual feared object or situation is confronted.*
2 *Imaginal or fantasy exposure – this entails imaging the act of dealing with the problem while in a state of relaxation. The behaviourist Joseph Wolpe pioneered the technique of pairing relaxation with the troubling conditioned stimuli.*

The client is given 'homework' in the form of tasks between sessions. Goals are discussed and negotiated. The client is also often asked to keep a diary to note progress and setbacks.

Stimulus and responses
The stimulus is the object or situation that stimulates and elicits the negative behavioural responses. The responses are the inappropriate, dysfunctional or maladaptive behaviour manifested in response or reaction to the stimulus. The object of the therapy is to neutralize the power of the stimulus to create the destructive negative response.

Avoidance and exposure
A person who suffers from panic attacks has become a passive slave to the fear the stimulus evokes and its incapacitating effects.

The reaction to the fear is avoidance of the feared object or situation (stimuli); the agoraphobic stays within the safety of home and the person who is terrified of crossing bridges, at great inconvenience, takes a much longer route home. Part of the treatment plan of action is what is termed exposure; that is, the client is gradually introduced to the feared stimulus. The therapist would suggest factors such as the length of time and amount of exposure to the object or situation at an appropriate learning stage, agreed to by the client. For example, a first stage for someone who is terrified of birds might be to look at photographs of birds, then at another time visit a menagerie to view caged birds at a distance, either with a friend or with the therapist (therapist aid). At a later session, when both the client and therapist consider the client to be ready, a bird may be let free to fly around the room or be held by the client.

Coping strategies

These are basically elements that help alleviate anxiety and stress and help keep stress levels down to a manageable level. Strategies are planned with targets and goals. Tasks are given between sessions, often to reinforce work achieved in the session or in therapist-aided outings. The ultimate goal is to give the client not only an understanding of the maladaptive behaviour, but also ways of coping with it, then modifying and overcoming it, so that passivity is replaced with assertiveness.

Systematic desensitization and relaxation

This method is based on the learning laws of operant and classical conditioning.

Joseph Wolpe wrote a paper called 'The Systematic Desensitisation Treatment of Neuroses' (1961), describing techniques to decrease, in an organized manner, levels of anxiety over the causal factors. The term 'neurosis', which was used to refer to a collection of psychological problems – the central characteristic being acute anxiety – has now come to be included collectively under the heading of 'anxiety disorders'.

Systematic desensitization, which Wolpe is accredited with perfecting, is used in the treatment of phobias, obsessive compulsive disorders and panic disorders.

Since phobias and other forms of anxiety disorder are accompanied by physiological ('fight or flight') responses such as sweating, heart palpitations and dizziness (see Figure 7.5), Wolpe suggested the use of relaxation in the form of progressive muscle relaxation to help the client gain control over the anxiety-producing condition. First the client would be trained during therapy sessions, by the therapist, in the relaxation techniques; then, when these became familiar to the client, they could be self-applied in stressful anxiety-producing situations. Wolpe recommended deep relaxation as an anxiety-inhibiting response because he believed that we can't experience deep relaxation and fear concurrently. The same practices are used in adapted forms today.

The anxiety hierarchy

Following a relaxation programme, the therapist constructs an anxiety hierarchy. The client makes a list of anxiety-producing situations or scenarios (in the case of phobias and panic attacks), listing them in order of manageability (e.g. those which cause mild discomfort, proceeding to increasingly frightening and therefore challenging situations, culminating in situations which would produce the most anxiety). The content of the list constitutes the number of steps in the client's hierarchy of 'tasks', which vary from individual to individual.

Description and imagination technique

Wolpe recommended the use of description and imagination in the treatment of certain anxiety disorders. The idea was to 'unlearn' the phobia that was learned through the process of association. Adopting this technique, the therapist begins by describing a first-step scene from the anxiety hierarchy list. The client imagines the scene while maintaining a state of relaxation. For someone suffering from acrophobia this might be sitting by a window in a room on the first floor of a building.

The description and imaging process proceeds through the steps of the anxiety hierarchy until eventually the client is able to hear the most difficult step described in detail and to imagine being in the scene while maintaining a state of relaxation; in the case of the acrophobic this might be standing at the edge of a cliff top.

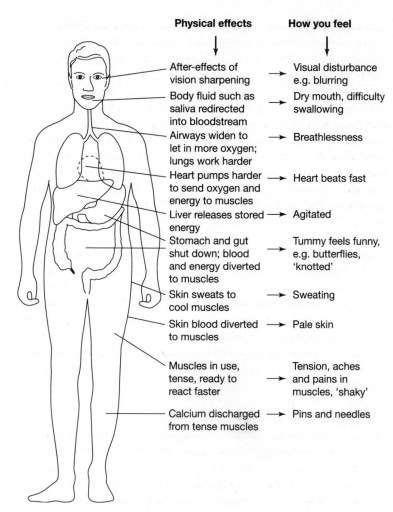

Physical effects	How you feel
After-effects of vision sharpening	→ Visual disturbance e.g. blurring
Body fluid such as saliva redirected into bloodstream	→ Dry mouth, difficulty swallowing
Airways widen to let in more oxygen; lungs work harder	→ Breathlessness
Heart pumps harder to send oxygen and energy to muscles	→ Heart beats fast
Liver releases stored energy	→ Agitated
Stomach and gut shut down; blood and energy diverted to muscles	→ Tummy feels funny, e.g. butterflies, 'knotted'
Skin sweats to cool muscles	→ Sweating
Skin blood diverted to muscles	→ Pale skin
Muscles in use, tense, ready to react faster	→ Tension, aches and pains in muscles, 'shaky'
Calcium discharged from tense muscles	→ Pins and needles

Figure 7.5 Physiological manifestations of an anxiety panic attack.

Cognitive behavioural therapy (CBT)

Insight

More than any other form of counselling, CBT therapists have collated empirical data confirming its efficacy in treating an array of psychological problems, which is why it is currently the therapy of choice by the National Health Service (NHS) in the UK. Other approaches believe the successes of their methods to be comparable. My belief is that no one approach has all the answers.

Cognitive science emerged partly in response to behaviourism's deterministic view of human behaviour, which some therapists criticized as reducing the human being and human consciousness to the level of the machine. The central focus of cognitive approaches is the individual's thought patterns and beliefs, and how these link with self-defeating behaviour. Clients are helped to change the way they think; irrational, self-destructive thoughts are replaced by more realistic and helpful thoughts.

The underlying principals of the cognitive behavioural theory (CBT) approach include:

▶ *A collaborative therapeutic relationship – as an active form of therapy, there is emphasis on therapist and client co-operation.*
▶ *Structure and goal orientation – CBT is a highly structured and problem-focused way of working, and goals and tasks are identified and agreed upon by clients and counsellor.*
▶ *Development of self-help – CBT relies on client motivation and willingness to take part in homework tasks. The client is coached in the techniques and skills of the approach.*
▶ *Cognitive techniques and behavioural experiments – elements of both approaches inform CBT concepts and practical application.*
▶ *Empiricism – based on experience, experiment and observation, the approach is well tested through extensive experiments, research and studies. Clients test for themselves the effectiveness of change, noting how their thinking affects their emotions and behaviour.*

AARON BECK

Aaron Beck, one of the founders of cognitive therapy, began his professional life as a psychoanalytic psychotherapist. In his work he came to the conclusion that an individual's cognitions (i.e. mental messages) affect both feeling and behaviour. He noted the irrationality behind self-critical cognitions, which he called 'automatic thoughts'. These are also sometimes termed negative automatic thoughts (NATs).

The psychoanalytic understanding of emotional disturbance, or behavioural dysfunctioning, is that it is rooted in unresolved trauma from childhood. In contrast, **the cognitive approach considers problems to arise not directly from the events themselves but from how the individual interprets and creates meaning for them.** Another difference between the two approaches is that while psychoanalysis considers thought to be dictated by emotional needs, cognitive behaviourists believe it is cognitive processes that govern the emotions. Cognitive behavioural counsellors use a model of cognitive processing called the cognitive distortion model devised by Beck. In this model Beck proposed that, when a person perceives a situation to be threatening, it results in a reduction in reasoning and functioning of normal cognitive processes.

Cognitive (thinking) distortions include:

All or nothing thinking – thinking in absolutes. Polarization of extremes, black-and-white thinking with no shades of grey.

Example: In cases of phobias something that is mildly risky may be perceived as highly dangerous. There is no gradient range between 'I'm OK, I can manage this' and 'This is really dangerous, I can't do it.'

Crystal ball gazing – negatively predicting the future.

Example: 'The last woman I asked out refused me so I'm sure to be rejected if I ask someone out again.'

Emotional reasoning – assuming negative emotions as reality.

Example: We feel guilt and therefore assume we are guilty. In the case of abuse we could think, 'I am guilty, I must have done something to deserve it.'

Discounting the positive – dismissing positive experiences.

Example: When something has been achieved, saying, 'It was just a fluke – anybody could have done that.'

Jumping to conclusions – making a negative assumption with no evidence to support it.

Example: Your boss has called an emergency meeting and you think, 'My work isn't satisfactory, I'm going to get the sack.'

Labelling – naming a behaviour as a personality trait.

Example: We don't manage to complete something and tell ourselves 'I'm a failure' or 'I'm a loser.'

Magnification or catastrophizing – blowing things out of proportion, exaggerating things.

Example: You've put on a little weight and say to yourself, 'I'll always be fat and no one will love me.'

Mental filter – thinking in a way that blocks reasoning. Ignoring positive information and concentrating on negative information.

Example: Thinking, when being mildly challenged by a very supportive friend, 'He always criticises me.'

Mind reading – thinking we know what others are thinking and not checking things out with them.

Example: A friend is talking about how funny and good fun another friend is and you imagine she's thinking that you're too serious and that she finds you boring.

Over-generalization – concluding from one negative event that everything is going wrong.

Example: Putting a dress on and finding it's got a rip and saying to yourself, 'Everything is going wrong.'

Personalization – self-blaming and taking responsibility for things outside our control.

Example: A teacher thinks 'It's my fault' when the school fails an educational standards report.

'Should' and 'must' statements – tyrannical demands we make of ourselves.

Example: 'I *should* always be kind to everybody and never be angry' and 'I *must* clean the house everyday'.

Do any of the above seem familiar? Most of us will identify with many of these kinds of distorted ways of thinking.

Insight

'Shoulds' and 'musts' can get in the way of our enjoyment of life. We forget how to be carefree and spontaneous. We frequently don't understand what drives us in this self-policing way and CBT is good for examining the source. More often than not, it is far and distant rules laid down by parents or authority figures that we have internalised and that, as adults, we really don't need to bend to.

MEMORY

Memory is another area associated with cognitive distortion. Research has shown that people suffering anxiety or traumatic times lose the ability to recall details of painful events accurately. The sufferer generalizes and the power of recall is diminished. This is thought to be because of a connection between the events and recalled negative emotions. In cognitive behavioural counselling this causes a problem because of the need for client contribution in the construction of micro-analysis of events which is used as part of therapy.

METACOGNITION

Metacognition refers to the ability of individuals to deconstruct and understand their own cognitive processes. This involves reflection and awareness of the various steps in thinking or problem solving; for example, in the use of strategies such as simplifying tasks to make them manageable by selection, planning actions and systems, creating order and so on. Parents pass on metacognitive strategies to children when they 'model' the use of strategies.

ALBERT ELLIS

Albert Ellis, who along with Aaron Beck is regarded as a founder of cognitive therapy, went on to establish rational emotive behaviour therapy (REBT). Ellis, like Beck, originally trained as a psychoanalyst. REBT (also referred to as RET) adopts a robust directive therapeutic style that challenges and confronts the 'irrational beliefs' of clients. 'Crooked thinking' governed by 'shoulds' and 'musts' was, in the opinion of Ellis, the cause of emotional problems and maladaptive behaviour. Internalized irrational beliefs lead to 'catastrophizing', anxiety and depression; 'catastrophizing' means to view things in an absolutistic, exaggerated or overstated manner – an 'it's the end of the world' scenario. In REBT and in CBT the client is helped to change their irrational beliefs to more rational statements, thereby enabling them to deal with problems constructively. Ellis's ABC theory is central to CBT.

The ABC theory of personality functioning
A – represents the activating event – a person's action, attitude or an actual physical event.

B – represents the belief the person has about the event.

C – represents the consequence of the event, in terms of the individual's emotions and behaviour in relation to their experiencing of the event.

The CBT counsellor or therapist teaches the client, through the ABC formula, how to engage in metacognitive processing of their thoughts in relation to events. Cognitive reactions to events can be monitored, reflected on and understood, giving the client more choice of perspective.

In Ellis's theory it isn't A, the activating event, that causes C, the consequence, but rather it is B, the client's beliefs, that colour the relationship between the event and the consequence (i.e. the resultant feelings and conduct). For example, one person might believe that a missed opportunity means that all opportunities are now closed to them and, feeling depressed, give up trying to achieve their goal; while another person might think the missed opportunity is one of many that will come their way and feels OK about the situation, continuing to work towards their goal.

Cognitive theories were added to the behavioural approach to therapy because therapists realized that cognitions (e.g. thoughts, beliefs, perceptions) played a major part in individual experiencing. Behavioural and cognitive practices have merged as the two are acknowledged to complement each other. The combined theories have produced a therapeutic approach for the treatment, in particular, of depressive and anxiety states. As a scientific therapeutic approach that relies on observation and monitoring (of behaviour and cognitions), the model has been widely endorsed and adopted by the medical professions. A central aim of cognitive behavioural therapy is to replace negative beliefs and automatic thoughts with realistic self-accepting beliefs that are more self-affirming. With the counsellor's help, the client learns to monitor and gain control of how they think and behave.

Cognitive contents are the components of our thinking that motivate us. Donald Meichenbaum, writing in 1986, drew attention to the effects of 'self-talk' and internal dialogue. Beck wrote about automatic thoughts as dysfunctional, and Ellis lists in *Reason and Emotion in Psychotherapy* 'irrational beliefs' as the main contributing factors of self-depreciating and defeating behaviour. The following are examples of irrational beliefs linked to situations or events:

- ▶ *I made a mistake – I am so stupid, I do everything wrong/ I can't do anything right.*
- ▶ *The end of a relationship – he doesn't love me. I am totally unlovable/unattractive to everyone.*
- ▶ *I was placed third in an activity that I always win – I am a complete failure.*

The cognitive behavioural counsellor picks up on these types of distorted belief statements and, with the client, questions the underlying assumptions that form them; for example, the counsellor might say: 'You are used to being the best at your subject; now you've come third, which is a very high placing, yet you think you're a total failure.'

ANXIETY-INDUCING AND REINFORCING SELF-STATEMENTS

Meichenbaum draws attention to the statements that accompany behaviour as internal dialogue. Internal dialogue involves talking to ourselves while we go through situations or events. In exams or interviews we might tell ourselves during the proceedings that we will fail or we're messing things up if any slight difficulty or hitch in the proceedings arises. The (negative) self-statements can sabotage hopes of success by 'feeding' feelings of anxiety; also, the inner dialogue distracts attention from external details, which might cause further incapacitation of 'performance' behaviour.

The therapeutic relationship

A criticism of behaviourism has been that, in an approach built on empirical investigation (knowledge based on experimental research), the therapist has taken a clinically detached and highly directive role. The client could easily be made to feel powerless or worthless. Although traditionally the client–therapist relationship has not been considered central to these modes of therapy, more recently in cognitive behavioural therapy it has been recognized that the relationship is important, for several reasons:

- ▶ *The co-operation of the client is necessary because the approach is task and target oriented requiring negotiation.*
- ▶ *In a supporting role, the therapist needs to demonstrate that they are trustworthy, warm and accepting, as well as directive, as the client's motivation could depend on encouragement and praise.*
- ▶ *Therapist-aided tasks (when the therapist accompanies the client on anxiety-inducing tasks) necessitate sensitive communication. Client and therapist work closely together and trust is essential.*
- ▶ *The therapist teaches or coaches the client in the use of skills and techniques, helping them gain insight into how they function and guides them towards 'self-therapy'.*
- ▶ *When a client chooses therapy, they might have had problems for some time. It might have been a huge step for them and they might feel frightened, embarrassed or angry. If they feel vulnerable, the first impressions of the therapy offered and the attitude demonstrated by the therapist might influence whether or not they continue.*
- ▶ *If a therapist demonstrates sustained empathic understanding throughout treatment, it will encourage a client through times of difficulty. Setbacks and lapses are less likely to be experienced as overwhelming.*
- ▶ *The therapist is highly active in the treatment. They are directive, taking on the role of coach, motivator and supporter – offering encouragement and praise, modelling behaviour, offering therapist aid and continually assessing the client's needs and monitoring progress.*
- ▶ *The therapist prepares the structure and content of each session between sessions and therefore is acutely aware of client particulars.*

Sometimes a member of the family acts as a co-therapist whose role it is to support and encourage. The co-therapist will be guided by the therapist and informed as to progress and difficulties.

(The therapist will advise the helper not to comfort or collude in ways that could encourage avoidance of difficult tasks.)

The lines of enquiry that the therapist is likely to pursue include the following:

▶ *Circumstances – what triggers (brings on) an attack or particular behaviour? What? Where? When? How?*
▶ *Levels of anxiety – what happens to the body in physical manifestation, e.g. sweating, shaking, numbness?*
▶ *Thoughts and feelings – those that accompany the behaviour while it is taking hold.*
▶ *Anticipatory factors – what the thoughts and feelings were directly before the onset of the episode (panic attack, tantrum, etc.), e.g. anticipating catastrophe, dreading confrontation.*
▶ *What is experienced after an attack? Is there relief or does the unease continue for a period of time?*
▶ *What the consequences of the behaviour are, e.g. antisocial; effects on work, play, relationships; self-defeating, restricting aspects.*
▶ *Variables – are anxiety levels or behaviour worse at particular times or do particular situations cause exacerbation? Is the situation fluctuating or constant? What factors contribute to improvement or deterioration?*

Strategies for coping with anxiety

Before
Picture yourself coping
Stay relaxed
Breathe slowly and calmly
During low anxiety
Stay as relaxed as possible
Stay in the situation
Breathe slowly and calmly
Don't add secondary fear (this situation need not lead to a worse situation)
Use distraction

(Contd)

> **During high anxiety**
> Breathe slowly and calmly
> Accept your feelings
> Notice your NATs – negative automatic thoughts
> Replace them with rational, coping thoughts
> Stay in the situation if possible – if not, return as soon as you are calmer
> Wait for the uncomfortable feelings to pass
> **Afterwards**
> Note the positive ways you coped
> Continue with what you were doing
> **The golden rules**
> Accept your feelings
> Try not to avoid situations

The cognitive behavioural counsellor uses various techniques to assess cognitions, including asking the client to apply methods of monitoring self-statements by:

▶ *thinking out loud while doing a task*
▶ *working with a tape recorder to record spontaneous talk*
▶ *completing worksheets to record, for example, details of the activating events, belief and behavioural consequences/outcome.*

Once the client becomes aware of their beliefs and automatic thoughts they can begin, with the guidance and encouragement of the counsellor, to experiment with alternative (more balanced) beliefs or self-statements in relation to particular events.

Aim of therapy

The focus of work is to bring to the client's awareness cognitions that can be either appropriate or inappropriate, functional or dysfunctional, constructive or destructive, rational or irrational, adaptive or maladaptive. In simple terminology, cognitions can either work for us or against us, and the cognitive behaviourist helps the client make changes to lessen, if not totally eradicate, negative self-messages and their effects.

Insight

CBT has given the world of therapy tools, techniques and strategies that work well with other models. I regularly encourage the client to challenge self-destructive, negative thoughts to help them change their thinking patterns and accommodate healthier, more balanced views.

Intervention techniques or methods

These are techniques or methods used to accomplish behavioural objectives after the initial stages of contracting, explaining the rationale for treatment, problem assessment and setting of goals or targets have been established. In *An Introduction to Counselling*, John McLeod has identified intervention techniques as including:

▶ *Challenging irrational beliefs.*
▶ *Reframing the issues – for example, perceiving internal emotional states as excitement rather than fear.*
▶ *Rehearsing the use of different self-statements in role plays with the counsellor.*
▶ *Experimenting with the use of different self-statements in real situations.*
▶ *Scaling feelings – for example, placing present feelings of anxiety or panic on a scale of 0–100.*
▶ *Thought stopping – rather than allowing anxious or obsessional thoughts to 'take over', the client learns to do something to interrupt them, such as snapping a rubber band on his or her wrist.*
▶ *Systematic desensitization – replacing anxiety or fear responses with a learned relaxation response, the counselling takes the client through a graded hierarchy of fear-eliciting situations.*

- *Assertiveness or social skills training.*
- *Homework assignments – practising new behaviours and cognitive strategies between therapy sessions.*
- *In vivo exposure – being accompanied by the counsellor into highly fearful situations; for example, visiting shops with an agoraphobic client.*

Worksheets are used to help the client gain insight into how their thoughts affect them (see Figure 7.6, an example of a thought record). Inventories help the client gauge their emotional state and its accompanying cognitive processes and their effects.

Insight

I find that some clients like to have homework – in between session tasks – to keep them linked with the counselling and give them a sense of being active in their problem solving. It engenders the idea of self-therapy, wherein clients learn to be their own therapist, which is the ultimate objective of CBT.

SCHEMAS

In CBT a schema is a collection of core beliefs (a kind of psychological profiling used to map out which core beliefs are maintaining our problems and 'what makes us tick'). A schema provides insight into cognitive patterns. The therapist helps the client build a schema conceptualization, and will challenge cognitive distortions and look for evidence against maladaptive schemas. Understanding schemas helps break unhealthy, distressing behaviour patterns. The client learns to categorize and interpret their experiences. Beck described a schema as 'the mode by which the environment is broken down and organized into its many psychologically relevant facets'. Building a schema involves several stages:

- *Identifying and examining NATs (negative automatic thoughts).*
- *Identifying and examining negative underlying assumptions and core beliefs (about self, others and the world) with an aim towards change.*

Situation	Moods	Automatic thoughts and images	Evidence that supports the 'hot thought'	Evidence that doesn't support the 'hot thought'	Alternative/ balanced thoughts	Rate your moods now
Who was there? What was happening? When was this? Where were you?	Describe what you were feeling. Use a word to describe each mood. Give each mood a rating between 0–100%.	Who was going through your mind immediately before you began feeling this way? Did you have other thoughts or images come into your mind?	Consider this hot thought and think about the evidence there is to support this thought.	What's the evidence that doesn't support your hot thought.	Write a different balanced thought. How much do you believe in the balanced thought? Give it a rating between 0–100%.	Now have another look at the moods you have noted in the mood column. Think about how you feel now and re-rate these moods – from 0–100%. Do you now feel differently in any way? Record any new feelings or moods that you are experiencing now.

Figure 7.6 Example of a thought record.

- *Making links between cognitions, behaviour and physiology (effects on the body).*
- *The use of cognitive techniques and behavioural experiments (e.g. noting old patterns and trying other ways) to restructure dysfunctional beliefs and assumptions.*
- *Problem- and symptom-focused interventions.*
- *Relapse prevention/management.*

Cognitive behavioural approaches address the problem of relapse with clients who have addiction problems, such as alcohol or drug abuse, by providing strategies and skills for dealing with periods of relapse. These are based around identifying typical situations such as times of emotional crisis, or a social situation that triggers a step back to pretherapy behaviour. This might be an alcoholic drink at a family get-together, encouraged by others (social situation), or a person with a drug problem (re)turning to drugs because of a painful or stressful situation which they feel unable to cope with (emotional crisis). Other techniques used include: reframing or redefining distortive self-statements to acknowledge that, although the client has lapsed this time, it does not imply total relapse; and the counsellor and client working out a plan of action for particular situations, given to the client as written instructions to use as a coping strategy if a temptation to lapse occurs. Social skills are also learned as a method of helping the client; for example, in declining invitations to join in (alcoholic) drinking sessions or handling a conflict situation.

AFFECT AND NON-CONSCIOUS PROCESSES

As we have seen, there was a development from an exclusively behavioural perspective to the recognition of the role of cognitions – it was realized that human behaviour was more than the sum of learning through experience; it also involved associated thought processes. More recently there has been a recognition of **affect** or feeling. It appears the various different schools of therapy have moved closer together. CBT acknowledges 'non-conscious states' that are similar to Freud's preconscious state. Material is accessible, not buried in the unconscious, but is not fully conscious. Individuals adopt 'defence manoeuvres' whereby affective (mood, feeling, emotion) states are avoided. 'Security manoeuvres' produce desired affective states. These are similar to Freudian defence mechanisms and the 'armouring' of resistance. The learned affective state (LAS) refers to the vicarious, learned imitating of parental emoting; in the same way as the child imitates the parental model of thinking and behaving, the child learns to express emotions. The environment becomes the controlling factor of the emotional process. As a means to understanding the origins of the individual's emotion reactions, cognitive behavioural therapies have acknowledged the need to explore the client's early developmental years of past experience. The individual's view of their life, with emphasis on the early years, is termed the phenomenological developmental history (PDH).

Characteristics of the Behavioural/Cognitive Approach

THE BEHAVIOURAL/COGNITIVE APPROACH...

▶ *is a highly structured approach that's effective in addressing problems*
▶ *is collaborative*
▶ *calls upon the therapist to act as an educator and coach*
▶ *encourages self-awareness and self-responsibility*
▶ *makes links between thoughts, moods and actions*
▶ *provides practical coping strategies and skills*
▶ *can be combined with other approaches.*

For a more in-depth exploration of CBT, see *Cognitive Behavioural Therapy* in the *Teach Yourself* series.

THINGS TO REMEMBER

1 *All types of counselling derive from three main approaches. These are: psychoanalysis, behavioural and humanistic.*

2 *The psychodynamic model of counselling has its roots in Freudian psychoanalysis. Psychodynamic counsellors work with transference, the client's defences and other unconscious processes. Important figures who have contributed to psychodynamic theory include: Sigmund Freud, Carl G. Jung, Melanie Klein and Donald Winnicott.*

3 *Developmental psychology, which studies the importance of different stages of human psychosocial development, from birth to old age, is also central to psychodynamic training.*

4 *The theories of psychoanalyst Carl G. Jung are an important part of the psychodynamic canon. His interests were extensive and from his studies of mythology, ancient cultures and spirituality he developed many theories including: the interpretation of dreams, psychological types, the shadow and the collective unconscious.*

5 *The founder of person-centred counselling, Carl Rogers, introduced the idea that it is necessary for the therapist to adopt core values or attitudes – empathy, congruence and unconditional positive regard as the fundamentals – for significant therapeutic benefit.*

6 *Rogers and his contemporaries moved away from medical models in psychology and introduced in their place the idea that, when people were truly listened to by an attentive and empathic counsellor, then they naturally find ways to self-heal.*

7 *Person-centred therapy, like other humanistic approaches, believes in what is termed 'the process of change'; that is, the client's ability to self-express and develop as an individual in*

the supportive and facilitative environment provided by the counsellor.

8 *The idea that our thoughts influence our emotions and behaviour – 'What we think is how we feel' – is central to cognitive behavioural therapy (commonly known as CBT).*

9 *The founder of cognitive therapy, Aaron Beck, took psychology down a new road when he noted the negative automatic thoughts (NATs) of depressed patients. He then set about helping his patients find more helpful and balanced ways of thinking.*

10 CBT, *which is a combination of cognitive and behavioural theories and practices, is a collaborative model of counselling where the client carries out tasks and homework between sessions.*

8

....

Demystifying the jargon

In this chapter you will learn:
- *how the different defences work*
- *some analytical terms and their origins*
- *what the commonly used terms of counselling mean.*

Many of the terms used in the psychodynamic approach derive from psychoanalysis. Psychology dictionary definitions give clinical meanings, and whether we understand these or not might depend on foreknowledge of other technical terms. While some therapists regard specific terms as necessary – useful for dialogue between therapists as a type of shortened language – others (like the ex-psychoanalyst Jeffrey Masson, who warns against diagnostic labelling) consider the jargon to have meaning for the particular exclusive world of therapists, and that the use of categories to describe clients' mental processes is actually dehumanizing.

Freud identified various categories of 'defences' that have become widely accepted in psychology, psychiatry, counselling and psychotherapy alike. Even therapists who don't consider themselves to refer overtly to psychoanalytic theories are usually familiar with the psychoanalytic theoretical meaning of defences such as denial, repression, regression and so forth. In fact, terms like these are also used in everyday life as a form of psychological language for the layperson, even if loosely used.

The traditional Freudian view is that a defence mechanism is a weapon employed by the Ego (the reality principle) to protect from anxiety, conflict, shame and other types of painful experiencing. The source of the potential anxiety is the Id (the pleasure principle), which motivates the person to satisfy its basic biological urges (including sexual impulses) in any way possible. The Id calls for immediate gratification, irrespective of logic or moral reasoning. The Ego and Superego develop ways of containing the deviant expressions of the Id. The function of the Ego, as the (predominantly) conscious part of the psyche that's aware of social restraints and consequences of behaviour, is to satisfy the demands of the Id by reasoned and socially acceptable means. As 'piggy in the middle' the Ego, in turn, is influenced and restrained by the Superego. The Superego (the conscience) demands that the Ego utilizes internalized moral and ethical views (rules and taboos) to regulate the rampant Id.

The psychodynamic counsellor treats defences with respect, acknowledging that most were formed many years before, possibly in early childhood. Although the defence was appropriate to the client's survival at the time (to withstand anxiety, trauma, shame, etc.), it may be limiting the person in the present – for example, interfering with self-development or the development of close relationships with others. The person-centred approach believes that, by offering unconditional positive regard to the client, their defences will gradually diminish as the client recognizes that they're acceptable to the counsellor as they are.

In a series of books on 'attachment behaviour', John Bowlby explored attachment and loss. He noted how a person who has experienced abandonment as a child attempts throughout life to protect themselves from further anxiety by distancing themselves from others. This results in an 'attachment anxiety' – further abandonment and the pain of separation and loss. It's at a later stage, as a spouse or parent, when the person finds it difficult to show affection or commitment in a relationship, that the defence mechanisms might prove to be most destructive.

The defences

DENIAL

The term 'in denial' is commonly used to describe when a person is refusing to face up to something about either themselves or what's happening in their lives. It's implied that the person has made a conscious decision to deny an unpleasant reality. In contrast, the psychoanalytical meaning of **denial** is that it's an unconscious mechanism that refuses to acknowledge thoughts, emotions, needs or wishes that cause anxiety. As an unconscious process its function is to deny difficulties that can't be dealt with consciously. In the therapeutic setting, something a therapist suggests to a client (an observation made or an interpretation offered) is rejected; denial is indicated when this is done with some speed, 'automatically', and without any consideration or reflection.

DISPLACEMENT

Displacement is another defence that involves the redirecting of feelings and impulses (see the glossary for an outline of the meaning of 'impulse') from the original source to another object, person or situation. An example is when a person feels angry with their boss but is unable to express it; on arriving home they become angry with their spouse (for no apparent reason). Displacement is evident in the transferential relationship between the counsellor and client when impulses or desires arising from the original sources (often the client's parents) are replayed.

In a behavioural context, displacement refers to the substitution of one response for another, particularly if the original response is thwarted or blocked in some manner.

FIXATION

Like regression, **fixation** is a defence that relates to earlier developmental stages. The term is used to explain when an individual gets stuck at a certain stage or fixed in their outlook, demonstrating failure to progress from one stage of development to the next – hence the term 'a mother/father fixation', used to describe a situation when an adult is highly reliant on nurturing, approval or guidance from the parental figure (e.g. 'tied to their mother's apron strings').

Erik Erikson's 'whole life' scheme of psychosocial development makes the point that movement to the next level of development (e.g. adolescence to young adulthood) requires the fulfilment of tasks in the resolution of the problems particular to that stage. In the adolescent stage issues and tasks that the young person has to grapple with are concerned with the establishing of an individual identity or development of a consistent self-concept. Incompletion of the task causes 'role confusion'. An individual who has failed to resolve certain issues and deal with the many challenges of the adolescent stage of development might in later life become a 'Peter Pan' figure, finding the ageing process particularly difficult to deal with. Inevitably there's always unfinished business regarding stages of development; it's extremes of these that are relevant to the fixation theory.

IDEALIZATION

Idealization is a form of denial where an object of attention (parent, partner, sibling) is presented as 'all good' to the therapist, masking ambivalent feelings towards them. So, instead of declaring feelings of jealousy and hatred towards the sister who excels at everything she does, the client says how clever and marvellous she is and how well the two have always got on; rather than stating that his father was a cruel, bullying megalomaniac, the dutiful son says that he was a kind, considerate father whom he adored. When the client talks about the person in exaggeratedly glowing terms, this could be a signal that opposite emotions lurk beneath the acceptable ones. The 'all bad' representation of illicit emotions of hatred and fear (products of the Id) towards the other person is too dangerous to acknowledge and has therefore been repressed, replaced – via the Ego as a mediator or by the moral internalized views of the Superego – by an idealized view of the person. Idealization as a defence applies to groups of people, nationalities or locations when the object of idealization is revered, idolized or elevated to extremes.

PROJECTION

Projection is the defence of attributing to others feelings or aspects of self that can't be directly owned. Projection takes the onus of responsibility from the one who projects by placing (often negative) attention on the other person where unconscious urges can be safely identified. An example of projection is when one person accuses another of being angry, unhappy or bad tempered, when it's really the speaker who's feeling the emotion. The anxiety-provoking feelings are externalized by disassociation from the self and by reallocation to another person.

In *Still Small Voice*, Michael Jacobs gives an example of a client-to-counsellor projection, common to the early stages of counselling. When the client says, 'I think I may be wasting your time,' Jacobs comments: 'Although this may indicate a difficulty in allowing themselves to claim attention, it can also disguise the client's feeling that counselling is a waste of time, because it has apparently got nowhere in the initial meeting.'

Insight
Jargon can be off-putting, but usually a fairly simple concept lies behind a fancy name or term.

PROJECTIVE IDENTIFICATION

This term, used by Melanie Klein to describe a type of object relationship, means the placing of part of oneself on to another person, then identifying with them. It has close associations with other defence mechanisms: denial, idealization and splitting (see later). Projective identification is the paranoid-schizoid position when the baby, and later the child, disown their own destructiveness, attributing it to someone else (originally the mother's breast as part object – good and bad).

Projective identification is a psychological interpersonal process in which the recipient begins to think, feel and behave congruently with the projections – the recipient gets pulled into the manipulations of the projector, identifying with what's projected on to them.

Another aspect of projective identification is that the projector reinternalizes the modified material when it has been 'psychologically processed' by the recipient.

RATIONALIZATION

As a defence mechanism, **rationalization** conceals the real motivations for the individual's thoughts, feelings or actions. Irrational, obscure and confusing material is 'rationalized', made sense of, by the client, as a defence against the therapist's probing, disapproval or interpretation. Rationalization can take the form of 'philosophizing', explaining away anxiety-producing material and 'staying in the head' (i.e. the realm of rational thought) rather than getting in touch with feelings. It's a process of making what's experienced as confusing, non-rational and hidden, into something clear, rational and ordered and therefore manageable.

Intellectualization is similar. The more highly educated client retreats 'into the head' to avoid deep feelings. The client might philosophize or expound 'life theories', or attempt to foil the counsellor with their analytical knowledge.

REACTION FORMATION

Reaction formation is a term used for a process through which unacceptable thoughts, feelings or impulses are controlled by creating opposing attitudes or behaviours to mask the feared ones. Anxiety is averted by outwardly engaging in behaviour urges of the Id. It may be helpful to think of reaction formation as a red herring detracting from qualities or attitudes of the self that seek expression, when a person has strong 'anti' opinions and feelings that indicate a 'fixed' position in reaction to the submerged urges. Reaction formations are so convincing a part of a person's personality that they become a permanent feature.

The psychoanalytic belief is that the original thoughts, feelings and impulses are repressed. Since they're stored in the unconscious mind, they emerge from time to time in free association and in the content and relating of dreams where the 'Id will out'. For example, a person who is fanatical about her appearance, who follows a strict diet regime, may dream about herself as plump and happy indulging in an orgy of food.

REGRESSION

Regression is another defence activated by the Ego. At a simple level it refers to a person resorting to actions that have provided security or comfort in the past. In psychoanalytic theories the implication is that anxiety or stress causes the individual to retreat from reality into an infantile state or pattern of behaviour. (Think about the young man in Chapter 7, Case study 3 who regressed to an infantile use of language.)

An individual might begin to display infantile behaviour when they haven't actually engaged in this particular activity in the (primitive) infantile stage of development; for example, an 11-year-old begins to suck his thumb, although he's never done this before, at any age. Regression occurs at times of adaptation when an unconscious aspect is brought up. Jung said, 'By activating an unconscious factor regression confronts consciousness with the problem of the psyche as opposed to the problem of outward adaptation' (*The Collected Works*). In this light, regression can be seen as a type of distracting device or a refusal to go forward at that point in time until unresolved material (held within the psyche) is satisfactorily addressed.

In the cognitive behavioural model of working and in cognitive-developmental theories, regression refers to when a client goes back to a previous mode of behaviour before learning how to cope with more complex issues or tasks. An example of this is when a person who has been terrified of flying has reached the point that she has taken a short journey in an aeroplane, but, when the time nears for her to embark on a longer flight for a family holiday, the old anxiety and panic returns and she reports to her therapist that she can't go anywhere near an aeroplane. This 'going back before going forward' is regarded as a temporary resting phase on an otherwise progressive pattern of cognitive processing.

REPRESSION

Repression, as a means of blocking an unpleasant experience from memory, is at the root of many other defences. The psychodynamic understanding of the term is when anxiety-laden thoughts, feelings and experiences have been totally forgotten, hidden away in the deep recesses of the unconscious mind. These might have been disturbing impulses that were experienced as dangerously threatening and were not allowed into consciousness, or painful memories that have been 'stored' so that the person can go forward with their lives as best they can. In the understanding of the working of defences, it helps to remind ourselves that they're always designed to protect, although in the long run they can work against the emotional development of the individual.

It's a psychoanalytic view that repressed material is stored in the body, causing psychosomatic symptoms. The psychoanalyst Wilhelm Reich, a contemporary and close associate of Freud, also believed that repression was a defence against unacceptable sexual desires. He designed a therapeutic system of 'bodywork' to release repressed (usually libidinal) pent-up thoughts, feelings and memories stored in the body as 'armouring', which manifested in psychosomatic symptoms. Reich identified a source of life energy that he called the 'orgone force'. His pioneering work included the patient exercising deep breathing and receiving massage from the therapist to encourage the release of blocked emotions and buried traumas. He noted that the breaking down of these tensions in the body was accompanied by a cathartic response from the patient of crying, spasms, laughter or screaming. Practitioners such as Alexander Lowen, the founder of a therapeutic technique called bio-energetics, developed Reich's work.

RESISTANCE

Resistance is a term that encapsulates the use of the various forms of defence (e.g. denial, projection, 'flight into health'). See Chapter 7, Resistances and defences, for an exploration.

SPLITTING

Splitting was a term used by Melanie Klein, who placed emphasis on the first few months of life and referred to the mother's breast as 'part object' to the infant, who experienced the breast as either 'wholly good' (e.g. an available source of comfort, sustenance and pleasure) or 'wholly bad' (when unavailable for gratification). The good/bad splitting occurs because the young infant has no appreciation of good and bad co-existing in the mother (the object in relationship to the infant). According to Klein, the infant experiences rage when the breast is absent and this leads to feelings of anxiety, guilt and fear of loss.

SUBLIMATION

Freud regarded this defence as normal and necessary as it serves a compromising, mediating function. **Sublimation** is usually defined as a redirecting expression of feelings and desires or impulses in a 'grown-up' manner. The individual who has reached a mature level of personal development is capable of expressing feelings openly, while at the same time appreciating what constitutes acceptable behaviour towards others (in the larger social context). Freud was of the view that excesses of feeling find expression in other socially and culturally acceptable constructs. He believed that the growth of civilization necessitated the sublimation of the primary expression of the Id, but that the Id asserts itself in science, technology, literature and art. The idea of the Id finding expression in art is evident in aspects of the work of surrealist artists like Salvador Dalí and Paul Delvaux who, inspired by psychoanalytic ideas, promoted dreams and the unconscious in their work. The surrealists experimented with 'automatic' drawing in an attempt to capture forms of art from the unconscious, inner world. Picasso's tortured *Guernica* might be seen as an example of the Id's *thanatos* (death drive) and another example might be the more recent works of art by Damien Hirst featuring animals preserved in formaldehyde. In technology, the urge to create, without addressing long-term consequences, manifests in its side-effects of pollution and ozone destruction. Currently in science we have the workings of the Id exemplified by the wish of some scientists to clone humans and genetically alter crop sources (sometimes referred to as 'playing God' – a moral and ethical Superego statement!). The Id is most often seen in its potentially destructive context but it's also powerful as a creative motivating force of individual (and Jung would say collective) expression.

Insight

Knowledge of 'defences' – first identified by Freud, his contemporaries and successors – is very useful when trying to understand a person's problems more fully. We can understand the defences or the defensive way people behave by exploring the anxiety beneath.

Other terms

ACTING OUT

This term is used to describe uncontrollable outbursts of behaviour. A 'problem' child might 'act out' for the rest of the family, in so much as they're the one who expresses or displays (in outbursts because the problems and feelings are denied by others in the family) the anxieties, conflicts and aggressions that are held within the family dynamic. Equally, **acting out** might be evident in the neurotic symptoms of an adult. In psychodynamic theory the term is used when a client is acting out (as in putting into action) some of the issues that are being worked out in therapy, outside of therapy. A young man might talk about being very angry with his father but never be able to confront him; instead, he becomes angry with another male authority figure 'out there' in his life.

BORDERLINE PERSONALITY DISORDER

The client or patient who is considered to be a borderline case lives in a precarious position between normal adaptive functioning and 'real psychic disability', which makes the forming of relationships with others extremely difficult. The therapeutic relationship is complicated by the client's dependency and reactive expression of anger.

The Kleinian view of **borderline personality disorder** is that he person's development has been arrested in the early years of the 'paranoid-schizoid' stage of development, when the infant experiences in terms of 'wholly good' or 'wholly bad' (splitting), and the persecutory anxieties of this stage persist.

CATHARSIS

From psychoanalytic theory, the term 'catharsis' refers to the release of tensions and anxiety experienced when repressed feelings from the past – memories, wishes and urges – are brought into consciousness through therapy. **Catharsis** often involves 'emotional discharge' – weeping or laughter. In 1893 Freud and his colleague Josef Breuer called their methods of psychoanalytic investigation 'catharsis'. Freud believed that psychoneuroses were based on sexual, instinctual forces that maintained pathological manifestation. Symptoms could be turned back into 'emotionally cathected ideas' brought into consciousness, thereby giving insight into the nature and origins of what were formerly unreachable unconscious processes.

COMPLEX

A **complex** is an idea filled with emotionally charged content which interrupts our attention and redirects our thinking and behaviour; also a cluster of feelings around an association with a person (like the mother) or an event. The terms 'inferiority complex' and 'superiority complex' are familiar to us all.

DEPRESSION

Depression is a mood state characterized by a lack of self-esteem, and by despondency, lack of motivation and decrease in activity with accompanying sadness and defeatism. Bouts of depression are considered normal when they're of relatively short duration. It is classified as a disorder in various ways in psychiatry, depending on the extremes and intensities of the moods and their effects. The two most useful classifications for counsellors to note are: neurotic depression – severe depression (in terms of depths and duration) which doesn't involve the sufferer's loss of contact with reality; and psychotic depression – the sufferer demonstrates a variety of impairments of normal functioning. The term 'clinical depression' is used to denote that the sufferer would benefit from medical or therapeutic attention.

FREE ASSOCIATION

Freud used the technique of **free association** to investigate the unconscious mind as an alternative to hypnosis, which was a method used at the time. In free association unconstrained associations between words, thoughts and ideas are encouraged as a method of accessing unconscious material. This technique is still used by psychodynamic counsellors, who let the client talk and express what is uppermost in their minds.

IMPULSE

Impulse, used in Freudian theory, means an instinctual act, an unconscious force arising from the Id. The cognitive behavioural use of the term refers to an event or an act that's 'triggered' by a stimulus (something that rouses into activity) over which the individual has insufficient or no conscious control. Impulses interest those of behavioural and psychodynamic orientation alike in the analysis of certain behaviour; for example, what makes a person who has never displayed antisocial behaviour experience a sudden incitement to act, uncharacteristically, with violence towards others? Both would acknowledge the activation of unconscious forces. A characteristic of an impulsive act is the speed at which it occurs.

INTROJECTION

Introjection refers to the internalization of parental and societal views, rules and taboos. Introjection has positive and negative aspects – positive qualities and attributes can be instilled through vicarious means. They might be modelled by the parents; the young child introjects a picture of themselves through parental views and opinions that can be positive or negative. A child might experience heavy criticism from a parent throughout childhood and internalize this as a self-view. Consequently, as an adult, they continue the internal criticism, considering themselves to be worthless, with resulting low self-esteem.

Paranoid-schizoid position
The **paranoid-schizoid position** refers to the earliest phase of development when the infant responds to the breast as 'part object', experiencing the breast as both 'good' and 'bad'. The 'splitting' in both the object and the Ego (internalized) is an expression of paranoid anxiety.

Part object
Part object refers to objects that are introjected into the Ego from earliest infancy, beginning with the introjection of the

part ideal (feeding) and part persecutory (withdrawn) breast. Part objects are the result of conflicts within early experiencing and are characteristics of what Melanie Klein termed the paranoid-schizoid position (as above). A glossary of Freudian terms, which includes those introduced by Melanie Klein, can be found in Hanna Segal's *Introduction to the Work of Melanie Klein*.

NARCISSISTIC PERSONALITY DISORDER

The original psychoanalytic term was **narcissistic** neurosis. Freud introduced the concept of narcissism, taken from the Greek myth of Narcissus, who fell in love with the image of himself reflected in a pool of water. The diagnostic description of the term is that the narcissistic personality is totally self-absorbed, having an exaggerated sense of self-importance and displaying an exhibitionistic need for attention. There is a propensity to fantasize about success, power, riches and so on, and a general grandiose self-glorifying attitude towards self. Freud wrote that the characteristic feature of narcissism was 'loving oneself'.

Psychoanalytic theory defines narcissism as primary or secondary.

Narcissism (primary)
Primary narcissism refers to the young child's libidinal drives being focused on the self, the Ego (in **autoerotic** satisfaction). This is a normal stage of development; only when this stage continues into adulthood does it become a neurosis.

Narcissism (secondary)
Secondary narcissism refers to the love of self that precludes love of others – emotional investment in oneself.

Narcissistic neurosis
Narcissistic neurosis is a neurosis characterized by extreme self-love that excludes normal feelings of love for others, thereby preventing the individual from forming a transference in therapy.

NEUROSIS

Freud used the term **neurosis** to describe a personality or mental disturbance due to a conflict involving the blocking of instinctual urges. Neurosis was once thought to be a neurological or organic dysfunction, and viewed as a disease of the nerves.

OPTIMAL FRUSTRATION

Optimal frustration describes feelings felt by the client in response to the blank screen or abstinent approach of psychoanalysis and the psychodynamic approaches. It refers to the frustration that the client experiences when the counsellor 'holds back' from comforting or reassuring, or from directly answering questions posed by the client. Instead the counsellor offers interpretation, addressing the underlying or unconscious meaning of a question. For example, the client might ask, 'Have you got someone coming here after me?' If the counsellor were to answer 'yes' or 'no', this wouldn't allow exploration of what lies behind the question.

Instead, the counsellor's response might be, 'Do I have a client coming here after you…? I wonder if what concerns you is that you might be one of many clients that I see and that you are not important to me?' The client's first reaction could be to deny that this is their concern and they might feel a frustration that the question has not been directly answered, but the frustration that the client experiences acts as a stimulant which causes inner conflicts to emerge and be discussed.

PHANTASIES/FANTASIES

Early childhood experiences mould our perceptions of our world. These perceptions, particular to each individual, affect how we process our thoughts and feelings in our internal world.

Freud termed these **phantasies** because of their idiosyncratic nature. The term 'fantasy' doesn't mean that the perception is untrue, but rather that understanding/experiencing of the world in infanthood, and as a young child, can be distorted as fantasy. Fantasy is best regarded as an idiosyncratic distortion. Fantasies are real to the individual, buried in the unconscious mind in association with other people, experiences, surroundings and so on. Fantasies relate to how we perceive ourselves, our inner world, and how we interact with the external world, others and our environment.

The counsellor who uses the psychodynamic approach might intervene with: 'What is your fantasy about...?' to help the client elucidate personal meanings.

The spelling 'phantasy' is used to distinguish the Freudian meaning from the 'fantasy' characteristics of daydreaming and wishful thinking. The *ph* spelling indicates the nature of the fantasy as an unconscious process.

PSYCHOSOMATIC DISORDER

Psyche originally meant 'soul' and the psychological meaning is 'the mind'. *Soma* pertains to the body or general physical components. **Psychosomatic** thus refers to the interaction between the two.

THINGS TO REMEMBER

1 *The psychodynamic approach originates from psychoanalysis and is more jargon laden than other types of therapy.*

2 *Some therapists are of the opinion that the use of categories and labels to describe client's mental processes are dehumanising and unnecessary.*

3 *We create defences (also called defence mechanisms) to protect ourselves from painful or traumatic situations and experiences as well as from the feelings they generate: conflict, anxiety, humiliation or shame.*

4 *Counsellors respect the defences of clients and the focus of their work is to address the associated feelings and behaviour that underpin the defences.*

5 *Freud identified a tripartite categorization of mental processes: the Id – the pleasure principle driven by basic instincts; the Ego – the reality principle that is the grown-up discerning self; and the Superego – the conscience, with its internalized 'shoulds' and 'musts'.*

9

....

Dealing with anger

In this chapter you will learn:
- *how to cope with anger – your own and the client's*
- *the cognitive behavioural and psychodynamic perspectives on working with the angry client*
- *exercises, including an exercise from the Gestalt approach*
- *from a checklist the 'dos' and 'don'ts' when confronted with anger.*

This chapter is concerned with anger and how to deal with it in an adaptive and constructive manner. It's easy to project outwardly about anger as a problem that other people have, and for this reason the trainee counsellor is advised to get to know their own anger. As I have pointed out elsewhere in this book, both stress management and assertiveness techniques help us understand and cope with our anger and the symptoms and underlying reasons, such as tensions and unrealistic self-goals and expectations of others. Anger can usually be managed by the counsellor and can even be used productively.

Anger and the trainee counsellor

....
Insight
Before I started counselling training and became more self-aware, it wasn't unusual that, when I was angry about

> something, I would interpret it as feeling sad (usually
> disappointment-type sad). Like many people I didn't like
> to own up to my angry feelings. Many clients say early in
> counselling 'I don't really get angry' only to get in touch with
> their anger at a later stage of the counselling.

Anger in itself is not bad – it's a human expression part of the age-old 'fight or flight' stress response. A certain amount of stress and angry impulse gives us the will 'to do', but inappropriately high levels of anger can be harmful to our self and others and violence is always unacceptable. Before being presented with the anger of clients, it's advisable to explore our own experience with dealing with anger – our own and others'.

- ▶ *What makes you angry – presses your triggers? Prejudice? Being ignored? Criticism? Insensitivity? Rudeness? Feeling vulnerable? Feeling humiliated? Incompetence?*
- ▶ *Who do you most commonly get angry with? Your partner, spouse? Friends? Your immediate family? People in authority?*
- ▶ *How do you express angry feelings? Do you tolerate so much, then 'blow up'? Accuse, blame, criticize?*
- ▶ *Do you take time out to assess the situation and approach the problem assertively?*
- ▶ *Do you ignore your angry feelings?*
- ▶ *Whom do you feel safe enough with to express angry feelings? With a close friend? With your partner or spouse? With a parent? Do you feel it's something you have to deal with alone?*

We're more likely to feel afraid of other people's anger if we're afraid of our own. If we feel we have no right to be angry ourselves, then our attitude to other people's expressions of anger is also going to be dismissive. As counsellors we need to self-challenge and accept our imperfections in the interests of being genuine with clients.

ACCEPTING RESPONSIBILITY FOR OUR ANGER

Expressions like 'You made me angry' and referring to ourselves in the abstracted second-person form (e.g. 'When that happens you feel so angry') allow us to avoid responsibility; we don't have to own our anger as we do when we state, 'I am angry.' No other person makes us angry as such; others behave in a certain way by doing or saying something, and if we have an opposing agenda, problem or issue, we might respond with anger. Our 'trigger' or 'button' is pressed – we react in a negative way. I say negative, but we need to be careful here because anger expressed appropriately, as a means of reasonable self-assertion, is both valid and necessary (and at times we need to acknowledge that a client has a right to be angry in relation to their experiences). This kind of anger is not aimed at hurting people or gaining revenge or winning an argument. It's more to do with expressing your right as an individual and it never threatens with physical violence. Before we meet the anger of our client, we need to recognize and understand the manifestations of our own.

Insight

The first step in taking control of anger problems is to mentally take responsibility. People experience relief when they stop making excuses and blaming others and instead try to understand their anger and begin to embrace anger-controlling techniques and strategies.

ASSOCIATIONS

As a way of getting in touch with your anger, take time to think of what associations you have. Complete lists like those below detailing your associations.

▶ *Other people – parents, siblings, childhood friends, bullies, etc.*
▶ *Metaphors and imagery – 'pressure cooker', 'bottled up', 'roaring like a lion', 'shouting like a fishwife', 'eaten up with anger', 'a whiplash tongue', etc.*
▶ *Symbols and archetypes – fire, war, animals (wolf, tiger, lion), bared teeth, demon eyes, warrior, devil, witch, destroyer, etc.*

Anger exercise

When you've added your own contributions, ask yourself which have most meaning to you. Are you able to put them into any specific context? For example: 'demon eyes' – as a child when certain 'grown-ups' were very angry with me their eyes appeared to me to bulge out of their heads.

Where do you hold anger in your body? What does it feel like?

Try to image your anger in a drawing or painting. What thoughts accompany your anger?

AVOIDANCE

Unless as counsellors we become familiar with and work at understanding and accepting our own anger, we might devise ways of avoiding facing the anger of our clients, as it presents itself, by deflection or collusion, or by other methods of keeping discomfort at bay. We could fail to pick up on angry statements, on body and facial expression and important associated feelings, or collude in the client's avoidance and efforts to keep angry material hidden. Perhaps we might encourage the client, through the use of reflecting skills and open questions, to explore their anger, only to find that our skills are insufficient to support the client through the expressed anger. The therapist's work includes dealing with hostile feelings in the 'here and now', making sure they are not avoided or acted out.

SAFETY PROCEDURES

Before we move on to helping techniques, remember the importance of safety procedures. When considering working with clients who have a history of violence or aggression the following points need to be established:

1 *Your suitability to work with the client – i.e. have you sufficient training and experience?*
2 *The client's suitability for counselling – i.e. do they require a more experienced counsellor than yourself? Would psychotherapy (of a longer duration than you can offer) or other medical help be a better option for them? Extreme aggression can be physically or organically based.*
3 *Is the client currently taking any medication?*
4 *Do you have sufficient support from a supervisor who can advise you?*
5 *An awareness of safety procedures and facilities in the building. If you work for an organization they will have specific safety policies and procedures; for example, an alarm system in each room and an understanding that at no time should a counsellor be working with a client alone in the building. There should always be at least one other counsellor as a backup or witness if anything goes wrong. Safety is equally important for those working in a private setting. If you're working alone, you might like to consider issues of personal safety.*

When working with clients who are experiencing difficulties with either expressing or controlling anger, reflecting feelings back to them is unlikely to be enough. The counsellor needs to encourage the client to talk about and express their anger in the 'here and now'; for example, saying, 'Tell me how you are feeling now as you talk about these past events.' This helps the client to bring past and present feelings together and to deal with them in an adaptive and constructive manner. The client can also be helped to own their feelings by being encouraged by the counsellor to say angry statements out loud, such as 'I feel angry when…' and 'I feel angry now because…' Expressive methods of therapy, like those used in psychodrama – techniques that involve imagining and role play – are useful because they help the client address their anger towards the actual person(s) or situation, rather than holding it inside or offloading it on to the counsellor.

A Gestalt method

This is a variation of the 'empty chair' method (see also Chapters 5 and 10). An empty chair is placed to face the client, at a distance of about two metres.

Begin by asking the client to identify the source of their angry feelings and then direct the client to imagine that the person (if it is a few people, they can be addressed one by one) is sitting in the chair. Let the client know what you are feeling; for example, 'I sense that you are very angry; I don't care to be the target of your anger, so rather than telling me how angry you are feeling, I would like you to express your angry feelings towards the imaginary person in the chair.'

You can then be alongside the client facing the empty chair. They may choose to sit or stand – standing when the imagined person sits gives the client an advantaged position, which they might prefer. In your role as supporter and coach you are no longer likely to be the recipient of the client's anger. They might, at first, find it difficult or embarrassing to talk directly to the imagined person and may turn to you, beginning: 'Well, I am really angry with my father, he's always criticizing me and interfering with my life.' As counsellor you can help the client by 'modelling' direct communication with the imagined person to help them get started; for example, 'I am angry with you, Father. I don't like how you criticize me and I feel that you interfere with my life.'

Another method of addressing the anger is to coach the client to be aware of physiological signals activated by anger (see Figure 9.1). Individuals react differently, but often reactions include a pounding heart, headache, tension in the shoulders, sweating and clenching of fists. It can also be useful to adopt methods used in cognitive behavioural therapy, asking the client to keep a journal and note what happened before an angry outburst, what they were feeling before and during it, what the consequences were and what they felt when the anger had

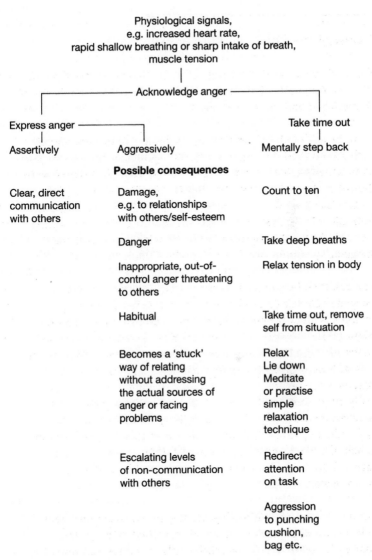

Physiological signals,
e.g. increased heart rate,
rapid shallow breathing or sharp intake of breath,
muscle tension

——————— Acknowledge anger ———————

Express anger ——————————   Take time out

Assertively   Aggressively   Mentally step back

Possible consequences

Clear, direct   Damage,   Count to ten
communication   e.g. to relationships
with others   with others/self-esteem

                     Danger   Take deep breaths

                     Inappropriate, out-of-   Relax tension in body
                     control anger threatening
                     to others

                     Habitual   Take time out, remove
                                                self from situation

                     Becomes a 'stuck'   Relax
                     way of relating   Lie down
                     without addressing   Meditate
                     the actual sources of   or practise
                     anger or facing   simple
                     problems   relaxation
                                               technique

                     Escalating levels   Redirect
                     of non-communication   attention
                     with others   on task

                                               Aggression
                                               to punching
                                               cushion,
                                               bag etc.

Figure 9.1 Anger chart – based on assertiveness training and stress management techniques and guidelines.

subsided (e.g. relief or shame). The before, during and after
assessment helps the client to make connections between
cognitions, emotions and associated behaviour, heightening
self-awareness.

Appropriate and inappropriate expression of anger

We express anger in many ways, ranging from raising our voices to threatening violence verbally or physically, or even carrying out violence. Feeling angry is normal. The suppression of anger is unhealthy, as we're likely to store anxiety in our bodies and develop aches and pains or more serious illness. We can learn to express anger in appropriate ways as opposed to giving vent to inappropriately high levels of anger.

Appropriate expression of anger includes:
Dealing with angry feelings assertively, being firm, raising our voice level, stating clearly what we feel, think and mean; taking action which does not involve physically hurting other people; being specific and concrete regarding our needs and wishes.

Inappropriate expression of anger includes:
Physical threats or actual harm to other people; destruction of other people's property, verbal bullying or harassment; making unrealistic demands of others.

Make a fuller list to help you explore what you consider to be appropriate and inappropriate expressions of anger.

ALTERNATIVES TO 'BLOWING A FUSE'

Look at Figure 9.1. Note body cues, what your body tells you. To use a behaviourist term, we can 'unlearn' destructive behaviour. We can learn to pause and think, and to redirect our energies by learning to stop when we recognize the physiological body changes. By reducing heat from the situation we can choose to step back mentally, following learned procedures to calm the mind and body. Count to ten, take deep and slow breaths and relax, 'self-talk' the body – tell yourself you can be calm, relax, lessen the tension in the body by shrugging your shoulders up to the count of three and then let them drop, circle your shoulders. Most importantly at this point, take 'time out' from the situation and try to get away from the anger-reinforcing environment. Give yourself a break – time to 'mull over' and assess the situation. This can be achieved by:

▶ *Taking time to meditate or practise a simple relaxation technique.*
▶ *Redirecting energy by engaging in physical exercise or energetic activity, such as scrubbing the floor, hammering nails into wood, etc.*
▶ *Redirecting attention or aggression by focusing on a task. Aggression can be redirected by employing a Gestalt technique of hitting a pillow or cushion, or similar, with fists or an implement such as a tennis racket while verbalizing the grievance. This method of expressing anger is safe for non-violent persons only (a violent person's anger can be further activated by an exercise like this, as it unleashes pent-up anger). The person who is angry is more likely to be in a position to assess what appropriate steps need to be taken when the heat is taken out of the situation. Everyone is different and needs to find something that works for them. Helpful tactics to let off steam include taking a vigorous walk, listening to music, screaming and shouting with the windows closed, singing at the top of the voice or writing a vitriolic letter – it doesn't have to be sent. None of these things hurts other people.*

The client is then in a position to be more objective about the situation and can decide what (if any) further action needs to be taken. Anger often escalates as personal relationships become more strained. The individual can feel increasingly misunderstood and unloved. Irrational thoughts and beliefs increase proportionally.

Examples of irrational and rational beliefs

Group 1 – Irrational (negative) thoughts:
1 *I've got too much to do, I'll never get everything done and they'll think I'm a failure.*
2 *I have been humiliated and I'm going to get revenge.*

(Contd)

3   I'm trapped and I'm powerless to change my circumstances – it's up to my husband to make decisions.
4   I've got to win this argument; if I don't then people will think I'm a fool.
5   He is ruining my life. He always lets me down and criticizes me.
6   It's just not fair; she got promotion when I am better qualified for the job – it's the story of my life.
7   Other people don't show me any respect, they use me and then when I need them they let me down.

Group 2 – Corresponding alternative (positive) thoughts:
1   I will do what I realistically can. What other people think doesn't matter. I know I am doing the best I can.
2   People are not always pleasant and I can learn from this experience and survive it. Thoughts of revenge are a waste of my energy and stop me enjoying myself.
3   I can decide what I want to change in my life. Not all the changes I would like to make may be possible right now. I can negotiate with my husband as a first step.
4   I don't always have to be right. I can respect my own point of view and respect other people's right to have different views.
5   My happiness comes from within me and is not dependent on other people's behaviour towards me or their opinion of me.
6   Life is not fair and it is unrealistic to expect it to be. I will have other opportunities, as I have in the past. This person's promotion doesn't diminish my abilities.
7   I am a worthwhile person. If people don't treat me with respect then that is their problem. I can't control the way others behave towards me. If I help another person in any way it is my choice and it doesn't mean that they have to reciprocate.

Let's compare the self-statements from each group.

Group 1
The negative, irrational thoughts are self-defeating, defensive and self-denying, demonstrated by words and phrases such as *failure, humiliated, trapped, powerless, I'll never get, I've got to win, ruining my life.*

Feelings from group 1
Overwhelmed with responsibilities, powerlessness, entrapment, humiliation, hurt, abandonment, loss, let down, expectations, dependency on others for happiness, approval, life's unfair. 'Shoulds' and 'oughts' of self and others. Irrational beliefs that accompany angry feelings reveal our high expectation of both ourselves and others.

Group 2
The positive, rational thoughts are self-affirming and responsible, demonstrated by words and phrases such as: *realistic, worthwhile, I can negotiate, I am doing the best that I can, I can learn and survive (from the experience), I don't always have to be right.*

Consider the statement, 'I don't always have to be right'. My own reaction is to give an inner 'Phew – what a relief!' I wonder what your reaction is.

Feelings from group 2
Relief – which comes from a dropping away of 'shoulds' and 'oughts' – targeted towards both self and others; humility, I'm human, it's OK to make mistakes/be wrong; tolerance – other people have their own opinions, it's OK if they don't agree with mine; self-respect – I am capable of making decisions, I do the best I can, I can survive, inner strength, I'm a worthwhile person; hope – in affirmation of self and capabilities.

Working with a video

Insight

I don't work with a video camera myself and, apart from in training, never have, but other counsellors have found it an effective aid in working with some clients with anger-related problems.

Some experienced counsellors have adopted the use of video work. The client can role play situations that they recognize as producing angry responses, practising appropriate adaptive and more constructive ways of dealing with other people and potentially problematic situations. This could be a past unresolved experience or a conflict that is currently taking place. The counsellor can practise with the client, 'modelling' adaptive behaviour and demonstrating methods used until the client is familiar with working with this medium. It won't suit everyone and, of course, the client must always be presented with a choice as to whether they would like to try this kind of work or not. People who have been physically, mentally or sexually abused may abhor the idea of working with a camera because of its intrusive probing nature. They could feel humiliated by seeing themselves 'performing' in an angry way. The client needs enough Ego strength to appreciate that their anger is the way they behave at times and isn't them as such. They also need to believe that their behaviour can change. The client with very low self-esteem might need to build up to working with a video recorder and might consider it as an option when they see some progress has been made.

Suitable candidates for video work usually enjoy the exploratory nature of it. Viewing the playback and trying out different responses and reflections can be a valuable learning process. By role playing a recent real situation that caused the client to be angry, the client will see their behaviour more objectively and see themselves as others could perceive them – as, for example, out of control, frightening or vulnerable. The client gains insight into the other person's point of view if they role play both themselves and the person they're in conflict with by alternating roles. Again, the counsellor first models this technique. By reviewing the video recording the client witnesses the dynamics of the relationship; they gain a sense of being angry and what it feels like to be on the receiving end of that anger. They can also examine the responses they anticipate. When challenging situations are looming that are known to the client to bring on anxiety, and are therefore likely to produce anger, then more appropriate responses can be rehearsed in preparation. The counsellor and client can discuss the recording together, replaying and homing in on particular parts. The counsellor can ask the client what they were feeling or thinking as both themselves and the other person in the role play. The video frame can be frozen while questions are asked: 'You look very sad here – what is going through your mind?', 'Your mood seemed to change at this point – what are you feeling?' The observation of body language is also useful.

The methods used in this chapter have been mainly of the directive cognitive behavioural approach, looking at behaviour and thoughts and beliefs (cognitions) and coaching in and modelling certain corrective thoughts and behaviours. The cognitive behavioural method teaches or 'coaches' the client to 'self-talk', replacing irrational incapacitating thoughts with more rational ones. The psychodynamic approach addresses causal factors and underlying (repressed) material. The counsellor will also be attentive to dreams and psychosomatic symptoms.

The psychodynamic perspective

The psychodynamic counsellor would approach the client's problems by considering anger in terms of the transference, introjections, defences – such as denial, repression and displacements – and working with the sensitive confronting of resistance. Childhood-related material, feelings associated with abandonment or loss, are likely to be re-experienced through the transference. The object relations concept of 'good enough mothering' and holding and containing the client's anger will come into play. The good enough mother can contain her infant's destructive rage while remaining loving and nurturing; she doesn't retaliate or take revenge on her child. The client who holds deeply rooted anger might not have had 'good enough mothering' (or adequate valuing from a significant other). The 'not good enough mother' might have been emotionally wounded and therefore stunted in her ability to demonstrate love, afraid of her own anger and possibly unable to control it, resulting in anger turned towards the self. This could manifest in various ways; she might desperately attempt to satisfy the infant's every demand promptly, behave inconsistently, be cold, punitive or rejecting, or place a rigid regime on the infant or child. The child of dysfunctional parenting has introjected many negative views of themselves and self in relationship to others; for example, 'I am stupid', 'I am not worth loving', 'I am responsible for my mother's inability to cope.' Families who avoid unpleasant topics or express anger by physical violence or abuse fail to 'model' appropriate methods of expressing and dealing with anger. The anger gets 'split off' as something to be feared because of its destructiveness and denigrating potential. Psychologists and sociologists alike are of the opinion that unresolved problems with anger can transfer from one generation to the next.

As we have seen, destructive anger is often displaced anger, directed towards someone other than the person or situation that provoked it. The angry client might demonstrate destructive idealization of the therapist, a form of splitting and acting out of destructive anger. The client could feel an emotional ambivalence towards the therapist, being unable to tolerate the therapist as having 'good' and 'bad' potential, and may attempt to make the counsellor manageable by assuming an idealized view of them. Feelings of strong need and helplessness can result in rage, which hides an impulse towards relational closeness. Extreme anger is often a defence against painful feelings of sadness, vulnerability or helplessness, linked to loss, abandonment and fear of separation, which will most probably be recalled in therapy and re-experienced in the negative transference as an echo of the client's past.

The main focus of the psychodynamic counsellor is to help the client get in touch with vulnerable feelings, bringing denied anger out into the open, which in itself can be a great relief to the client. The dangers are that the client hides behind defences and verbal and non-verbal manifestations of defensive reactions: being vague, becoming silent, changing the subject, offering rationalization or fending off feelings with continual chatter; the anger felt towards the therapist is reallocated to other people outside the therapy (acted out); defences are acted out through resistance to therapy (not turning up for the session, being late); and hidden destructive anger will be detrimental to the therapeutic process. The 'angry client', who initially finds it difficult to communicate thoughts and feelings, most probably lacked parental 'mirroring' and the counsellor's support and willingness to face the source of the destructive impulses can be reparative.

The need to be mirrored, brought to our attention by Heinz Kohut in his developmental theory of self-psychology, is a grandiose-exhibitionistic need of the child. Kohut was of the opinion that to develop a healthy self-concept the child needs to be shown that at least one of the parents derives great pleasure in having them around. The parent demonstrates love and regard for the child from the subtle cues of gesture, expression and tone of voice. The child looks into the mirror of the parent's face and, seeing love, approval and pleasure, forms a picture of themselves. The self-concept then is positive – I am a lovable, worthwhile person. However, the parent can't always be the mirror that reflects a positive self-image. Kohut said that, when the parent fails to 'mirror', it presents an opportunity to draw on the memory of the positive experiences, when the child can be their own mirror. Kohut called this process 'transmuting internalizations'. Over time the transmuting internalization contributes to part of a 'strong and cohesive self'. By conveying a genuine interest, acceptance and empathic responding, the counsellor 'mirrors' self-worth to the client, accepting the mothering role in the transference. While appreciating the effects and importance of past relationships and experiences, the counsellor keeps the client's attention in the emotional experiencing, in the here and now in relationship to the counsellor, encouraging them to be both more responsive to their own feelings and emotions and attentive to their emotional interaction with other people.

THE REPARATIVE RELATIONSHIP

Insight

Clients can feel very vulnerable talking about their anger and how they express it. It can be extremely self-affirming when they are able to talk freely with a counsellor about the strong emotions they experience and feel that the counsellor – seeing the bigger picture – is accepting of them as a person.

People who have been well mirrored as children appreciate themselves to be acceptable, lovable and attractive and are not solely reliant on others for their self-esteem. The child of dysfunctional parenting, with parents who exhibited low self-esteem and a disposition towards angry outbursts, has rarely received enough positive messages. The grandiose-exhibitionistic needs, which sought fulfilment at the early developmental stage, are frustrated and repressed since there is no opportunity for these wishes to be satisfied. The counsellor's work can be seen to attempt to repair some of the lack experienced. The idea of reparative relationship is useful for working with anger. Therapy can provide nurturing and a form of corrective reparenting, supplying an emotional experience lacking in childhood. It's the re-experiencing of old conflicts and impulses in a non-judgemental, non-threatening supportive, empathic environment that makes reparation possible. The counsellor mirrors a self-worth by valuing the client and extending positive regard. The reparative model encompasses person-centred qualities and values of warmth, acceptance and empathy. The client experiences in the 'here and now' of the therapy that anger can be confronted, can be talked about, explored and understood. Rather than being devastatingly destructive, the outcome is positively constructive.

General checklist when confronting anger

Do:
Be caring and empathic
Confront sensitively and tentatively
Confront the defence, not the client
Accept and respect the client's true feelings
Be supportive and strengthen the client's Ego
Be optimistic and realistic
Hold the boundaries
Have adequate supervision

Beware of:
Becoming aggressive, punitive or defensive
Colluding with the client's resistance
Losing yourself in the transference/reparative intention

THINGS TO REMEMBER

1 *It helps us understand others when, as counsellor or helper, we own and familiarize ourselves with how we feel and behave when we are angry and what presses our own triggers.*

2 *As counsellors we need to look after ourselves too and make sure that we are working at a level of anger problem we are equipped to work with. We need to think in terms of safety, too.*

3 *There are techniques and exercises that the client can learn and practise to defuse, contain or express their anger in healthy ways.*

4 *Being able to express oneself in an appropriate assertive manner and having good communication skills can counter the need to vent anger in inappropriate outbursts.*

5 *Some things aren't helpful while working with people with anger problems. Learning the 'do's and 'don'ts' of what is appropriate or not is crucial.*

10

....

Underlying issues

In this chapter you will learn:
- *what can help when a client brings difficult issues, such as prolonged grieving*
- *about client and counsellor views of suicide*
- *how to help those who are self-harming*
- *the definition of abuse.*

When people decide to have counselling, they've decided that they need specialized help, recognizing that they have problems or difficulties that they're presently unable to cope with alone. Having made the decision to do something about the situation, the prospect of talking to a stranger about intimate problems can still be daunting and often it's difficult for a person to open up in the first session – no matter how sensitively the counsellor handles the intake session, the 'presenting problems' (i.e. the problems that the client openly expresses to the counsellor) may be only symptomatic of more deeply rooted troubles. Sometimes the client presents problems as generalizations – they are depressed, or not getting on well with others in a close relationship, or dissatisfied with life. These feelings are very real and sometimes the clients themselves aren't fully aware that 'bigger' issues lie below the surface manifestations. But the client who initially says they're depressed might, a few sessions into the therapy, intimate or tell the counsellor directly that they have been considering suicide; or the person who at the onset of therapy cited their main problem to be trouble in close relationships may eventually reveal that they're suffering from a form of unresolved grief. With this in mind, the focus of this chapter is the client who suffers from unresolved grief, the suicidal client, the self-harming client and the client who has been abused – all real-life situations that people go through and present with in therapy. On occasions these surprise and sometimes incapacitate the inexperienced counsellor or willing helper.

Insight

People often have high expectations of counselling and sometimes think that the counsellor can fix the most serious of problems in a short span of time. It's important that hopes and expectations are talked about and that the counsellor is realistic about what might be achieved.

Grief

Grief is always associated with some form of loss that involves change. The person who grieves is attempting to acclimatize or reorientate themselves to the new circumstances that they find themselves in. This is not always straightforward, for a variety of reasons. When we think of someone as grief-stricken we usually associate the condition with the death of a loved one (bereavement), yet there are other sources of grief to consider which require deeply challenging readjustment. These include:

- ▶ *Change of circumstances – e.g. loss of job, ongoing financial problems that are status/security related.*
- ▶ *Change in relationships – e.g. death of a loved one, a child growing up or moving away, divorce or separation.*
- ▶ *Change in body/health – e.g. loss of limb, internal organ, persistent or serious illness.*
- ▶ *Change in physiological functioning – e.g. due to ageing, fitness deterioration, loss of mental faculties, deafness, eyesight deterioration.*

People grieve for many reasons and in differing ways. Through grief, we work out and eventually resolve our deeply felt loss and the accompanying pain and anxieties. Grief therapists such as William J. Worden and Elizabeth Kubler-Ross have, in their writings, greatly enhanced the understanding of grieving processes. One of the main reasons a person suffers prolonged grief is that they have been unable to express, in their own time and in their own way, all the complexities and stages of their grief, their thoughts and emotions; they might not have felt heard, acknowledged and supported. It follows that counselling can help enormously because they can talk about all their feelings, including a yearning for the deceased, blaming other people, or guilty feelings. When a person is trying to cope with a fundamental change (physical or in life circumstances), feelings of frustration, anger and depression can contribute to a prolonged grief.

Insight

Working with grieving clients can trigger grief in the counsellor over their own past losses. When this has happened to me I have made sure that I have taken it to the support of supervision.

AN EXAMPLE OF UNRESOLVED GRIEF

If grief is not fully expressed at the time of the loss, it can lie submerged as a source of pain and inner conflict. An account follows of how a client was helped with problems originating from unresolved grief.

In this example we see many of the known symptoms of grief: shock, denial, guilt, anger, emotional withdrawal and physical symptoms accompanying the psychological effects. The client had become 'stuck', suffering acutely from the death of the child because she hadn't been able to go through the grieving process fully and at her own pace. There was what the Gestalt approach terms 'unfinished business'; the infant's death hadn't been accepted and integrated as part of her life experience that would allow her to move on and live in the present. Susan commented that what helped her in counselling was being able to 'say anything I felt like saying'. She felt supported because nothing she said or felt was dismissed but was explored with interest. She felt that she had been 'given permission' (when everyone else expected her to be stoic) to talk about feeling angry and how depressed and 'dead' she herself felt; and it helped. She was able to identify fears and misconceptions, recognizing that sudden infant death syndrome (SIDS) is a *bona fide* medical problem that affects families across the social cultural spectrum, and occurs in the families of doctors and other medically trained individuals.

Case study 4

Susan was a woman in her late 20s. Her presenting problems were: she felt generally depressed, she had no interest in sexual relations with her husband, she felt that their relationship was on a downward spiral, she had no energy or enthusiasm for anything, suffered from severe headaches and had heavy, painful menses. During the first few sessions of counselling Susan was composed and appeared somewhat distant both from what she was saying and the counselling experience. Although she talked openly about her deteriorating relationship with her husband and her lack of sexual drive, she spoke without feeling, completing most statements by rubbing her eyes. I sensed an underlying sadness that was incongruent with her matter-of-fact outward manner. When I related this to her, she told me that two years previously her four-month-old son had died in a 'cot death' (also termed Sudden Infant Death Syndrome). When I asked her how she had felt at the time of the death she used the word 'numb'. She related that she cried at the time but there had always been an air of unreality about it, especially when her husband and relatives kept telling her to 'try for another baby as soon as possible' as if the infant was replaceable. She began to cry when I asked her the baby's name, saying that neither her family nor her friends ever referred to him any more. For everyone else's sake she had tried to behave as if she had fully recovered but she never had. Instead, to protect herself, she had cut off from her feelings and this had inadvertently caused close relationships to suffer.

In the sessions we had together, Susan experienced the grief that she had clearly repressed. She talked about the initial shock, the pain, guilt, sadness, anger and helplessness she had felt and continued

(Contd)

to feel. She felt immense guilt – blaming herself for the infant's death. Visits from various sympathetic personnel, including a police interview, only confirmed her fears. She was angry with herself and others 'for letting it happen' and angry towards the child for going, as if he had changed his mind about accepting her as a mother. She recalled the way those around her had adopted a 'hush hush' approach to the tragedy, which left her feeling rejected and 'lost'; she yearned to hold and touch her baby.

By acknowledging and re-experiencing the grief she had originally been unable to express fully, she began to understand why she had distanced herself sexually from her husband. She acknowledged that she was terrified of the possibility of having another child; she also felt that she had no right to experience love or pleasure, judging herself to be a bad, neglectful mother who deserved punishment.

NORMALIZING THE GRIEF

What is needed to work with someone who is suffering from unresolved grief? It's important to acknowledge what they're going through, to help the client to actualize the loss. Another important factor is the 'normalizing' of their feelings, thoughts and behaviour. The grieving person who hasn't come to terms with the death of a loved one will inwardly ask themselves what is wrong with them, why they can't get over it. There can be many reasons, including disbelief about what has actually happened. The reason a person has not actualized the death is more often than not because they have never been allowed to experience it fully in their own way.

The counsellor can help with this, encouraging the client to fully express their grief in whatever way they choose. The person might like to bring in photographs of their loved one to show the counsellor; they most certainly will want to talk about the person and can be encouraged to share their memories with you. Susan brought in some of her baby's clothes and toys to show me. Because people are very sensitive and vulnerable when they are grieving, there's a tendency for them to think that what they experience is abnormal. For example, some people talk to the deceased person or hear their voice; experience bouts of copious crying or moments of spiritual euphoria; feel unconnected from what's going on around them, becoming increasingly alienated from their own experiencing and from other people. Counsellors may choose to self-disclose to help the client to appreciate that they are not alone in thinking 'different' thoughts or feeling extremes of emotion. The counsellor, if they think it will be useful to the client, might say something like, 'I felt like that too when my mother died' or 'It took me a long time to accept my friend's death' – just enough to share a little of the counsellor's own experience without distracting the focus from the client.

The counsellor can help the client to:

▶ *actualize and accept the reality of the loss (whether this is bereavement, broken relationships or physical change)*
▶ *identify, focus on and experience the pain of grief*
▶ *adjust to life as it is now, without the loved one or in the changed circumstances*
▶ *get in touch with inner resources, e.g. by reality testing and drawing attention to achievements*
▶ *redirect emotional energies from the deceased one or 'life as it was', and reinvest energies in new relationships and life interests.*

Insight

It has been my experience that, when people are in the throes of grief, they rarely think that they will ever feel differently, and some reassurance from the counsellor that they will feel differently in time can help. I sometimes explain that it is not so much time that is the great healer, as the saying goes, but all the emotions and stages we go through in our grief that eventually bring us to some resolution.

Stages of grief

Grief therapists writing on the subject have identified various stages of grief. There can be considerable movement between the stages – all of which are normal. Variously they have been described as follows.

Stages of grief

The initial stage

In the first stages of grief recognized normal reactions include: shock, denial, unreality, emotional outpourings, psychological and physical symptoms (e.g. inability to think straight, feeling panicky, bodily aches and pains, depression).

The middle stage

While the first stage consists of immediate, shocked grief responses, the middle stage relates to expectations and disappointments of ourselves and others. These include:

▶ **Guilt** – *e.g. we could have done so much more for the other person.*
▶ **Anger** – *e.g. at self and deceased for envisaged inadequacies in the relationship.*
▶ **Resentment** *towards the deceased* – *e.g. they have left behind the one who is still living.*
▶ **Idealism** – *the deceased was a 'perfect' person.*

The last stage

The final stage represents the resolution of grief – a realistic coming to terms with the life and death of the loved one:

▶ **The realistic overview** – *e.g. 'I did what I could' for the deceased; 'She was a lovely person but could also be difficult at times,' appreciating both positive and negative aspects of their lives.*
▶ **Acceptance** – *e.g. understanding of the person's death, that they are no longer physically present in the person's life, letting go.*
▶ **Readjustment and emotional investment** – *e.g. moving on.*
▶ **Personal growth** – *the client's development of a stronger inner self, acknowledging, appreciating and cherishing the contributions the deceased person made in the client's life and an internalization of the person.*

SUPPORTING ROLES

It's the opinion of grief therapists that no specialized skills are needed when working with grief. The process of grieving requires time and the free expression of thoughts and emotions. The main thing is just being there with the client, acknowledging and supporting them through their expressions of grief, listening, using reflecting skills and gently encouraging them to get in touch with and explore their feelings to assist with actualizing the loss. Person-centred skills are particularly important, especially empathic responding. Because people are vulnerable when they hold on to deeply painful emotions, the counsellor's ability to convey acceptance and to hold and contain the client's catharsis of grief is all-important. In the Western world we tend to hurry most experiences along, including those in the areas of self-care and reflection. 'Normal' life calls us back to work, to relating to others – even those close to the person who mourns might give a time limit, expecting the person to recover from the loss in as short a time as a few weeks. Individual need and expression is, more often than not, dismissed in favour of conventional ideas of normality and 'getting on with life'.

In *Death – the Final Stage of Growth* by Elizabeth Kübler-Ross, Rabbi Zachary I. Heller gives examples of the support systems religious communities offer. For example, he writes about the Jewish way of mourning as a collective experience. Jewish tradition confronts death directly; the loved ones of the terminally ill person 'surround, comfort and encourage the patient'. The deathbed confessional as a rite of passage allows the dying person to express any residual concerns and fears. The ceremonial involvement of family and community is a comfort to those who survive, children included. The Jewish tradition of maintaining a vigil at the bedside of the dying is of immense value, both for the dying person and those about to face bereavement. Judaism shields mourners from being overwhelmed by guilt because the community shares in the care of the dying. The Jewish mourner isn't protected from the death of the loved one, being called on to make funeral arrangements at the beginning of the grief process.

Religion might or might not be a comfort to the mourner, but it's important that the counsellor respects the person's religious beliefs. When the client is from a different culture it would be helpful if the counsellor familiarizes themselves with the practices and customs surrounding death. It can be a source of distress to the surviving members of a family if the person hasn't been treated with respect in accordance with the traditions of their culture, in hospital, on their deathbed or in funeral arrangements. For example, the dying Muslim will wish to face Mecca to die, and may wish to have a relative whisper the call to prayer or family members to recite prayers. If none of this is carried out it can complicate the grief process.

As we have seen, many complex feelings are involved in loss of any kind. These include abandonment – being left behind; anxiety – about coping without the person or with the disability or the impoverished circumstance; sadness – at the loss and the separation, yearning for and missing the person; and fearfulness – of facing life in this new situation. The subject of fear isn't widely addressed in association with mourning, yet it's a primary emotion that feeds the other emotions. People might fear that they'll be alone, will have no one to love them, that they can't look after themselves, can't manage financially; or they might fear their own impending death.

Depression

> ### Insight
> Symptoms of grief and depression are very similar and in fact it is natural and normal to feel 'down' for a while following a bereavement. We would expect a grieving person to feel sadness but other symptoms may suggest depression. Signs to look out for include: despondency, lack of energy and motivation, loss of sleep, loss of appetite, constant fretting and negative thinking, and an inability to concentrate.

The depressed person is likely to be fearful about life ahead and could be constantly defeated by irrational thoughts and beliefs such as 'my life is over'. The woman who has recently undergone a hysterectomy might consider herself to be no longer fully a woman. Underneath these thoughts lie fears of leading a lonely, meaningless or impoverished life. The elderly survivor might feel that since their spouse has died they have nothing to look forward to but joining the deceased. When a person's spouse dies, they often have real worries that they might be unable to cope alone with day-to-day practicalities of life, such as paying bills, mending appliances and running a home. This is exacerbated by physical symptoms such as listlessness. Feelings of dependency may result in anger: 'How could he leave me with this financial mess?', 'I don't know where anything is; my wife used to do all that.' A child whose parent has died may fear that they have somehow killed the parent. Fear issues need to be addressed before a person can move on; the counsellor can challenge these thoughts by normalizing the person's beliefs as normal and appropriate to hold, but also help the client to 'reality' check. The term 'irrational' is perhaps misleading in this context because feelings of inadequacy and dependency are a normal stage to go through. The counsellor's acceptance of these, conveyed by empathic responding and verbal acknowledgement of fears, frees the client to express associated emotions.

REALITY TESTING

This is a method of challenging the client to look at their one-sided thinking. For example, someone who experiences guilt turns in on themselves and believes that they have been neglectful of the deceased, telling themselves that they should have done more, even to the point of thinking that their neglect has indirectly or directly caused the death. In relation to the example of Susan, who blamed herself for being a bad mother, the reality testing came in the form of asking her what she did for the child and what her relationship with him was like. By re-exploring many details of occurrences in his short life she could appreciate that she had on the whole been a very attentive, loving mother. Sometimes reality testing may involve the counsellor (sensitively) providing specific information that contradicts an irrational belief or challenging the client to check medical facts with a physician. For example, Susan may have thought she was physically unable to have another fully healthy baby (genetic factors), and a woman who has had a hysterectomy may believe that her sex life is over.

The letter and the empty chair technique

The letter and empty chair are simple techniques that have been used effectively to help the grieving person to resolve 'unfinished business' and say goodbye to the person who has died. As a first step the counsellor can ask the client if they would like to write a letter to the deceased to say all that they want to say, identifying unresolved issues – perhaps what they wished they had been able to say to the person when they were still alive – as a way of saying goodbye. It's important that the counsellor doesn't give too many suggestions about what the letter might contain – it needs to come from them. It's up to the client what they do with the letter. Some people might find the writing down of their thoughts, feelings and wishes enough to bring relief, but bringing the letter to a counselling session is also presented as a possibility.

The technique of the empty chair has been explained in Chapter 9, but, to recap, the client addresses an empty chair as if the person they're addressing was sitting there. The client is then able to talk to the person. In the letter and empty chair technique the client can read out the letter, addressing the person who is imagined to be in the chair. The client can express strong emotions such as anger, resentment, bitterness, guilt, love and tenderness through these media. This technique is particularly helpful to clients who are finding it difficult to get in touch with their grief and are harbouring complex and debilitating emotions.

An example from my own counselling experience was a young woman whose brother had killed himself in particularly tragic circumstances a year before she sought help. The letter writing, followed by reading out the letter in therapy using the empty chair method, released an immense amount of guilty feelings (she should have helped him more) and also angry feelings (how could he do that to her and the rest of his family) – which proved to be cathartic for her. Often grief is hard to resolve because of the ambivalent feelings felt towards the deceased person; this is especially true when a person has taken their own life.

To sum up, there are many reasons for unresolved or complicated grief. Possible reasons include:

▶ *Cultural issues – not being able to mourn or carry out ceremonies in a way that is appropriate to a religion or culture.*
▶ *Shut-down time – not enough time has been allowed (because of self-censuring or the requirements of others) to grieve.*
▶ *Lack of support and understanding from others – a lonely experience, accompanied by emotional withdrawal.*
▶ *Ambivalent feelings towards the deceased person – resulting in an idealized view of the dead person – or unresolved issues between the two at the time of death.*
▶ *Complicated guilt feelings – often related to those above; watching the dying person suffer; in cases of suicide, not being able to say goodbye – the person who is left behind wishes they had been able to tell the dying person that they loved them or to say goodbye in a way that would be meaningful to them (e.g. having input in the funeral ceremony).*
▶ *Inability to accept the person is gone – related to shock and denial, especially with sudden death through accident or illness.*

The suicidal client

In the spirit of a mini-research project over a period of time, I asked a number of people what they thought a counsellor's role was with regard to people who say they are contemplating suicide. All but a few said, in varying ways, that it was the counsellor's job to stop those persons from killing themselves by making them feel better about themselves or their life situation. Some said words to the effect that the suicidal person should be made to understand how devastated the people they leave behind would feel; a few advocated strong intervention strategies. Generally, people have strong reactions to the subject of suicide. The question 'Does a person have the right to choose to end their life?' brings up uncomfortable feelings for most of us. Having someone say to us, 'I really don't want to live any more,' is a challenging situation. It would be wise to examine our personal attitudes and beliefs with regard to suicide before we are faced with a client who says just that. Take time to think over the following questions.

▶ *Do you think it's a person's right to choose?*
▶ *Do you think that intervention – e.g. hospitalization, psychiatric treatment – is justifiable when suicide is inferred?*
▶ *Do you think the person contemplating suicide is incapable of making a considered choice?*
▶ *Do you think suicide is wrong, an act of selfish self-pitying?*

Now, replacing the word 'think' with 'feel', work your way through these questions again.

THE COUNSELLOR'S ANXIETY

Insight

It is crucial that a counsellor has adequate supervision for their support needs when counselling a suicidal client. They may need to see or speak over the telephone to their supervisor more frequently. The supervisor can provide ongoing practical advice on appropriate action as well as emotional support.

It's a normal reaction to feel anxious at the thought of another human being ending their life. Not surprisingly, counsellors can feel swamped by feelings of responsibility for the fate of the client. Anxiety can cause the counsellor to collude with the client by intervening with a change of subject or promoting a positive attitude towards life. Anxiety is often linked to impossible expectations of ourselves as counsellors. Individual counsellors need to assess their experience and training and accept their limitations. We actually do the other person an injustice if we attempt to work at levels beyond our experience and capabilities. It might be appropriate, for new counsellors especially, to refer the client on. The first time a client reveals that they intend to kill themselves, the new counsellor might be impeded by 'self-talk' such as 'If they kill themselves, I'll be blamed.' Other irrational self-statements may go something like:

▶ *'I am personally responsible if the client takes their life.'*
▶ *'If I am a competent counsellor I can persuade them to change their mind.'*
▶ *'Through the therapeutic relationship I can give them a sense of self-worth and save them.'*

Are these types of self-statements realistic? Examine any irrational beliefs you might hold on the subject of the counsellor's responsibility towards suicidal clients and replace them with more balanced ones, taking into account the client's responsibilities and free choice. All talk containing suicidal intention needs to be taken seriously. People do attempt to kill themselves and some succeed. They could be cries for help or they might equally be considered decisions that the person has made having weighed up the pros and cons of their life situations.

SOME OF THE REASONS AND SITUATIONS OF SUICIDAL INTENTION

The suicidal cry for help
This might come from the person who repeatedly thinks of killing themselves but has not attempted to do so to date. Suicidal references

are a plea to be heard and responded to. The person is likely to be in emotional pain and inner turmoil and they can only express it in imagery of self-destruction. They feel alone and may be holding a great deal of unexpressed anger, resentment and frustration towards themselves and others. They might feel persecuted or unloved. There can be an underlying wish to control or manipulate the behaviour of those close to them – 'I'll make them see what they've done to me', 'I'll make them sorry.' It would be a mistake to dismiss the person as merely attention seeking. The number of young males who commit suicide is disproportionally high in most societies. This could be due to many reasons, but is likely to be related in some way to internalized pressures and expectations of family and society. The pressure to 'succeed' in life can cause tremendous stress and the person who in his own eyes consistently underachieves, failing to live up to his own or others' expectations, can suffer from chronic low self-esteem. The suicidal person usually feels that they, and their lives, have little value or meaning.

The crisis situation
Another reason a person might have suicidal thoughts is a desperate reaction to trauma or a crisis situation. For example, they may arise when a person close to them dies; they feel they 'can't go on' without them. The survivor could be in a state of shock and feel that the only solution to the desperate psychological pain they're experiencing is to end their life. A further instance of this crisis category is the person who loses all material wealth or is shamed or outcast by their community and has no sense of place or worth.

Example

An example of the latter was a client I saw, an Indian woman who had been ostracized by her community for leaving her husband, taking their two children with her. Her husband had been abusive – physically, sexually and mentally – and her self-worth was very low. Her decision to leave the material comforts of their middle-class family home meant that she was, along with her two young children, living under great duress, with Social Security funding, in temporary accommodation. In this atmosphere she felt she couldn't go on; she felt diminished in the eyes of her community and of society, and she had no self-respect and no hope of providing adequately for her children. She felt doubly oppressed and discriminated against: as a member of an ethnic minority group, by society as a whole, and as a rejected member of her community and culture.

Quality of life

Those who experience poor quality of life and who have no chance of improving their situation – including the heavily disabled person, people who are terminally ill and those who live with continuous terrible pain – may have weighed up their situation and having taken into account all considerations decided that they want to put an end to their lives. What's the position of the counsellor in this case? You might be tempted to try to buoy the person up or to deflect what they're conveying, to make both of you more comfortable, when what's needed is to stay in the feeling world of the client, to give them a full opportunity to state their desperate state of mind and the pain and hopelessness they're feeling.

It can also be helpful to explore with the person what they do value in life, what it might be hard to leave behind if they did decide to end their lives. Appropriate questions could reveal, for example, that the person feels that they're a terrible burden on a carer and it might be appropriate to 'reality test'. The client might also like to talk about dying and religious beliefs. The topic of dying is still a taboo subject for most people and a person contemplating dying can find much relief in talking to another person who doesn't shy away from the reality. Details like these could be enough to highlight that there are some ambivalent feelings about living. The people in the above situations are liable to be depressed because of their dire conditions; some types of depression require medical treatment. If depression is linked with indications of mental illness such as hearing voices that instruct the person to end their lives, then the client should be urged to see a doctor immediately. The counsellor needs to be aware of the medical history and any medication the client is currently taking. Mostly, people who talk about suicide have a considerable ambivalence about wanting to die – some regard it as the only solution at the time; others, who have considerable physical difficulty and live with continuous heavy pain, make a considered and conscious decision to end their lives.

Possible reasons for the client to relate suicidal intentions:

▶ *they feel overwhelmed by their problems and are unable to see any other solution*
▶ *they feel alone and unloved*
▶ *they see no value in themselves or their life*
▶ *a 'cry for help' – they're emotionally disturbed, fearful that they may kill themselves and want to be stopped*
▶ *a way of saying goodbye, a preparation for death*
▶ *an imploding expression of anger – revenge on others*
▶ *the person is suffering from mental illness and needs medical help – e.g. referral to a psychiatrist; they may hear voices telling them to kill themselves, suggesting schizophrenia*
▶ *to manipulate the actions or attitudes of others*
▶ *because they have decided to end their life, having considered it carefully – they're sure they want to do it and would like others to understand, respect and accept the reasons for the decision*
▶ *to have supportive contact with another person before dying*
▶ *to 'admit' to suicidal thoughts/considerations – bringing them out in the open (there may be ambivalence about dying)*
▶ *to seek help and affirmation or confirmation of self-worth*
▶ *a reaction to crisis.*

How can a counsellor help?

First, the counsellor can keep in focus how vulnerable the client is and strike a balance between sensitivity and mild challenging. The counsellor can help the client to clarify and make thoughts concrete, in particular by being aware of 'clues' – what is being implicitly said and asking the client about feelings, especially angry ones. The counsellor can be direct and say, 'Are you saying that you are having thoughts of killing yourself?' Without trying to change the person's mind about whether their life is worth living or not, the counsellor can help them to explore relationships or the problems they are experiencing. Because there are many taboos generally around the subject of suicide it's helpful to encourage the client to talk about their self-destructive thoughts, bringing them out into the open. Empathic, attentive responding will give the client a sense that what they reveal is acceptable, that you are able to hear it and contain it, being neither shocked nor overwhelmed by it. Be aware of both the client's body language and your own; look for signs of stress, awkwardness or withholding of feelings. It may be appropriate to self-disclose; for example, if you become aware that the client has become very anxious, you might say, 'I'm aware it's very difficult for you to talk about your feelings and I'm aware of my anxiety too.' The person who feels suicidal usually feels very isolated and genuineness and warmth from the counsellor may be the only nurturing they receive. Your conveyed concern will give them a sense of being valued, which is likely to be something they are presently lacking.

Self-harm

Insight

It's important that counsellors try to expand their understanding of complex issues like self-harming and abuse by reading up-to-date material and attending regular training. Reasons for self-harming are wide ranged but there do seem to be many young people who suffer through feeling a misfit in their peer group and having low self-esteem. With the young, it can begin at times of extreme stress such as exams, parents splitting up, losing a parent from their lives, or being the victim of bullying or abuse.

Self-harming comes in many guises, but always involves some form of sustained injury such as cutting, bruising or burning. It is not an easy means of self-expression for others (non-harmers) to understand. What makes a person cut their own arms or burn holes in parts of their bodies, or bang their head repeatedly against a wall?

A high percentage of young people who have been abused go on to self-harm. It has been described as an attempt to express the unspeakable, a way of 'letting bad out', of telling the world what has happened to the victim. Although the injuries are usually hidden under clothing, the abuse experienced is re-enacted in a different form and 'written on the body'. Some women will cut or burn themselves on parts of their bodies where the initial abuse and injury was carried out.

WHO SELF-HARMS?

At one time medical health professionals thought that it was predominantly young females between the ages of 15 and 25 who self-harmed, and variance from this pattern seemed rare. Psychiatrists, clinical psychologists and others working in the mental health field regarded self-harm to be linked to the young women's maladaptive approach to sexuality. Yet a considerable number of men self-harm too. It affects both sexes across the age groups.

A counsellor who worked in a telephone crisis centre told me that she had experience of women in their 70s calling when they had self-harmed. Author Diane Harrison worked as a counsellor with people who self-harm and is herself a survivor of many years of self-injury. She has talked with carers of the elderly who told her that some older people, who have become highly dependent on others, begin to self-harm, possibly as an expression of frustration, in the form of scratching themselves or knocking and bruising their hand or legs against bed frames or pulling their catheters out. Lack of self-worth, loss of autonomy or having little regard or respect from others are possibly contributing factors.

In an article in *Open-mind*, a British mental health magazine, Diane Harrison expressed some of the complex feelings associated with self-harm:

> *Self-harm is about getting through each moment. It's a symbolic language from the unconscious where you are trying to tell yourself what is going on inside even though you can't make the conscious links. It can be a way of trying to rid yourself of dirty feelings inside that seem to take over, like a poison. The pain and rage finds an outlet through self-mutilation, even though women are often unaware that they are angry at all. Men who self-injure tend to be more overtly angry and may be more open to talking about it.*

ISSUES OF CONTROL

Some people who self-harm have spoken of letting something out from their inner world. Others see self-harming as a way of taking control; their body or mind was hurt by other people in the past and by doing something to themselves they then appropriate the ability to injure by owning the act. Instead of 'our secret' of sexual abuse, the injury becomes 'my secret'. It is also a way of feeling 'alive'. A young client told me that after she cut herself (usually on her lower arms), 'I know that I exist – I see the blood coming out and I feel better.' The person often experiences signs of acute disassociation with their feeling world of emotions, and from other people who know nothing of their experiences. Self-harming is, for some, a way of registering and controlling boundaries between the internal and external world. The 'marking' or scarring that ensues after injury is also regarded as a form of branding, saying, 'This happened – I am affected for life.'

A person might self-injure several times in the same day or once a month – frequency is variable, depending on situations, triggering events and emotional reaction.

SHAME

Self-harm takes on many forms, involving cutting, burning, scratching or injuring the body in any way. Sometimes people will bang their heads against the wall or punch themselves when they're depressed. Injuries are usually carried out on parts of the body that can be hidden such as the inside of arms or legs, and for this reason it can be kept secret.

Often people feel great shame and hide their injuries. Although great relief often follows the act, the effects of the act perpetuate self-disgust. To the outside observer self-harm or injury might seem punitive and self-destructive, but we must remember that it's a mode of survival. Sometimes when an individual is rushed to hospital with a severe cut or burn, doctors and nurses mistake the act as a suicide failure or dismiss it as a manipulative attention-seeking behaviour.

ANGER AND DEPRESSION

Counsellors and other therapists working with clients who self-harm say that self-hate and self-disgust are always contributing factors. The client experiences numbing depression and loss of a sense of self. They may be stuck on self-thoughts of 'Who am I?' or 'I am worthless.' The initial harm done to them has been taken into their bodies (internalized) and there they hold the anger until they 'let it out'. The survivor of sexual, physical or emotional abuse might be angry at themselves for 'allowing' the injustices to happen to them, as well as angry at the perpetrator. Instead of 'acting out' the anger on the person or persons involved, they express it towards their own bodies.

Because children are often the targets of abuse of various kinds, being defenceless and malleable, they have no resources to deal with either the perpetrator of the act or the act itself. Subsequently feelings of powerlessness extend into adulthood and the revenge is enacted on the victim's own body, reflecting the accumulation of self-hatred. As a child they may have had no one to talk to, or no other way to relieve their distress and confusion.

THE CYCLE OF SELF-HARM AND SELF-CARE

For some people the post-care of their injury offers solace – a nurturing they lack in their lives. Just as the body has become a focus of punishment, it then becomes a focus of caring in changing bandages, cleaning the wounds, applying ointments. Although another person might initially do this, perhaps a nurse or helper, some people take comfort in nursing their wounds. A 'split off' part of themselves – a part that loves and respects themselves – comes into play to care for the abused, hurt part of the self.

SOME OF THE REASONS GIVEN FOR SELF-HARMING

Feelings that precipitated the action:

▶ *Painful emotions – grief, sadness, desperation, helplessness, hopelessness.*
▶ *Anger – rage, frustration, powerlessness, injustice.*
▶ *Anxiety – fear, panic, stress, tension.*
▶ *Self-hatred – shame, 'contaminated', dirty, guilt.*
▶ *Unreality – numbness, dead, unconnected, alienated.*
▶ *Loneliness – unsupported, lack of contact, unheard, unloved.*

Effects of the act of self-harm:

▶ *Outlet for feelings – relief, expression, externalization of pain, soothing, distracting.*
▶ *Control – of body or self, owning the anger, repulsing the abuser.*
▶ *Self-punishment – cutting out 'bad' or 'dirty' parts, atonement (linked to guilt).*
▶ *Feel alive – reconnecting with feeling world.*
▶ *Communication – way of telling others about emotions and problems.*

What can help the counsellor?

To help you manage the feelings that cutting, or other forms of self-injury, evoke in you:

▶ *Use supervision and group support to discuss difficulties.*
▶ *Try to respond – not react.*
▶ *Recognize powerful feelings evoked – be prepared to look at them, not deny or push them to the back of your mind.*

- *Ask yourself questions about your feelings such as:*
  - ▷ *What is it about self-harm that threatens me?*
  - ▷ *What do I bring to this experience from my past?*
  - ▷ *What does being in control of oneself mean to me?*

You may hold polarized views about rescuing or rejecting. Part of you might want to rescue the person; another part might want to reject them. You could feel repulsed or afraid. Try to see the whole person, not just the injury or scars. Appreciate that the self-harm is there for a purpose and has helped the individual survive.

A clinical psychologist would use behavioural techniques such as asking the client to keep a diary as a means of monitoring self-harming episodes, noting thoughts and feelings that precipitate the injuring, what the client is feeling during the actual harming and what feelings follow on, and finding other channels of expression. Some counsellors consider these methods to be superficial, that emphasis on 'cure' and methods of stopping the behaviour ignores underlying associated feelings. Failure to comply with behavioural programmes can, where the symptom is regarded as the problem, lead to the withdrawal of help. If the person were to continue to self-harm in this climate of expectancy, the feelings of self-disgust and failure become reinforced.

Above all, make sure you're working at a level you're comfortable with. You'll be working with distressful and powerful feelings. It's important to acknowledge your own limitations and refer the client to a more experienced therapist if necessary. It might be necessary to give the client information about other agencies and crisis services.

Clients express their emotions in different ways; anger, hostility, emotional pain and sadness can be expressed overtly or as a baseline. The client might seem detached, sullen or depressed. The counsellor can easily be drawn into the client's feelings of hopelessness, or feel overawed by the client's problems and feel inadequate. In the countertransference the counsellor can feel weighed down or that they have to be all-powerful for the client or a nurturer. Nurturing can be useful, but a counsellor needs to be realistic about what they (or the agency or organization) can offer; otherwise they will be restricted by an unrealistic wish to fulfil all the client's needs. The counsellor probably can't be with the distressed or suicidal person for more than an hour a week and therefore a network of support is needed for the client. In this case the counsellor can make sure that they and the client have identified other support systems. This could involve a key social worker, a doctor or a specialist agency. Counsellors can prepare themselves for demanding client work by building an awareness of helping techniques, strategies and interventions to give the client the feeling of being therapeutically 'held'. Counsellors also need to look after themselves when counselling people who have experienced deep trauma and who emotionally act out during sessions. Adequate supervision is necessary for the holding quality it offers the counsellor. The supervisor will be aware of the potential impact of working with high levels of client distress.

Examples of responses to self-injury

Unhelpful responses include:
- *shock*
- *anger*
- *criticism – regarding self-harm as attention-seeking or manipulative*
- *any kind of punitive measure*
- *contracts that insist that the person agrees not to self-harm*
- *bombarding with questions*
- *avoidance – minimizing or dismissing self-injuries.*

Helpful responses include:
- *being warm, accepting and supportive of where the client is now*
- *maintaining clear boundaries – be clear about what you or your agency can offer*
- *taking the self-harming seriously – facing it with the client*
- *empathic responding, conveying concern*
- *thinking of self-harm as a consequence of trauma and an expression of a trauma continuum*
- *being clear about agency policies and guidelines*

- *being 'real', honest, congruent with the client (holding negative feelings)*
- *exploring 'buttons' or 'triggers' – patterns of behaviour*
- *exploring existing coping strategies and establishing new supportive ones*
- *helping the client bring the 'secret' world of self-harm into the room, in relationship with the counsellor*
- *developing a trusting environment for client exploration and disclosure.*

Abuse

Insight

My experience working with clients who have been abused physically, mentally, emotionally or sexually is that it can take some time for the person to trust in me as the counsellor, and in the counselling itself, enough to open up about the abuse in any detail. Trust, shame, anger, control, the fear of humiliation and being in the vulnerable position of talking about emotional experiences are all issues that can affect the counselling.

The person who thinks about or attempts suicide, the person who self-harms, the person who has problems with their expression of anger and the person who has suffered abuse all usually have low self-esteem and sometimes feel extremes of self-hatred. Past abuse could be at the root of their problems. Prolonged repeated abuse is likely to seriously damage a person's sense of self-worth. In *Counselling Adults Who Were Abused as Children*, Peter Dale draws our attention to the fact that 'there are no commonly accepted definitions of abuse'. The main categories given below (Definition of abuse) can be extended to include mental abuse and others more specific to the individual experience. Dr Alice Miller, who was a practising psychoanalyst for 20 years, holds the conviction that methods of conventional child rearing and education effectively thwart self-expression in the child, and that it's commonplace and in fact an accepted part of Western societal norms that adults bully, criticize and humiliate children.

Those who suffer abuse from others are often children or adults who are physically and mentally less strong than the perpetrator of the abuse. The victims have learned first hand, sometimes at an early age, that adults and other people are untrustworthy, cruel and unpredictable. The most difficult aspect of the abuse is that it usually comes from the people who are expected, by society and by the child, to love, care for and protect the child. The child who sustains physical injury or endures sexual abuse feels 'all mixed up' (as one client put it) in their feelings towards the perpetrator, who might be a parent or some other member of the family. Because of the complexity of feelings the sufferer experiences – which might include love, hate, anger, helplessness, vulnerability and self-disgust – the child or young person keeps the abuse hidden. After all, if they can hardly believe it's happening, then how will others believe it?

DEFINITION OF ABUSE

Four main categories of child abuse are commonly cited by child safeguarding agencies: neglect, physical abuse, sexual abuse and emotional abuse.

The NSPCC defines physical abuse and sexual abuse in the following ways:

> *Physical abuse includes hitting, shaking, kicking, punching, scalding, suffocating and other ways of inflicting pain or injury to a child. It also includes giving a child harmful substances, such as drugs, alcohol or poison. If a parent or carer reports non-existent symptoms of illness in a child, or deliberately causes illness in a child, this is also a form of physical abuse.*

> *Sexual abuse can take on a number of different forms including: enticing or forcing a child to engage in fondling, masturbation, oral or anal intercourse; making a child observe inappropriate sexual behaviour; showing a child pornographic books, videos or photographs or engaging them in inappropriate discussion about*

sexual matters; meeting a child following sexual grooming which is when an abuser builds up a relationship with a child with the intent on abusing them at some stage .

(The NSPCC website, 2009)

Confidentiality and client disclosure

The law protects children under 17 and other social constructs are also in place to safeguard the child. A counsellor needs to be aware of legal obligations and implications of working with those who have been or are presently being abused in any of the above categories. Remember too that these categories can merge; for example, a person might suffer physical, emotional/mental and sexual abuse.

Counsellors, whether working with young people privately or with an agency within Social Service settings, are required to have the relevant skills and knowledge of appropriate procedures to implement action if abuse is disclosed. It is ethical practice, during an intake session, to give information about the service offered, and what might be involved. At this stage the counsellor addresses the where, when and how practical matters of the counselling. The client's history, family details and other relevant details are taken. The issue of confidentiality also needs to be raised. It should be made clear to the client that, although the service offered is in the main part confidential, there are circumstances when confidentiality may not apply. It should be explained in advance of any disclosure that, if the counsellor thinks that something the client has told them suggests that the client or another young person in the family is in immediate or potential danger, then other authorities might have to be involved. The client would be assured that, if the counsellor decides that a situation necessitates the passing on of disclosed information to other parties, which could be consulting with a colleague or supervisor as a first step, the client would be told prior to it happening.

Working with young children who have experienced abuse is highly specialized work, requiring specific training in how to respond sensitively to the problem. The newly trained counsellor who's setting up in private practice needs to consider carefully the responsibilities inherent in working with children and young people. It's a complex area of counselling and there are many issues to get acquainted with; for instance, how and when it's necessary to pass information on to child protection agencies within Social Services – which could lead to police involvement and giving evidence in court proceedings.

Survivors of abuse

The remainder of this discussion will focus on the adult client who has experienced abuse either in childhood or as an adult. Some clients decide to have counselling following the advice of a social worker or a doctor; some self-refer. The reasons they give for deciding to have counselling sometimes conceal a history of abuse; as we've seen, self-harming and suicide attempts or suicidal thoughts can be a consequence of abuse. In the case of sexual abuse, the victim might never have told another person. Multiple physical abuse is hard to conceal; usually others in the family, friends or neighbours are aware of it. A social worker or doctor who's unaware of the abuse history may refer the person to counselling because they demonstrate antisocial behaviour, or are suffering from depression.

Insight

Abuse issues can lie dormant for years and then be triggered by an event. For example, someone who has suffered sexual abuse as a child may revisit the abuse when they themselves become parents.

TRUST

Trust is a central issue with most people who have experienced abuse of any kind, and possibly more so when the abuse experienced was sexual. It's acknowledged that children are unable to fend for themselves or stand up to their abusers. The victims of abuse often have to rely on the people who abuse them to 'care' for them in fundamental ways – to feed, clothe and house them. The result is an uncomfortable dynamic between loving and hating the perpetrator of the abuse. The child's perception of what's appropriate behaviour becomes blurred as boundaries and roles are transgressed. It can be difficult to form a working alliance with the abused child part of the adult client who demonstrates a low tolerance level for intimate personal interaction. The client might find it difficult to trust a warm, positive regard from the counsellor if they've been consistently humiliated and criticized or have had their trust betrayed. The consequence is an inability to trust or a tendency to trust indiscriminately. It's necessary to maintain clear boundaries because the client could have little sense of what's appropriate behaviour. They might demonstrate a compliant 'learned helplessness', being unable to assert autonomy and remaining highly dependent on others in meeting the challenges of everyday living; or reveal the 'care taking syndrome', compulsively assuming responsibility for the needs of others as a way of attaining self-worth and control. The abused child sometimes displays a pseudo-maturity at a cost to their own developmental needs. Learning assertiveness skills can be useful for the client in identifying and understanding personal needs, boundaries and how to assert the self positively.

SEXUAL ABUSE

The experience of sexual abuse in childhood can lead to sexual dysfunction later in life, manifesting as promiscuity, oversexualization or the repression of a sexual identity. The stress is on the word 'can' because there is documented evidence that not all individuals who have been abused experience these problems. Some people are fortunate enough to establish loving relationships with others, including satisfactory sexual relationships, but many others have difficulties in establishing a sexual identity that they themselves are happy with. As children their experience of sexuality was confusing and frightening, often involving secrecy, threats and hostility. There can be a propensity to self-blame: 'I could have stopped it', or 'I sometimes had an orgasm, so it was my fault too.' They might consider themselves to be 'damaged goods' and associate sex and sexuality with hostility, fear and guilt. As an adult the victim of sexual abuse could find it very difficult to trust both their own expressions of sexuality and those of their partner in a loving context. Parenting can also bring back past complex associated anxieties; for example, a mother who was sexually abused by her father might fear that her husband will do the same to their daughter.

POWER ISSUES

The person who's been abused physically, emotionally or sexually is likely to have reservations about trusting authority figures – including a counsellor, whom they might experience, in the transference, as either a potential abuser or another link in a chain of bureaucracy, part of a system alongside social workers, doctors and other 'official' figures. One of the key rules is that a counsellor avoids putting words into a person's mouth, even when they think that the client is giving strong hints that there has been abuse in their background. Rather than ask probing intrusive questions, the counsellor should let the person unfold what has happened to them in their own way. Since they haven't been able to own what happened to them emotionally, physically or sexually in the past, it's important that they can disclose what they choose to. For example, when the client says, 'My father refused to put a lock on the bathroom door and when Mum wasn't around he would come in when I was having a bath,' an appropriate response from the counsellor could be: 'He didn't respect your privacy...' or 'It seems to me completely understandable that at that age you would expect to be able to take a bath in privacy' (the second response 'normalizes' the client's feelings, encouraging her to go on if she chooses to). An inappropriate response would be if the counsellor asked, 'Did he touch you?' or 'Was he sexual with you?'

While a counsellor needs to be aware of the dangers of being intrusive, too direct or voyeuristic, they also need to convey to the client that the material is bearable to hear. The countertransference feelings can be the 'good parent' who won't abuse but neither will they engage enough with the client to encourage them to talk as freely as they would like. Another possible countertransferential response could be that the counsellor feels abusive or powerful in response to the client's expectations of potential abuse. Abuse experienced in the counselling setting by the client can include feeling humiliated, criticized, punished or having their feelings dismissed. These issues need discussing and careful monitoring with the supervisor. In *Against Therapy*, Jeffrey Masson, who was a practising psychoanalyst for some years, has chronicled details of how eminent analysts have abused their position with their patients or clients. Counselling organizations stipulate the inappropriateness of a counsellor engaging in a sexual relationship with a client and a counsellor member who does so invites official disqualification from membership and accreditation. It's recognized that a client is in a disadvantaged position when they put their trust in a counsellor, because they are in a disempowered and vulnerable state.

An integrative approach

Increasingly it's acknowledged that no one approach to therapy is complete in relation to depressive states. The person who has been the victim of abuse suffers 'real harm' – mental and emotional distress. Since mind, body and spirit are all involved, various approaches contribute to healing. The psychoanalytic/ psychodynamic models, survivor/recovery models (which encourage group support) and eclectic/integrative models are among the theoretical approaches described in clinical literature. The psychodynamic model offers an object/relations insight through 'attachment theory', transferential material and the sensitive working with defences; for example, denial – 'It didn't affect me much'; repression – 'I don't remember a lot about what happened in my childhood'; minimizing – 'It wasn't full sex; other people have to put up with much worse'; rationalization – 'I must have encouraged it'; disassociation/splitting – 'I used to think about something else when it was happening; I didn't feel anything.'

The person-centred core conditions model provides a safe environment, a warm non-judgemental and accepting relationship that encourages the client to talk openly, exploring the reality of their experiences. In contrast with the abstinent stance of the psychodynamic mode of counselling, the person-centred paradigm offers an opportunity for the client to improve on interpersonal and social skills. Adopting the person-centred values, the counsellor reassures and encourages the client to be more self-affirming; for example, 'It wasn't your fault – it was wrong of the person to take advantage of you. You were a child.' An adult, perhaps a woman who is the victim of her husband's violent aggression, who rationalizes the situation by saying, 'It's probably my own fault, I make him go mad – I deserve it,' is likely to feel reassured by the counsellor who tells her that she's not responsible for her husband's aggression.

The cognitive behavioural approach addresses the learned and maladaptive responses the victim (because of their past abusive experiences) might have towards people generally, not only those who are aggressive or exploitative. Cognitive states (including dysfunctional ways of relating to other people) are challenged by focusing on the self-defeating, distorted thinking patterns and replacing these with more realistic perceptions of what happened. This process also addresses the individual's low self-esteem. Behavioural difficulties, learning difficulties and lack of social skills are all possible effects of abuse.

There are four themes of therapy to consider:

1 *Physical*
   ▷ *The individual's ownership of and respect for their own body.*
   ▷ *Developing a sense of appropriate boundaries and ways of relating to others in interpersonal contact.*
2 *Emotional*
   ▷ *Helping the client to express freely and explore their emotional inner world.*
   ▷ *Helping the client to release and express anger.*

> *Helping the client to express and accept ambivalent feelings with regard to the abuser.*

> *Conveying to the client that they're valued and accepted as a worthwhile person.*

> *Providing a holding and containing safe environment in which fear is reduced.*

> *Helping the client make contact with the survivor or resourceful side of themselves.*

> *Developing a capacity to trust self and others.*

3 *Mental*

> *Changing distorted thinking, perceptions and imaging (e.g. not 'damaged goods' or a 'despicable person') and negative automatic thoughts.*

> *Clarifying responsibility issues – who did what to whom?*

> *Developing a survivor consciousness – proud of their achievements in surviving.*

> *Increasing self-esteem/self-worth.*

> *Increasing contact with adult coping self and inner locus of evaluation.*

> *Developing autonomy and personal integrity.*

4 *Social context*

> *Increasing social skills.*

> *Use of appropriate boundaries.*

> *Appropriate behaviour.*

> *Self-mastery.*

> *Increasing interpersonal skills.*

> *Encouraging assertive behaviour.*

THINGS TO REMEMBER

1 A client may come to counselling for one reason but during the counselling other more serious issues are revealed. Unresolved grief, suicidal intent, self-harming and childhood abuse are all issues frequently disclosed to counsellors, sometimes after a few or many sessions have passed.

2 Unresolved grief can occur for many reasons and isn't always about the death of a loved one. Generally, what helps the grieving client most is providing a place where they can express their grief in their own way and in their own time. Talking about the deceased and reflecting on their life is also hugely healing to the bereaved.

3 The suicidal client can bring out complex feelings in the counsellor, not least of which is fear. It's a good idea to examine your own attitudes towards suicide and read about the kinds of life situations or health issues that can push a person towards suicide. Attentive, empathic and respectful listening and responding are the skills that help the most.

4 Self-harming has become more commonplace in the young and the reasons for this are varied. However, self-harm is an expression of inner mental pain and turmoil which is registered by harming parts of the body, hereby externalizing and localizing the pain.

5 People who have suffered childhood abuse usually have trust issues with figures in authority (who symbolize adults who could further abuse). Abuse comes in various forms: sexual, physical, mental, emotional and neglect. As with clients who self-harm, issues of power and control are likely to emerge during counselling. Taking an integrative supportive stance and groupwork are recommended when working with abuse.

11

Cultural issues

In this chapter you will learn:
- *how to gain an insight into other cultures*
- *about aspects of the counsellor–client relationship in a cross-cultural setting*
- *about other cultural perspectives from first-hand accounts.*

Background

Cultural concerns came to the attention of the counselling and psychotherapy world in the 1960s and 1970s in the climate of equal opportunities, when racial inequalities also became a focus of concern. At this time counsellors attempted to develop and integrate cultural considerations in training and practice. It was acknowledged that in multicultural societies counsellors often work with clients from a variety of cultural backgrounds. Working within counselling with people from a different culture has been termed 'transcultural', 'cross-cultural' and 'intercultural' counselling. The multicultural approach recognizes that membership of a particular culture influences psychological development and personal identity, and acknowledges that emotional or behavioural problems can reflect the cultural milieu of the client. It rejects an ethnocentric approach – where cultural differences are regarded as deviations from the 'norm' of a dominant culture.

The concept of culture

The concept of culture is complex and multidimensional. The cultural dimension of human experience affects behaviour and relational patterns, and the way an individual constructs 'selfhood' in relation to how they perceive; for example, reality or morality, both of which are likely to be viewed differently by a collectivist or individualistic culture. The complexities of cultural diversity therefore have important implications for counselling. Counselling calls for sensitivity to the possible ways that different cultures express themselves in their outer and inner worlds. It's unrealistic to expect counsellors to be experts in different cultural orientations. Social anthropologists say that, unless a person is immersed in a particular culture for a considerable length of time, they won't be able to fully understand the social networks, use of language, religious rites and myths particular to it, or to have a sensory perception of the environment. In reality a counsellor will have few or no opportunities to see the client interacting within their own culture. Observation and experience of the client is likely to be restricted to the client–counsellor relationship, the counselling process and what the client chooses to reveal. However, it's possible for the counsellor to become sensitized to the nuances of language and to the structures and traditions – through input gained directly from the client, from relevant reading matter, from other members of the culture and through art, dance, religion or other expressions of the culture. It might help if the counsellor enters into the client's world; by attending a ceremony, for instance. The possibility of this could first be discussed with the client, demonstrating a genuine interest and a willingness to engage in a dialogue of cultural difference.

It would be useful to create a working framework that encompasses elements of the client's world view, so that counsellors can understand how the client relates to others in their social behaviour, their perceptions and their assumptions with relation to health, help and cure. Although there's no one right way to understand a culture, working guidelines can help counsellors understand the complexity of cultural identity and influences. While guidelines can't offer expertise in any given culture, nor be specific to any school of counselling, they can provide a way of raising awareness about clients' cultural differences and help the counsellor to demonstrate a willingness to engage fully.

To work transculturally, counsellors (and therapists in general) need to build an awareness of the intricate and complex dynamics of the relationship between personal issues and cultural context. A counsellor working across cultures needs to understand which of the client's cultural experiences will be useful in moving the therapeutic process forward. It would also be helpful to be aware of the family and social networks of the client's culture; the religious, spiritual and ethical background of that culture; and its approach to health care, education and employment. The counsellor can work at avoiding stereotyping or making assumptions, and appreciate that if the client perceives family ties or religious affiliations as liberating forces, then they must accept this. Different ways of perceiving the world might manifest in non-verbal behaviour, family patterns, gender relationships, expressions of emotion, theories of healing and issues around power.

The concept of self

White-dominated Western cultures have a dualistic view of reality. Western perceptions of reality assume that there is a sharp distinction between mind and body. Eastern thought, on the other hand, senses reality holistically, generally perceiving body, mind and spirit as being aspects of a single unified reality. The healing process is directed towards the whole person – body, mind and spirit. Healing can be a combination of various forms; for instance, yoga, chanting, meditation, relaxation techniques and diet. In contrast, counselling belongs to the individualist view of mental cure based on Freud's 'talking cure'.

Differences in outlook are also evident ontologically, in views of selfhood and the sense of self. While Western thought views the person in an individualistic sense – each person is seen as an autonomous separate individual with strong boundaries – non-Western collectivist cultures tend to see selfhood as being created and re-created through relationship, connectedness and interaction – the self exists in and through these. Individualistic concepts such as autonomy and achievement might appear alien to someone socialized by a collectivist culture where social systems and religious commitment drive personal decision. Conversely, virtues such as honour or duty might seem restrictively traditional to the individualist Western mindset.

NON-VERBAL AND VERBAL BEHAVIOUR

Cultural practices can differ in eye contact, facial expression, touch, proximity, the giving and receiving of information and gestures. For example, while in Western culture direct eye contact is considered a sign of openness, in some cultures it's regarded as inappropriate in some situations; similarly the shaking of hands is not always appropriate as a greeting in some cultures. Also, issues of modesty may restrict both the giving and receiving of specific information.

Clients conditioned by a culture that cherishes individualism might express themselves in linear or logical ways, displaying a strong sense of self as an individual with an autonomous identity. A person might say 'I'm a lawyer, my hobbies are…'; whereas the collectivist culture's form of self-expression might be more abstract, reflecting family and community orientation and collective responsibilities. Storytelling, dreams, symbols and myths are media used to relate individual experience in relation to community, identity and culture.

People from different cultures have different ways of demonstrating emotions. Emotion is a way of communicating, and what is considered appropriate in one culture could be inappropriate to another. Arab people, for example, can be elaborate and poetic in their interactions. People of non-Western cultures might hold a longer or shorter gaze than is usual in Western-oriented social interaction. In some cultures, people display strong levels of emotion at the funerals of their loved ones, while at Western funerals, people generally try to contain their grief. Conversely, Westerners could appear disrespectful and inappropriately forthright to people from a different culture. There are many variants and it's best not to make assumptions about knowing. Instead, take the position of a learner. A healthy curiosity and an appreciation of differences form a foundation to build on. At best the interaction can be mutually enriching.

Insight

I have found that I ask more questions when working cross-culturally. I think it's better to ask if unsure of the other person's meaning than fail to understand. I may say something like: 'Forgive my ignorance about this but would you mind telling me about…' or 'Sorry I don't understand, do you mind explaining that to me again?'

Family, community and gender roles

Community patterns of bonding and living together can vary considerably from culture to culture. These encompass notions of family, extended families, arranged marriages, childcare, inheritance and so on. It's important to take account of the structures within the client's community that strengthen and support them as natural support systems crucial to healing or problem solving; in Western societies the strongest bond or source of support is likely to be a spouse but in other cultures the strongest bond might be that of the parent and child. Gender roles differ in various cultural settings. In some traditional Asian communities the woman's role is primarily in the home as a nurturer and she has secondary status to her husband. A younger white professional woman counsellor might intimidate a middle-aged Indian woman visiting a counsellor for the first time. Equally, an older Asian female counsellor could intimidate a white male client. Age, race, culture, professional standing and social status are all factors that need to be taken into account, as well as the conventional or traditional gender relationships in the family and community within the context of the majority culture of society. We have to listen to and be respectful of our client's cultural norms, leaving our own values to one side. We can be of help only from the 'frame of reference' that the client normally functions within. A feminist approach to counselling, where the client might be asked to reject patriarchal constraint, could prove totally inappropriate to a female from a culture where masculine supremacy is the norm. Issues of gender inequality might be the last thing on the client's mind and would be introduced only as the counsellor's (inappropriate) agenda.

PAST/PRESENT ORIENTATION

A similar tension sometimes exists between individualist and collectivist notions of time. Western society is generally more future and goal-oriented. A sense of progress is important in the West and the past is often dismissed as old-fashioned or defunct. Time is perceived as linear, forward-looking and clock-oriented, work and leisure being divided into distinct parts of the day or week. Collectivist cultures, on the other hand, are more likely to be past-oriented, with a sense of continuity pervading the present. Ideas, values and belief systems might be expressed through oral tradition, and parents, grandparents and ancestors are often honoured and revered. Time is circular with less distinction between work and play. Leisure is a largely individualist secular notion. Muslims, for example, pray six times a day, preceded by washing their hands, feet and other parts of the body. During the festival of Ramadan eating is forbidden between sunrise and sunset. Tensions can be created when the counsellor doesn't appreciate the important role of family and heritage in the client's life. In their lack of understanding, white counsellors might inadvertantly invite the client of another culture to free themselves of past influences and internalized values/roles of past generations, to challenge, confront and even reject authoritarian and parental demands, which might seem like anathema to a client who has been immersed in a reverential attitude to the past, family and tradition.

BELONGING

Just as concepts of time can differ in cultures, so can attitudes of spiritually belonging to a specific place. In the modern, mobile societies of the industrialized world, community has suffered. A cultural identity is inextricably affected by past and origins and an awareness of a homeland or ancestral roots. Few people in the huge cities, where most of the world's population now live, interact within the same community – dominated by extended families, clan or tribe – as their grandparents did. For counsellors brought up in this mobile world where pride is taken in being part of a European community or the ability to globe-hop, the acute sense of place experienced by the collectivist sense of reality – the profound emotional, social and spiritual attachment to a particular place – might be difficult to grasp.

Also, we need to consider the relationship between personal problems and political socio-economic realities. It might be necessary to embrace the historical perspective to make sense of current experience. The way that someone feels could be a response not only to what is happening now but also as a reaction to loss or trauma that occurred in earlier generations. A client can be understood as a participating member of a culture and not just perceived in psychological terms. The identity, experience and emotions of the client must be set against the backdrop of their cultural milieu. Feelings of loss and expropriation (the taking away of land or property) might be the legacy of an imperialist or colonialist past, and this might need acknowledging and working through. Sometimes it might be important that the counsellor helps the client to explore the possibilities of political or social activity as a way of coming to terms with their heritage.

Insight

Sometimes during my work with people of different nationality and culture to my own, clients can become frustrated with me (perhaps in my lack of knowledge of what they are talking about) and I find it helpful to bring my sense of their frustration out into the open, apologise if I am unable to understand and ask them to explain things more fully. As with all counselling, it's about connecting with the other human being.

There is no single concept of 'normal' that applies across all persons, situations and cultures. Mainstream concepts of mental health and illness need expanding to incorporate the religious and spiritual dimension that influences the lives of those brought up in Hindu, Muslim, Sikh, Jewish, Rastafarian and other cultures. It's important to take a flexible and respectful attitude towards other therapeutic values, beliefs and traditions. Counsellors can assume that their own view of reality is culturally based. Counselling theories have been developed from white Western therapists (mainly European and American), inextricably influenced by Judeo-Christian morality. Ideas of morality, formed by religious belief, could differ between the majority culture and minority cultures. Beliefs and values might be strongly influenced by religious convictions.

A creative integrative approach

Counselling across race and culture requires an openness, flexibility and spontaneity on the part of the counsellor. The counsellor would benefit from learning about the client's world and focusing on what's important in their life. For example, it might be possible to work with other traditional philosophies or healing methods; acknowledging that beneath the client's cultural identity are beliefs and assumptions that sometimes merge with and sometimes challenge the counsellor's own. Cross-cultural counselling can be delivered through individual or couple therapy, family or group counselling, and can employ specific interventions (e.g. relaxation training or empathic reflection). The counsellor would consider the cultural appropriateness of what is being offered and at the same time be prepared to adopt an integrative approach, drawing on ideas and techniques from existing theories or therapies including those that hold meaning for the client.

Each cultural group has its own methods and techniques for helping people who suffer emotional or psychological disorders. There is likely to be a rich diversity of healing methods available that might include traditional healing techniques and spiritual perspectives. Counsellors can explore different cultural perceptions of well-being, illness, normality and cure. Different therapeutic systems are not always worlds apart and there is a growing awareness that an integrative approach (including the application of techniques such as yoga, meditation, body work, dreamwork, dance and sound) can have enormous possibilities and benefits. Psychosynthesis and the transpersonal approach to counselling embrace Eastern religion and philosophy and many of the above techniques.

SKILLS

A counsellor would have reached a level of proficiency in the use of theory and skills before embarking on work with persons of a different culture, which requires additional skills. Clearly, working with people of a different race and culture requires a flexibility of approach. The counsellor would be prepared to negotiate mutually acceptable ways of working. Considerations might include how important is it for the client that the counsellor is able to communicate in the client's first language or whether an interpreter is required and what would constitute helpful boundaries and the inclusion of family support during sessions. In *Transcultural Counselling in Action*, Patricia d'Ardenne relates how she held an assessment session with a Bangladeshi couple in the company of their grandmother, two uncles, an aunt and a small baby. The couple had sexual problems. All the adult family members present at the session contributed to the assessment, offering practical help at home regarding babysitting and more privacy for the young couple. This is an example of how counselling can be adapted to meet the needs of clients' collective culture.

Language use is important. Abstract middle-class therapeutic discourse, as a product of the dominant majority culture, is likely to be inappropriate when addressing people from ethnic minority groups. Any reference to psychotherapeutic terms such as 'fantasy', 'projection', 'transference' and 'denial' could be experienced (as indeed it may by many Western people) as clinically 'foreign', over-intellectualized, and as a cold, detached, superior stance. Humanistic terminology such as 'being real' or 'phoney' is also unlikely to be helpful. The counsellor can try to match the cultural and cognitive manner of the client by initially 'modelling' culturally flexible behaviour, enabling and encouraging open forms of expression.

Insight

In one of my counselling jobs I have talked over the telephone with people of many nationalities. On occasions I have found it difficult to understand what someone is saying because of their strong accent or their limited use of English. I have felt frustration rising in me and at these times I remind myself that I don't speak a word of their language and that they are doing really well.

The therapeutic relationship

The client from a minority group can establish a positive identity within the therapeutic relationship when the white counsellor acknowledges the difficulties they and their community encounter through prejudice and discrimination. To form a working alliance with the counsellor, the client needs to feel that they can trust the counsellor's integrity by experiencing them as genuine, sincere and open to the client's perceptual world and the complexities of another culture. At the same time, the counsellor, if a white person, is a member of the race/culture that discriminates against the client's race and culture. As a representative of a majority 'host' culture, and as a person who sees themselves as a helper, a white counsellor might adopt an attitude that denies oppression. In an attempt to promote a positive white identity the counsellor might cut off from certain aspects of themselves and project other aspects that they hope are more acceptable and productive. The relationship with the client of different racial or cultural origin could be restricted by feelings of guilt, shame and fear of difference. Both the white counsellor and the black client are psychologically impoverished when inequality is upheld rather than addressed. Personal development and consciousness raising are the fundamental tasks of those who accept that as advantaged members of society they bear some responsibility for the oppression of disadvantaged groups. Research evidence suggests that the liberal use of self-disclosure on the part of the counsellor helps build trust in the client–counsellor relationship because it demonstrates openness.

In an article in *Counselling* (a British Association for Counsellors magazine which has since been replaced by *Therapy Today – The Magazine for Counselling and Psychotherapy Professionals*) called 'Working with Issues of Race in Counselling', Aisha Dupont-Joshua stresses the importance of personal developmental work in transcultural counselling, in understanding the dynamics of the client–counsellor relationship:

> **Until white counsellors start owning their whiteness as part of their identity, and working on their racial identity development, they will be ill-equipped to work across cultures, because their attitudes, who they are and what they represent to their black clients, are vital ingredients in the counselling relationship.**

Dupont-Joshua points out that the black person's view of what it means to be a 'normal' white person is likely to be that, as part of the majority, they are used to 'being historically dominant, having access to privilege, being considered aesthetically attractive, being in control'. These factors can be acknowledged in the relationship so that the black client can comfortably air their views in an exploration of self-identity. This requires a non-defensive attitude from the counsellor.

Differences in belief and value systems – for example, notions of dependency, individuality, emphasis on history taking or the abstinent stance (blank screen) of the counsellor – might be totally puzzling and disorientating to clients who do not originate from the dominant culture. Counsellors sometimes think that caring, respectful core conditions – positive regard, empathy, genuineness and warmth – are the only requisites for working cross-culturally and ignore other methods of engagement. Areas of difference are covered by a benevolent 'we are all the same under the skin', which might mask uncomfortable feelings of awkwardness or hostility. Counsellors can demonstrate actively to their clients that they take responsibility for their own historically held attitudes by conveying a willingness to examine difficult cultural conflicts and prejudices within themselves.

Patricia d'Ardenne and Aruna Mahtani (*Transcultural Counselling in Action*) suggest practical issues for the counsellor to consider:

▶ *how your cultural or racial background affects your attitude to your client;*
▶ *whether or not you see the client's culture or race as a cause of the present problem;*
▶ *whether or not you see the client's culture or race as part of the solution to the present problem;*
▶ *whether or not you can accept, acknowledge and understand your client's culture;*
▶ *whether or not your expectations about the client's culture affect the counselling outcome;*
▶ *whether or not your cultural prejudice has a bearing on the counselling relationship;*
▶ *whether or not any cultural prejudice or racism experienced by you affects the counselling relationship.*

Insight

I have found that it helps when the counsellor is transparent about the way they work, offering information about the kind of service they normally provide and asking the client if that fits with their expectations and hopes for the counselling. It also makes for a good working relationship, when working cross-culturally, to ask the client how they would like to work and give assurance of flexibility.

TRANSFERENCE

Transference, in the usual sense of the term, occurs when the client brings unresolved issues from past experiences with significant others (usually parents) into the relationship with the counsellor. In the counselling relationship the counsellor becomes the parent, giving the client an opportunity to re-experience and work through the original complex emotions. When the client is from a minority culture the usual parent–child transference is likely to occur but another dimension of transference will also occur, that of the counsellor representing the oppressor/dominant or rejecting parent. The parent in this cultural context might also be the 'state', society, colonialism or some other dominant force that has been experienced as racist and rejecting. A white counsellor, for example, might at times be experienced by a black client as a white oppressor, who regards themselves as superior to them. Since the counsellor is experienced as racist at this point in therapy (in fact, the counsellor is likely to be experienced as potentially racist from the onset), the counsellor needs to draw attention to and willingly face these feelings with the client.

What follows is an example from my own experience.

Case study 5

A young male client (20 years of age) of mixed-race origin whom I will call 'L' came for counselling because of what behaviourists call an obsessive compulsive disorder. The training I had at this point was an integrated mix of psychodynamic with Rogerian values. I knew very little about cognitive behavioural theory and technique, so rather than dabble I decided to stay with the approach I was familiar with. He was spending up to four hours a day washing and cleansing himself. He locked himself in the bathroom for sometimes two hours at a time. Without going into too much unnecessary detail, I will outline some of the language and imagery he used in relating to me in the client–counsellor relationship.

His self-image was such that he thought that people perceived him as 'thick' – he talked slowly as if deliberating and he understood this mannerism to stem from early schooldays when he tried to extend his teacher's attention. It became a habit that backfired on him (one

(Contd)

CASE STUDY

wonders if the teacher's attitude was racist). The pupils at the school he had attended were almost exclusively white and he was always the only child of mixed race in his class. His appearance was akin to his mother's Afro-Caribbean background. People regarded him as black. He was very confused about his identity. He described himself as neither black nor white – and as having 'no chance' with women. He treated his mother with disdain at times.

My hunch was that we were working with issues (among others) relating to race and internalized racism, manifest in his negative self-image. His black origins were a source of self-disgust but the point was that it was learned disgust – a product of (probably covert) racism. Imagery that he used also spoke of despair, loneliness and unexpressed anger. One example was a repeated image of himself spinning for ever in time, all alone, in a 'black void'. He had described the time he took cleansing himself as 'filling in time' because he said each day went on for ever. Since early childhood he had experienced trouble making friends, being convinced nobody would like him. Focusing on the imagery of the friendless, helpless state of being in a black void gave an opportunity for us to explore his experiences of rejection from both black and white groups of people.

L's view of young black men was that they were 'fast talking' (unlike himself) and 'a lot of trouble'. When I asked him if he saw himself as a lot of trouble, he said, 'No, cos I never do anything – I stay·in.' His washing regimes could be not just a way of expressing self-disgust or washing the 'black away', but also a way of keeping himself occupied or out of trouble. My attempts to address his white origins were usually deflected. The issue of having a white counsellor came up when L came to a session following a job interview. He was surprised to find that the interviewer was a black woman, who reminded him of his mother. He talked about his problem in getting a job, which led to discussion of how black people are often allocated menial work. During this session I asked him what it felt like having a white female counsellor. This was not the first time I had posed the question but it was the first time that he was able to make use of it. He replied that he initially expected me (like others) to dismiss him as a black person. He also had the opinion that a counsellor would be a white middle-class 'do-gooder' with no sense of what it was like to be of mixed race.

This was a turning point in the counselling work because I realized that I had been colluding with L's denial of his white identity for two reasons: first, because it brought up my own uncomfortable feelings of being part of the majority (dominant) race/culture; and second, because he looked black; I saw him as predominantly black. I didn't consider myself racist but clearly there were race issues here.

Insight

The problems of first-generation immigrants and their second-generation offspring may differ greatly. The younger generation often have problems that arise from having a foot in each culture when, for instance, parental and familial expectations are traditional – as in an arranged marriage – and are at odds with their children's ideas, immersed as they are in the culture of the country they have been brought up in.

Similar mistakes can be made when as white counsellors we view other Europeans – or other white people – as culturally similar. One of my first clients as a new counsellor was a young Eastern European woman. Unaware as I was at the time of the significance of cultural issues, I missed a relevant source of understanding her experiences and her problems. I would now, being more experienced as a counsellor and I hope more culturally aware, be more interested in her experiences as a person who was brought up in a communist totalitarian state where there were (she told me) police guards in her university on the lookout for subversive student behaviour. This and other culture-related factors had connections with problems she was having relating to people she had met in England, including myself in the client–counsellor relationship. She felt 'watched' and criticized, and wanted to run away from responsibilities. While I was at the time sufficiently aware of her abandoning mother as a source of transference, I missed a second potential source, myself as counsellor whose inquiry paralleled the cold observer of the totalitarian state she had lived under.

The forming and maintenance of a therapeutic relationship depends on finding ways of working together that are mutually agreed. Culturally sensitized counsellors are flexible up to a point, but boundaries can be clearly outlined at the beginning – for example, timekeeping, location and duration of therapy and ways of working can be agreed. The client from another culture might want to show appreciation of the counsellor by extending an invitation to visit their home or meet outside the counselling setting. Situations like this can be avoided if the client has been given clear guidelines concerning boundaries and the reasons why they exist (e.g. issues of convenience, availability, protection of the client and maintenance of the therapeutic role) at the onset of the therapy.

A fear of being politically incorrect, being unconsciously prejudiced and being regarded as racist can seriously undermine the counsellor and the counselling work. But the discomfort experienced, owing to being part of a privileged group, is to some extent a tables-turned situation that can give the counsellor a sense of the client's culturally biased experiences (e.g. of being judged/stereotyped by race or culture, or by presumptions about the other culture). A willing attitude can be shown if the counsellor acknowledges the client's angry feelings in response to racist attitudes and discrimination, by giving the client permission to express the injustices and their effects, and when the counsellor is prepared to look at issues like stereotyping, power and inequality.

Institutionalized racism

One area where good practice in counselling is evident is the willingness to talk about cultural issues and by not succumbing to race-avoidance or race-neutralizing interventions. It's essential to acknowledge the reality of institutionalized and overt racism and discrimination in the lives of clients. Power imbalances between therapist and client might reflect the imbalance of power between the cultural communities to which they belong. Failure to address the racial context of the client's concerns will restrict or destroy the client's ability to express themselves. Avoidance of race issues could lead to the client concurring with the counsellor's definitions of what is important to address. Institutionalized racism permeates many agencies – the police, education and health. To quote the MacPherson Report (1999):

> *...the collective failure of an organization to provide an appropriate and professional service to people because of their colour, culture, or ethnic origin is institutionalized racism. It can be seen or detected in processes, attitudes and behaviour which amount to discrimination through unwilling prejudice, ignorance, thoughtlessness and racist stereotyping, which disadvantages minority ethnic people.*

It's essential for counsellors from all backgrounds to be aware of their own stereotypes, attitudes and feelings in relation to people from other ethnic groups. Many ethnic minority clients will have experienced institutionalized and overt racism and will carry the scars of these experiences into the therapeutic relationship. As part of any training programme, therefore, counsellors need to confront and challenge their own prejudices and ignorance. This could be a very painful process as trainees might find themselves challenging their own core beliefs and assumptions as well as those of their peer group and families.

So that the needs of ethnic minority clients are met, counselling agencies can ensure that their services are accessible to all; for instance, by being willing to work in ethnic minority community locations. As well as publicity drives they could employ outreach workers, hire bilingual or bicultural staff and provide crèche facilities. There may be issues of ethnic representation of staff, and setting up agencies that are run by and for members of specific groups – for example, Muslim women counselling female Muslim clients – might be a consideration.

A black Rastafari woman called Morowa gave an account of experiences in training and working as a counsellor.

Case study 6

At the start of my training I was very sure of wanting to recognize where I stand in my concept of my own identity. I fiercely wanted to protect and retain my identity, which I've struggled to gain through my own awareness and appreciation of the 'Black Consciousness Movement' of the 1960s and the Rastafari movement which I became part of in the later 1970s.

I was conscious that in the area of counselling, which is so under-represented by black people – less so Rastafari women – that I didn't want to be a 'token black' or be considered as 'one of them', as a black person who becomes part of a profession that is viewed as 'white' (such as counselling) is often perceived to be.

I was also aware of assumptions I had of not wanting the 'white' psychology to 'mess up my brain'. The structure of the course wasn't culturally biased and I was one of only two black 'counsellors' (the other was a male) out of 20. This number seems to reflect the percentage of potential black counsellors entering the area of work.

At times, in isolation within group discussion, when I raised issues around race, it was often met with great feelings of unease; even so there were usually a few members who were willing to engage with it by working with feelings it evoked in them and with the dynamics it created.

Through my experience of working in a women's counselling service I've seen the lack of black women who use this form of therapy as a healing process. When I began working there I was the first and only black counsellor. This realization came with ambivalent feeling. I also experienced feelings of isolation and it seemed I was expected to be the 'expert', have all the ideas and answers to anything to do with 'recruiting' black women to the service.

Almost immediately I experienced feelings around my worthiness to be there in the agency; for example 'I cannot fail', 'Am I good enough, as good as the white counsellors?' I felt many of these feelings were actually to do with my limited experience of the 'real counselling relationship'.

How much was really internalized racism? I had to struggle with the reality of being a 'novice' and detach it from any negative internalized feelings. I also had a feeling of responsibility around being 'good enough', as a failure on my path would, I assumed, affirm any negative feelings that might be around (from managerial staff) regarding the ability of a black person within this field of work and therefore influence any future developments.

As a black counsellor I feel a satisfaction that I can be part of the process of the 'provision of choice' within the service in trying to encourage and accommodate people of my race and culture.

I feel nevertheless that there is no point making a service accessible for ethnic minority groups if the theoretical approach remains rigid and doesn't continue to strive to become flexible to account for cultural needs of such users.

Morowa Selassie

Summary

There are a number of considerations required for cross-cultural practice:

- *The counsellor's awareness of their own cultural bias and values.*
- *The counsellor's willingness to engage with the client's frame of reference/world view.*
- *Learning about your client's culture – don't rely on your client to inform you.*
- *The possibility of internalized oppression and self-rejection wherein the work would include affirming a positive self/group identity.*
- *The counsellor's ability (and that of the organization or agency providing a service) to be flexible, adaptive and open to self-challenge, e.g. offering a matched counsellor or interpreter.*

- *Becoming familiar with specialist literature on working with particular client groups.*
- *The acknowledgement of societal inequality and discrimination as well as the subjective reality of the client.*
- *Cultural transference – the significance of the counsellor's identity for the client and power inequalities, e.g. the counsellor might say, 'I wonder what it's like for you to be telling this to a white person.'*
- *The counsellor's ability to be non-defensive in exploring their own racism, which many regard as an inevitability among those who are members of the majority culture.*

THINGS TO REMEMBER

1 *Cross-cultural issues came to the attention of the counselling world in a response to ethnocentric ideas which treat cultural difference as 'other' and the dominant country as 'the norm'.*

2 *Culture is hard to define but can be identified by religion, history, myths, language and social structures. Counsellors working transculturally can familiarise themselves with elements of the client's environment by, for example, reading about their culture, learning from clients' accounts or attending a religious or celebratory ceremony.*

3 *It helps when the counsellor is willing to examine their own learned prejudices and assumptions of dominance in relation to the client's nationality, race or culture, as well as to acknowledge institutionalized racism.*

4 *Individual cultures have their own orientation and concepts relating to selfhood, social behaviour, family and gender, religious adherence, and home and belonging, which the counsellor has to respect.*

5 *Person-centred core conditions of respect, genuineness and empathy are the cornerstone of cross-cultural work, alongside the challenging of white-dominated, Western cultural ideas and a willingness to embrace the client's culture and way of being.*

12

....

Working online

In this chapter you will learn:

- **the differences between face-to-face counselling and counselling via the internet**
- **the advantages and disadvantages of internet and telephone counselling**
- **professional considerations for these types of work, such as contracting, supervision and accreditation.**

Increasingly, counselling is being offered through the internet and over the telephone and some people prefer these methods of communication to face-to-face contact. People started using the internet to access therapy in the mid-1990s and many therapists now have their own websites. Some use the websites exclusively to advertise face-to-face services, while others also offer counselling, psychotherapy or other types of therapy on the net. Demand for what is sometimes referred to as 'cyber therapy' or 'e-therapy' is growing and subsequently the number of counsellors working online offering counselling through e-mail or chat rooms is also increasing.

Counselling over the telephone is another alternative to face-to-face counselling. The counsellor working over the telephone may be part of an organization or practising privately. Employee Assistance Programmes (EAPs) are companies that provide counselling to the employees of a wide range of organizations from multinational companies to government agencies and small businesses. Among a variety of services, they provide support or short-term contracted counselling sessions over the telephone. Counselling via the telephone is also available through many charitable support organizations and help agencies. In this chapter we will be looking at the issues around, and benefits of, these particular ways of working.

Therapy on the net

The booklet *Guidelines for Online Counselling and Psychotherapy* (2nd edn, 2005), published by the British Association for Counselling and Psychotherapy (BACP), gives practical guidelines on subjects such as: practitioner practice, contracting, confidentiality, data protection and storage. It validates online therapy work in its various forms and compares it favourably with face-to-face practices:

> *BACP recognizes the importance of online provision for a wide range of psychological therapies and the potential for significant benefits to clients, especially those who have difficulty in accessing traditional face-to-face services or those who, for whatever reason, prefer not to use them.*

WEBSITES

Therapy can now be found through internet websites, where the therapist (the provider) offers different services and packages to the client (the user). Counselling on the internet is made possible through e-mail, forums (using web-based forum software) and chat room communication. Therapists often use message boards and interactive self-help material to enhance the work. Counselling online follows the same ethical guidelines as face-to-face work. Clear contracting and agreements safeguard both the provider and user and set the scene for a working partnership. As we will see, there are many benefits of this kind of therapy and it's flourishing.

You'll need good IT skills to get a website up and running – many of us will need help with this. A knowledge of website design, broadband technology, computer networking and online communication is a must. If you are not particularly computer savvy then there are internet companies that can set up a website for you for a fee. You might like to use a consultancy service to help you to design and set up a website to a professional standard. Internet service firms advertise in *Therapy Today* – the monthly professional journal for counsellors and psychotherapists published by BACP – and a consultancy service is available from www.onlinecounsellors.co.uk. A website that is professionally presented can be well worth investing in. As J. Fink points out in *How to Use Computers and Cyberspace in the Clinical Practice of Psychotherapy*: 'The tools are simple: a computer, a good modem, and an internet service provider. A website can be programmed, hosted, and publicized for the cost of a few sessions.' The website for the International Society of Mental Health Online (ISMHO), www.ismho.org, is a useful resource for those planning to work online.

Insight

It's not compulsory to adopt telephone or internet counselling methods of counselling. Many counsellors, especially older ones, whose education didn't include the use of computers, choose to have as little as possible to do with computers and therefore the thought of counselling online is anathema. I currently counsel on the telephone and online in my job at an EAP company but not in my private work – as yet.

Important issues to consider

THE DEMANDS OF INTERNET WORK

Counselling associations such as BACP and ACA recommend that counsellors are experienced and proficient in their face-to-face practice and have had further appropriate training in the area before considering online work. Other considerations are how skilled practitioners are in computer and internet use and how suited the model of therapy is to this type of work. BACP recommend that counsellors should, ideally, have a minimum diploma-level qualification and also have accrued the 450 hours experience of counselling in face-to-face work as required for accreditation before they branch into specialist areas such as telephone or internet work. The work can be challenging and counsellors are likely to be presented with a wide range of issues. On a positive note, online work can be another string to your therapist's bow in what is a very competitive profession.

Websites should give information about the counsellor's credentials, training and experience. They may also give details of other resources, information, self-assessment material and articles relating to topics such as how counselling works, as well as further sources of support for specific problems such as depression, anxiety or panic attacks.

ASYNCHRONOUS E-MAIL AND FORUM COMMUNICATION

Counselling sessions can take place through e-mails or forums (a software option), and after a preliminary contact and agreements are set up – these can relate to fees, response times and other ways of working – the counselling can begin. The client and counsellor correspond through writing e-mails to each other. E-mailing doesn't take place in 'real time', which allows some flexibility in the correspondence. When counselling takes place outside of real time, it is referred to as an asynchronous method (that is, the communication is not synchronized). One of the benefits of e-mails is that it gives both the client and the counsellor time to read, consider their response and compose their replies. Text can be deliberated over and altered in a way that perhaps the spoken word can't.

SYNCHRONOUS CHAT ROOM COMMUNICATION

Unlike e-mailing, chat room communication or internet relay chat (IRC) does happen in real time and is referred to as synchronous. Because of this it's recommended that the counsellor has accurate and speedy typing skills. They also need to be able to respond quickly. The term 'chat room' sounds deceptively casual but the same rules of counselling apply to chat room activity as any other reputable form of counselling or therapy. Confidentiality, clear contracting, boundaries and client/counsellor roles are all areas of consideration.

CONTRACTS

Clear contracting offers important protection for both client and therapist and the counsellor will set up a contract for the client to read and agree to. This can be done by asking the client to enter their name, the date and to tick an 'I agree/disagree' or 'Yes' or 'No' box (to the aforestated terms). Contracts will cover areas such as fees/payments, ways of working together and issues of confidentiality. The client needs to be informed that, although overall their details and correspondence are confidential and treated with respect, there may be some situations (for instance, company fraud or when a person's life is believed to be in danger) where official bodies (such as the police) might have access to internet communication.

CONFIDENTIALITY

When offering counselling over the internet, it's crucial to confidentiality that optimum protection is set up through technological tools such as anti-virus and spam blocking software, firewalls and anti-tracking devices to minimize the risk of interference and interception of communication. The use of passwords or codes will protect the anonymity of the client. The keeping of client notes is also a confidentiality issue. The therapist and clients can discuss what will happen to their correspondence and agree to a timescale for the deletion of notes. Some therapists question the safety of keeping notes on the hard drive and prefer to keep paper notes only. Others will keep notes for a certain period of time before destroying them.

PAYMENT

The counsellor will set out fees and payment methods in the contract. The payments are usually made by cheque or by credit card online or a secure internet payment method like PayPal. Websites offering online counselling by e-mail or chat sessions have varying packages and fees – it's usually cheaper than face-to-face counselling. E-mail exchange might be a one-off or a package of six or more. Payment might be made monthly or in advance or at the onset of counselling. Chat sessions can be scheduled as half-hour or hourly sessions.

ACCREDITATION

Insight

I have always found the staff at BACP extremely helpful with my queries, either as a signpost to other agencies or as a provider of their own produced information material.

Counselling hours accrued by internet work can be used towards professional accreditation at the discretion of professional associations such as BACP and ACA if there is evidence to show that the counsellor is suitably qualified, experienced, is working ethically, efficiently and effectively, and that the association's guidelines have been followed. Internet counselling hours can also be included as part of the counsellor's professional development. (Check with the association for up-to-date requirements.)

SUPERVISION

Supervision is an important support in counselling work and supervision will be required for online practice. When working online supervision can take place either face-to-face or online; the supervisor will need to have experience and training relevant to this type of work to understand the issues and ethical concerns particular to it. Online supervision is a relatively new method of support and guidance and new guidelines are emerging. Counsellors need to assure that the supervision is adequate to support their online work. Supervisors ideally have expertise in the particular area and therefore are able to advise on issues like confidentiality, storage of notes and data protection.

Benefits and drawbacks of internet therapy

BENEFITS

- ▶ *Economical – fees are usually cheaper than face-to-face work.*
- ▶ *Accessible to those with disabilities (e.g. mobility or hearing problems) and to those who live in rural or remote areas (this applies to clients and counsellors).*
- ▶ *Clients can choose to remain anonymous (e.g. they may be shy or have a high public profile).*
- ▶ *They feel safer and less exposed.*
- ▶ *Suits people who have problems expressing their emotions – like adolescents.*
- ▶ *Convenient – can be accessed from own home, college, library or any location when accessed through a laptop (true for both clients and counsellors).*
- ▶ *Both the provider and user can keep messages to refer back to.*
- ▶ *Counsellors can fit internet work around other counselling.*
- ▶ *It's another source of income for the counsellor.*

DRAWBACKS

- ▶ *There is no visible body language or facial expression to read (which changes when visual tools like video link are used, though even then the reading of visual cues may be limited).*
- ▶ *Can't tell the age of the person (the client may be under age and there are child protection issues to consider).*
- ▶ *There's a lack of non-verbal cues, which can convey warmth or concern.*
- ▶ *Internet work is less intimate than face-to-face work (technical and distant); the client–therapist relationship is harder to set up and it's harder to maintain a working alliance.*

- ▸ *It facilitates both client and counsellor fantasies about the other.*
- ▸ *The online 'disinhibition effect' on the client, where the client is less inhibited and can write about things that they would find hard to say – such as suicidal thoughts or sexual abuse. The client doesn't have to look the counsellor in the eye. (This effect can be difficult or positive depending on the counsellor's ability to respond effectively.)*
- ▸ *It can be harder to detect mental health problems.*
- ▸ *Works better with some therapeutic models than others – for example, the psychodynamic model works with silences and the 'rule of abstinence', which wouldn't work online.*
- ▸ *The counsellor only has the information that the client decides to give (no way of checking).*
- ▸ *The internet can connect counsellors to clients worldwide and they may be expected to understand cultural particulars or to write in a different language.*
- ▸ *There may be problems with communication in what meaning is given to words. Every now and then it could be important for the counsellor to check that they are interpreting the client's particular meaning. The counsellor needs to be (to a certain extent) up to date with slang or new meanings of words or phrases or regularly check their understanding with the client.*

Who uses the internet for therapy?

Research shows that the majority of people using internet therapy comprise two groups, the young (20–30) and the middle-aged (40–50). There is evidence to suggest that, while in the younger bracket both sexes use this method of therapy fairly equally, the middle-aged clientele are predominately women. Many initially expect the counselling to be free on the net and the main presenting issues are relationship problems.

THE THREE MAIN ISSUES PRESENTED IN ONLINE WORK

1 *Relationships – anonymity may be preferred and difficult feelings might be easier to write than speak.*
2 *Self-esteem – shyness or self-consciousness may be a factor; sometimes people who think that they are unattractive, or who have facial or body disfigurement, prefer that they remain unseen and aren't judged on their appearance.*
3 *Bereavement – the client might be frightened that if they see someone in a face-to-face relationship they might be 'too emotional' and 'lose control' and prefer a less intimate mode of relating.*

Internet technology is now part of most of our lives. We adapt to new technology and find ways to make it life enhancing. We use it for gaining information, shopping, to contact each other and to access emotional support. The internet has opened up new ways of working for the counsellor where different skills from those used in face-to-face practice can be used. This adds to the experience of the counsellor and has also made emotional help easily accessible for the client.

Insight

Many of my counselling colleagues use the internet solely to advertise their services and they say that it's a good source of clients. The positive things about advertising on the net is that you can personalise your webpage and communicate your counselling style, professional details and give a sense of your personality if you so choose.

Telephone counselling

EMPLOYMENT ASSISTANCE PROGRAMMES

Employee Assistance Programmes (EAPs) are companies that provide an array of services to the workplace, such as counselling sessions over the telephone, face-to-face counselling, management support, mediation and conflict management, and critical incident support. The number of EAPs offering this kind of service has expanded over the past 10–15 years. It is now a very competitive market and these companies employ trained and experienced counsellors (who are usually accredited by a professional body such as BACP). EAPs offer an ever-growing range of facilities. Telephone counsellors (TCs) are usually the initial point of contact for the caller. After a first assessment call, the TC might contract with the client for a number of further sessions over the phone. Telephone work is usually short-term focused work of around six sessions. Many charitable organizations also supply structured telephone counselling services (as opposed to crisis intervention or advice and guidance); whether it's a bereavement support organization such as CRUSE or the National Drugs Helpline, they either offer telephone counselling themselves or can signpost callers to other local organizations that can provide this service (see Taking it further). Research has shown telephone counselling to be very effective.

PRIVATE PRACTICE

Insight

My experience is that it is harder, with some clients, keeping the session focused and staying within the time boundary over the telephone than in face-to-face work. Some people see it as 'having a chat' about their problems and it is necessary to keep to a structure throughout the session.

Some counsellors offer counselling over the telephone in their private practice. Counselling over the telephone requires attention to the same criteria as other methods of counselling. Ideally, the counsellor (as suggested by BACP) should be trained and experienced to a level of competency in face-to-face work before embarking on the specific area of telephone work. They would, ideally, take further training relevant to the medium, have sufficient supervision and provide the client with information about their credentials and ways of working before the counselling starts.

Clear contracting at the onset of counselling is crucial and being crystal clear about boundary issues, for example when and in what circumstances the client can call the counsellor outside arranged session times, is very important. A contract and relevant information can be sent in the post to be read and signed by the client. Telephone counselling, perhaps more than other ways of offering support, is open to misuse. People might think that the counsellor 'is just at the end of the phone' and feel it's OK to call at any time when they need support, so it's critical to be clear about boundaries. It helps to set up a separate telephone line for professional use when working from home so that client confidentiality is assured. It would also be helpful to identify other support systems the client could turn to in times of crisis.

HOW TELEPHONE COUNSELLING DIFFERS FROM FACE-TO-FACE WORK

- ▶ *As with the internet, there is no body language or facial expressions to interpret (although cues such as shifting around, voice intonation, hesitations and coughing may give clues to gestures).*
- ▶ *Other (auditory) cues become important – (speed of breathing, sighing, background noises).*
- ▶ *The client might hang up or say suddenly that they have to go.*
- ▶ *The client is in a more powerful position.*
- ▶ *The client can choose to disclose only what they want to.*

AREAS COMMON TO BOTH INTERNET AND TELEPHONE COUNSELLING

As with face-to-face counselling, counselling via the internet and over the telephone necessitates a clear framework for a contract. This could include:

- ▶ *verification of the counsellor's credentials and experience*
- ▶ *their declared model of therapy*
- ▶ *agreements about working together – professional boundaries; number, duration and frequency of sessions; review of the work at certain intervals; cancellation arrangements*

- *policies around interventions*
- *payment methods*
- *confidentiality and disclosure policy*
- *the law and data protection.*

TEXT MESSAGES VIA MOBILE PHONES

The mobile phone is another way that modern technology has been incorporated into client/counsellor use. Although mobile texting is unsuitable for actual structured counselling sessions, both the therapist and the client can use text messages, via mobile phones, to briefly contact the other; for example, when they need to rearrange a session. Another example is when a client, who has been unable to attend a last appointment, has written a short 'thank you and goodbye' type message to the counsellor.

If you'd like to find out more about online or telephone counselling then it might help to look at the BACP or ACA websites where codes of ethics and practice and ethical framework for good practice can be obtained (see Taking it further for these and for details of helpful booklets).

THINGS TO REMEMBER

1 *Counselling is available online by e-mail, forums and chat room communication.*

2 *Telephone and online counselling present the counsellor with their own particular challenges and there are disadvantages and advantages of working in these media.*

3 *Counselling over the internet or by telephone appeals to some clients more than meeting with a counsellor face to face. This can be due to a number of reasons such as: shyness, embarrassment, self-consciousness, disability, living busy lives or living in remote areas.*

4 *Companies like Employee Assistance Programmes (EAPs), which offer counselling to employees, increasingly offer online services as well as telephone counselling support.*

5 *BACP has produced booklets of guidelines for both telephone and online counselling, covering supervision, training, contracting and ethical concerns.*

Glossary

Active imagination A technique pioneered by Carl Jung, where the Ego engages with the unconscious mind through imaging.

Acting out A person displays strong emotions as a way of expressing pent-up feelings that exist in their environment.

Affect Emotion or feeling attached to an idea, a cluster of ideas or objects.

Assertiveness training Uses assertive models to help the client change patterns that might involve low self-esteem, dependency or other dysfunctional ways of communicating with others.

Attachment theory Refers to the work of John Bowlby, namely his three-volume work called *Attachment and Loss*, on the subject of human attachment in the context of personality development.

Autoerotic The use of one's own body for sexual pleasure – e.g. masturbation and also dreams and fantasies.

Behaviour therapy A therapeutic approach that focuses on human behaviour using experimentation it helps the client develop adaptive behaviour through 'unlearning' and modifying techniques.

Body language Involuntary gestures, facial expressions and body positioning that communicates inner feelings and emotions.

Borderline personality disorder Refers to a personality disorder where a person is no longer able to function in a normal adaptive way. They may be over-dependent on others or react angrily to intimacy of any kind and therefore have difficulties forming relationships with others.

Catharsis Originates from Freud's 'cathartic method' and refers to the emotional release of tensions and anxieties from the past.

Classical conditioning The pattern of Pavlov's experiments which were based on the observation of conditioned and unconditioned responses to various stimuli. Example: Pavlov's dog (see Chapter 7) – the dog continues to salivate when a light comes on although food is no longer being dispensed at the same time, and the dog associates the light coming on with food, causing it to salivate.

Cognitive behavioural therapy (CBT) Comes under the umbrella of both cognitive therapy and behavioural therapy and is concerned with a person's cognitions (thoughts), core beliefs and assumptions about themselves, others and the world. The client is taught to challenge their automatic negative thoughts and replace these with more balanced thoughts.

Collective unconscious Jung believed this phenomena to be common to all human beings. It manifests in dream imagery, fairy and folk tales, in religions, and in the mythologies of diverse cultures at different times throughout history.

Complex An idea or a related cluster of ideas associated with strong emotions that have been buried by the unconscious (repressed) but are evident in behaviour.

Conscious mind The part of the mind that is aware of thoughts, emotions and actions.

Countertransference Describes the displacement of affect by the therapist on to the client or the therapist's emotional involvement in the interaction of therapy.

Defence mechanism The unconscious mind protects the Ego from anxiety, conflict and other undesired effects.

Denial Unconscious refusal to face the reality of a situation.

Depression A mood state characterized by despondency, sadness and defeatism. Considered normal in short spells, it becomes problematic when the condition persists.

Developmental psychology A field of psychology concerned with the different developments or changes that occur within a human lifespan.

Displacement The redirecting of feelings and impulses from the original source to another object (person) or situation.

Eclecticism The selective use of ideas and techniques from a variety of theories or models.

Ego (I) Copes with the external world and mediates between the primitive instinctual urges of the Id and the moralizing prohibitions of the Superego. It is also the means by which we mediate with others and assert ourselves. (**Ego, Id** and **Superego** form Freud's tripartite model of the psyche.)

Electra complex Where a girl wishes to take her mother's position so that she can become the prime focus of her father's affection.

Eros Love or self-enjoyment, life-preserving instincts including sexual instincts.

Fixation The individual gets 'fixed' at a stage of development (in Freudian terms – sexual development).

Free association Method adopted by Freud and his colleagues to explore unconscious associations. The analyst would say a word and the patient invited to say the first thing (uncensored) that came into their minds.

Gestalt therapy A form of therapy developed by Laura and Fritz Perls, based on the Gestalt concepts of unity, wholeness and the integration of body, feelings and intellect. 'Unfinished business' from the past is brought into awareness. Focusing on past experiences, emotional states and bodily sensations, it broadens the client's self-awareness. It's a creative approach, using techniques such as 'the empty chair' and 'the letter'.

Humanistic psychology An approach concerned with self-development or 'personal growth', self-motivation and self-understanding. Both Abraham Maslow and Carl Rogers have been credited as being 'the father of humanistic psychology'.

Id (it) The human psyche starts at birth with the chaotic Id that incorporates the basic instincts governed by the pleasure principle. It gradually becomes controlled by the Ego (socializing force) and the Superego. (**Ego, Id** and **Superego** form Freud's tripartite model of the psyche.)

Idealization An idealized view of a person or place that masks ambivalent feelings towards them.

Impulse The term, as defined by Freud, means an instinctual act, an unconscious force arising from the Id.

Integrationism Elements of different theories and models are brought together to form a new working model.

Introjection Describes when the views and rules of others, particularly parents and society, are taken into the individual's psyche.

Johari window A four-part model representing an individual's self-awareness.

Latency period The time from four to five years of age to the beginning of puberty when sexual activity is sublimated.

Narcissism Taken from the Greek myth of Narcissus, it means the love of self that precludes love of others. In psychoanalysis it refers to a period when the young child's libidinal drives are focused on the self (in autoerotic satisfaction) as a normal stage of development.

Neurosis Freud's original meaning was that neurosis was a personality or mental disturbance due to a conflict resulting from the blockage of instinctual urges. Neurosis was also thought to be a disease of the nerves.

Object relations A British-based school of further-developed Freudian theory. Object relation theorists included Melanie Klein, Donald Winnicott, Ronald Fairbairn and John Bowlby. The object relations school moved away from the classical Freudian libidinal theories, placing emphasis on human contact and relationship.

Oedipus complex The name derives from the Greek hero who unwittingly killed his father and married his mother. Freud used the term to describe the boy's unconscious wishes to possess his mother and eliminate his father. Initially, Freud used the term Oedipus complex to refer to the male complex. He named a female complex the Electra complex.

Operant conditioning Describes behaviour that is largely determined by its consequences. Operant response is brought under stimulus control.

Optimal frustration A term used to describe feelings that the client has in response to the blank screen or abstinent approach of psychoanalysis and the psychodynamic approach. The client experiences frustration with the counsellor, which offers opportunities for exploration.

Paranoid-schizoid position A Kleinian term related to splitting and part objects. Splitting occurs in the Ego (self) and the object (mother and breast), causing the infant to experience paranoid anxiety.

Part object Refers to objects that are introjected into the Ego from earliest infancy, beginning with the part ideal, and the part persecutory, breast. It's a characteristic of the paranoid-schizoid position.

Personal growth A humanistic term meaning the ongoing development of a person.

Phantasy/fantasy Relates to the inner world forged by early childhood experiences. Fantasies are idiosyncratic by nature.

Preconscious Ideas and memories that are not conscious but are easily accessed.

The process The ongoing changing content of therapy, client–counsellor relationship and client development.

Projection Projection of unwanted parts of the self, which can't be owned, on to another person.

Projective identification A Kleinian term – the projection of part of the self on to the other person results in the person being perceived as having taken on the characteristics. Also, identification with the person takes place. The person who is receiving the projection may also begin to identify with the characteristic being attributed to them.

Psyche The soul, the essence of life or the mind.

Psychoanalysis A branch of psychology which originated from the work of Sigmund Freud in the late nineteenth century and beginning of the twentieth century.

Psychosis Severe mental disorder.

Psychosomatic Psycho means the mind/soul and somatic refers to the body. The term refers to the interaction of the two elements and the effect of one on the other.

Rationalization Hides the real motivation for the individual's thoughts, feelings or actions achieved through the rationale of the Ego.

Reaction formation Unacceptable thoughts, feelings or impulses are controlled by the Ego, creating opposing attitudes or behaviour which hide the feared ones.

Regression going back to an earlier stage of development – evident in behaviour.

Repression A means of blocking an unpleasant experience from consciousness. The memory has been shut out but remains in the unconscious mind.

Resistance A means by which an individual protects themselves from the uncovering of unconscious material.

Rogerian Of or pertaining to the work of Carl R. Rogers – the same applies to Jungian (Jung), Freudian (Freud), Kleinian and so on.

Shadow, the One of the archetypes of Jungian psychology. It refers to the alter-Ego of the person. It can be the under-developed side of a person or a primitive or negative side of their personality.

Social learning theory A theory that views human behaviour in terms of a reciprocal interaction between cognitive, behavioural and environmental determinants.

Splitting A Kleinian term that involves the Ego and the object (e.g. mother, breast). Infantile splitting occurs between the 'good' and 'bad' self and the 'good' and 'bad' object.

Sublimation An unconscious redirecting of libidinal desires or impulses. Freud saw this as a necessary defence action, as part of growing up and becoming a member of society.

Superego (higher I) The conscientious part of psychic processes that contains internalized societal and parental rules and taboos. The Superego is the source of ideals and guilt. (**Ego**, **Id** and **Superego** form Freud's tripartite model of the psyche.)

Thanatos The Greek god of death. Freud used the term to refer to an instinct for death that rejects pleasure.

Transference The displacing or 'transferring' of feelings and attitudes from persons from the past (often parents), or from other relationships in the client's life, on to the therapist. The transference can be positive or negative depending on whether the attitudes towards the therapist are hostile or amicable.

Unconscious Mental processes of which we are unaware. Freud assumed two types of unconscious processes – those that are easily accessed (preconscious) and those that have been subject to repression. The latter are more difficult to access and are evident in the client's use of resistance as protection.

....

Working alliance The agreement between the counsellor and client about how they will work together. It can also refer to the constructive relationship between the counsellor and client when trust is established.

....

Taking it further

Contact details

AFRICA:

Eastern and Southern Africa Counselling Association
Sanoda House, Kamunde Road, North Kariobangi,
Box 39086, Nairobi, Kenya
Tel: 2542 786 310
Web address: www.esaca.or.ke
E-mail: info@esaca.or.ke

ASIA:

Asian Federation for Psychotherapy
Head Office B.D.S. – 1 University Campus Sugar,
470003 (MP) India
Tel: +91 (07582) 26539
Fax: +91 (07582) 20916
E-mail: gshankar2002@hotmail.com
(Ganesh Shankar – president)

AUSTRALIA:

Australian Institute of Professional Counsellors
Head Office: Locked Bag 15, Fortitude Valley,
Queensland 4006, Brisbane, Australia
Tel: (00) 617 3112 2000
Fax: (00) 617 3257 7195
Web address: www.aipc.net.au
E-mail: headoffice@aipc.net.au

Australian Counselling Association
Thomas Street Grange, Queensland 4051, Australia
Tel: +61 (0) 7 335 64255
Fax: +61 (0) 7 335 64709
Web address: www.theaca.net.au
E-mail: aca@theaca.net.au

CANADA:

Canadian Counselling and Psychotherapy Association
16 Concourse Gate, Suite 600, Ottawa,
Ontario, K2E7S8, Canada
Tel: (613) 237 1099
Fax: (613) 237 9786
Web address: www.ccpa-accp.ca
E-mail: reception@ccpa-accp.ca

The Counselling Foundation of Canada
18 Spadina Road, Suite 200,
Toronto, Ontario, M5R 2S7, Canada
Tel: +1 (0) 416 9238953
Fax: +1 (0) 416 9232536
Web address: www.counselling.net
E-mail: info@counselling.net

IRELAND:

Irish Association for Counselling and Psychotherapy
21 Dublin Road, Bray,
County Wicklow, Ireland
Tel: 00353 12723427
Fax: 00353 12869933
Web address: www.irish-counselling.ie
E-mail: iacp@iacp.ie

Hong Kong Professional Counselling Association
c/o College of International Education, Hong Kong Baptist
University (Shek Mun Campus), 8 On Muk Street, Shatin, NT
Tel: +852 23347172
Fax: +852 23561469
Web address: www.hkpca.org.hk
E-mail: enquiry@hkpca.org.hk

New Zealand Association of Counsellors
PO Box 2015
Hamilton
New Zealand
Tel: +64 (0) 7834 0220
Fax: +64 (0) 7834 0221
Web address: www.nzac.org.nz
E-mail: execofficer@nzac.org.nz

Survivors of Bereavement by Suicide
National Office: The Flamsteed Centre, Albert Street,
Ilkeston, Derbyshire, DE7 5GU
Tel: 0115 944 1117
Web address: www.uk-sobs.org.uk
E-mail: sobs.admin@care4free.net

British Association for Counselling and Psychotherapy (BACP)
BACP House, Unit 15, St John's Business Park,
Lutterworth, Leicestershire, LE17 4HB
Tel: 01455 883300
Text: 01455 550243
Web address: www.bacp.co.uk
E-mail: bacp@bacp.co.uk

BACP will send publication lists on request including, for example, resource directories: Counselling and Psychotherapy Resources Directory, Training in Counselling and Psychotherapy Directory, information sheets, booklets, training information, journals, newsletters and articles.

British Psychoanalytical Council
Unit 7
19–23 Wedmore street,
London N19 4RU
Tel: +44 (0)20 7561 9240
Fax: +44 (0)20 7561 9005
Web address: www.bcp.org.uk
E-mail: mail@psychoanalytic-council.org

United Kingdom Council for Psychotherapy (UKCP)
2nd Floor, Edward House, 2 Wakley Street,
London, EC1 7LT
Tel: +44 (0)20 7014 9955
Fax: +44 (0)20 7014 9977
Web address: www.psychotherapy.org.uk
E-mail: info@ukcp.org.uk

CRUSE (Bereavement Care)
Central Office: CRUSE Bereavement Care,
PO Box 800, Richmond, Surrey, TW9 1RG
National Office Tel: +44 (0) 208 939 9930
Freephone: 0844 477 9400
Young People's freephone helpline: 0808 808 1677
Web address: www.crusebereavementcare.org.uk
E-mail: info@cruse.org.uk

Frank about Drugs (Frank)
Frank is also referred to as the National Drugs Helpline. It is a government-funded organization that provides information and support to anyone who is affected by drug use, whether directly or indirectly (such as family members and partners). They signpost callers to local services, some of which include counselling over the telephone.

Frank about Drugs
Freepost PO Box 4000,
Glasgow, GL3 8XX
Tel: +44 (0) 800 776600
Web address: www.talktofrank.com
E-mail: frank@talktofrank.com

UNITED STATES:

American Counseling Association (ACA)
ACA has many branches covering the whole of the United States. To find the addresses, telephone numbers, websites and e-mail addresses in a particular area, consult the main web address: www.counseling.org

American Counseling Association (ACA) online information includes: ACA news, employment, government relations, information for consumers/media ACA branches and division. Members of ACA can access information on expanding skills, ACA World Conference, Student in Counsellor Education, resources and books.

ACA Members Services Tel: +1 (0)800 3476647

Visual aids resources

Concord Media
22 Hines Road, Ipswich, IP3 9BG
Tel: +44 (0)1473 726012
Fax: +44 (0)1473 724531
Web address: www.concordmedia.co.uk
E-mail: sales@concordmedia.org.uk

This company will supply their catalogue, *Counselling and Psychotherapy*, which details a large selection of videos available covering a range of topics; for example, group therapy, grief therapy, counselling the drug abuser, Carl Rogers in action (conducting encounter groups, counselling an individual and facilitating a group). Also offers the 'Three Approaches to Psychotherapy' series; Part 1 is a film of Carl Rogers, Fritz Perls and Albert Ellis individually engaging in therapy in their different orientations with a client named Gloria. Most titles are available for hire or purchase.

Suggested further reading

AN OVERVIEW

Douglas, T., *Groupwork Practice* (Basingstoke: Palgrave Macmillan, 1993).

Presents information about the kinds of experiences people have in groups, both as a participant and a group facilitator. No particular theoretical approach is emphasized; instead Douglas uses an eclectic approach, drawing on many sources. The material he describes ranges from the forming of a contract to the issues of threat and trust within the group setting. It is a popular book that makes the processes of groupwork understandable.

Dryden, W. (series ed.), *Dryden's Handbook of Individual Therapy* (London: Sage Publications, 5th revised edn, 2007).

A worthwhile read as the book acquaints the trainee counsellor with the various schools of counselling and psychotherapy. It can be 'dipped into' if one (or more) orientations interest you. There are, for example, chapters on person-centred therapy, transactional analysis and Gestalt therapy. The psychodynamic approach is represented by chapters on the Freudian approach, the Kleinian approach and the Jungian approach. This is useful as it gives the reader insight into the individual views of each psychoanalyst. Windy Dryden contributes with a chapter on comparative reflections on the different approaches.

Dryden, W. (series ed.), *Questions and Answers on Counselling in Action* (London: Sage Publications, 1993).

As the title suggests, critical questions relating to counselling are tackled by well-established therapists such as Michael Jacobs, who writes on 'The Use of Audio Tapes' in the counselling setting and 'Client Resistance', and Dave Mearns, who writes on 'The Core Conditions'. The subject matter is diverse – for example 'Against Self-Disclosure' by Julia Segal and 'Spirituality and the Counsellor' by Brian Thorne. There are also chapters giving advice on starting your own private practice and the issue of how to make a living as a counsellor.

Hinshelwood, R. D., *What Happens in Groups* (London: Free Association Books, 1988).

A more scholarly account of the processes inherent in groupwork from a psychoanalytic viewpoint. Hinshelwood is a psychoanalyst and psychotherapist with many years' experience of working in groups. Good topic coverage of, for example, 'splitting off a role', 'the silent member' and 'the persecuted victim'.

Masson, J., *Against Therapy: Emotional Tyranny and the Myth of Psychological Healing* (London: Harper Collins, 1992).

This is a controversial book. Masson's view is that therapists are full of prejudices and shortcomings, and he warns against the pitfalls of therapy. He attacks all forms of psychotherapy from the psychoanalysis that began with Freud to the humanistic psychology of Carl Rogers. The chapters have titles such as 'Jung amongst the Nazis', 'Sex and Battering in Psychotherapy' and 'The Problem with Benevolence: Carl Rogers and Humanistic Psychology'. He believes that therapy diminishes the dignity, freedom and autonomy of the person who seeks help.

McLeod, J., *An Introduction to Counselling* (Buckingham: Open University Press, 3rd revised edn, 2003).

This is more than an introduction to counselling, in its thoroughness to detail. It is comprehensive in its range of counselling-related subjects, from the origins and the main approaches, to cultural concerns and morals, values and ethics, training and supervision. It is an excellent account of contemporary counselling.

THE RELATIONSHIP

Clarkson, P., *The Therapeutic Relationship* (London: Whurr, 2nd edn, 2003).

The relationship between client and therapist has come to be considered the most important element in the success of therapy. Petruska Clarkson offers five modalities (or relationships) which can be used as an integrative framework for different approaches. A chapter is devoted to each of the modalities, explaining them in depth. Other chapters cover supervision, training and ethics and how the five modalities may be applied to organization, group and couple therapy.

Khan, M., *Between Therapist and Client: The New Relationship* (New York: Owl Books, revised edn, 1997).

This examines the compatibility of the psychoanalytic and humanistic theoretical points of view. 'The New Relationship' between the therapist and client calls for an integration of the two models. Humanism offers warmth and respect for the client and the spontaneity of the counsellor, while psychoanalysis provides theories of the unconscious. Khan outlines the work of Merton Gill and Heinz Kohut. Kohut merged elements of psychoanalysis and humanism in his developmental theory of self-psychology.

OBJECT RELATIONS

Bowlby, J., *Attachment and Loss* (3 vols) (London: Pimlico, 1997).

Volume I – *Attachment* – deals with the nature of the child's dependency on the mother.

Volume II – *Separation* – deals with separation anxiety.

Volume III – *Loss* – deals with childhood grief and mourning in relation to the loss of the mother figure.

Written within the framework of psychoanalysis, Bowlby's epic work embraces object relations, separation anxiety, mourning, defence, and trauma theories. A central theme is the importance of a continuous intimate and loving relationship with the mother (or a permanent loved other) and the resulting anxieties and problems experienced when continuity is broken.

Gomez, L., *An Introduction to Object Relations* (Free Association Books, 1997).

The work of the main object relations therapists is introduced; Melanie Klein, Ronald Fairbairn, Donald Winnicott,

Michael Balint, Harry Guintrip and John Bowlby. A section on Sigmund Freud places the object relations movement in context. Part II of the book is concerned with the application of object relations in the counselling/therapy setting.

Phillips, A., *Winnicott* (Fontana Press, 1988).

Winnicott was part of the British psychoanalytical school of object relations. He was the first paediatrician in England to train as a psychoanalyst. He revised the work of Freud and Klein. He wrote about the mother–infant relationship and the significance of the early environment in the infant's development. Phillips' writing gives the reader a sense of the idiosyncratic style of Winnicott – what he was like as a therapist and as a person.

Segal, H., ed M. Masud and R. Khan, *Introduction to the Work of Melanie Klein*, (London: Karnac Books, new edn, 1998).

Melanie Klein contributed greatly to the object relations movement. She psychoanalysed children using play materials. This introduction covers the main theories and themes of her work; for example, phantasy, the paranoid-schizoid position, envy and the depressive position. In the introduction Hanna Segal intimates that a thorough knowledge of the work of Freud is necessary to fully appreciate Klein's contribution and some knowledge of Freud's theories would certainly help. The text is fairly academic. The glossary of terms can be referred to when theories/terms become puzzling.

Winnicott, D. W., *Playing and Reality* (London: Routledge, 2nd revised edn, 2005).

Playing and Reality is a further exploration of a paper D. W. Winnicott wrote called 'Transitional Object and Transitional Phenomena'. The book is a product of his extensive studies of babies and children. The text explains the role that transitional objects play in a child's development. He believed that 'everything is expressed in the play' and that play is the therapy.

Kirschenbaum, H. and Land Henderson, V. (eds), *The Carl Rogers Reader* (London: Constable, 1990).

This begins with a personal account from Carl Rogers, of his upbringing, his marriage and what it is like to be 'growing old', or 'older and growing'. The purpose of the book was to capture an essence of his work in one volume. The chosen selection represents the range of his life's work from 1942 to 1987 (i.e. shortly before his death in 1989). The volume includes previously published material, excerpts from journals and more specialized work.

Mearns, D., *Developing Person Centred Counselling* (London: Sage Publications, 1994).

A sequel to *Person Centred Counselling in Action* that Mearns wrote with B. J. Thorne. The book demonstrates the position the person-centred ethos holds in the therapy world and how the approach has evolved and been integrated into other approaches, since its embryonic stage in the 1940s, beginning with Maslow and Rogers and their contemporaries.

Rogers, C. R., *Client-centred Therapy* (London: Constable and Robinson, new edn, 2003).

If you're studying person-centred counselling or an integrative approach, then this book is likely to be on your reading list. The volume spans a decade, during which time the techniques and philosophy of the client-centered approach to counselling were being developed. This book is a product of research based on scientific and experimental techniques carried out by psychotherapists at the Counselling Center of the University of Chicago. The subject of the work includes the attitude of the counsellor, the experience of the client in therapy, groupwork and teaching methods/attitude.

Thorne, B. and Rogers, C. R., *Key Figures in Counselling and Psychotherapy*, series editor Windy Dryden (London: Sage Publications, 2nd revised edn, 2003).

This book begins with coverage of the life of Carl Rogers from childhood to his professor years and his involvement in the encounter group movement in the 1960s – and beyond. The subsequent chapters cover Rogers' main theoretical and practical contributions to the therapeutic world and the criticisms that his theories and practices have attracted. The final chapter discusses his overall influence.

SKILLS

Egan, G., *The Skilled Helper: A Systematic Approach to Effective Helping* (Belmont, CA: Brooks/Cole, 1986).

This is a widely used book and is currently in its tenth edition. Egan offers a three-stage model in this problem-solving approach, for example, in the sixth edition the three stages are: **Stage 1** – (getting the) story; **Stage 2** – (looking at the) possibilities; and **Stage 3** – possible actions. *The Skilled Helper* offers a wide variety of counselling skills useful to those working in the caring professions and indeed anyone who would like to learn interpersonal skills.

Nelson-Jones, R., *Human Relationship Skills: Coaching and Self-coaching* (London: Routledge, 4th edn, 2006).

Richard Nelson-Jones has had the experience of working as a counselling psychologist, a counsellor trainer and a human relationship trainer. The book contains numerous, clearly presented, skill development exercises. The exercises are designed to help the reader/participant to relate more effectively to others and to develop self-understanding. It covers many subjects concerned with relationship skills, including anger and stress management. Includes a useful glossary.

Nelson-Jones, R., *Practical Counselling and Helping Skills* (London: Sage Publications, 5th edn, 2005).

Contains useful training exercises for working on your own, with a partner, or in a group. The life skills theory produces a five-stage model of practice, which is demonstrated with a case example. The model is a problem-solving, skills and goal identifying solution-oriented method of counselling. Based on cognitive behavioural processes, it advocates a good counselling relationship as a base for applying the techniques.

PSYCHOANALYSIS

Erikson, E., *Childhood and Society* (Vintage, N. W. Norton & Co., 1995).

This is a product of psychoanalytical theory and Erikson's own clinical experiences as a psychoanalyst. He builds on Freud's developmental stages in his eight ages of man-stages of psychosocial development. Other subjects include a discussion of anxiety in young children, childhood in two American Indian tribes, Hitler's childhood and young Nazis.

Freud, S., *The Essentials of Psychoanalysis – The Definitive Collection of Sigmund Freud's Writing* (Hogarth Press, 1986).

The contents are selected from the canon of work that Freud produced. It includes his writing on dreams, the unconscious, essays on the theory of human sexuality and the pleasure principle and the reality principle. In the Foreword, Clifford Yorke points out that Freud continually revised his theories. Anna Freud recommended 'The Question of Lay Analysis' as a good introduction to his work. Anna (Freud's daughter and also a psychoanalyst) wrote the introduction and commentaries.

Jung, C. G., *Memories, Dreams, Reflections* (Vintage Books USA, 1989).

Mainly autobiographical, it is a fascinating read – offering a panoramic view of his life, his work and his religious beliefs. It details Jung's early childhood, his school and university years and his professional life. He speaks candidly about his personal and private relationship with Sigmund Freud, where their theories merged and diverged. He relates and translates many of his dreams and tells of his travels to countries such as Kenya, Uganda and India, in search of the 'primitive' soul. Most intimately, he writes about his personal experience of God.

Snowden, R., *Freud – The Key Ideas* (London: Hodder Education, 2010).

This covers Freud's principle theories such as those of the unconscious mind, the defences and transference as well as his take on civilization, religion, war, art and literature. There are fascinating insights into Freud's personal life and personality. The book also contains a useful glossary of terms to help the reader understand psychoanalytical terms.

Snowden, R., *Jung – The Key Ideas* (London: Hodder Education, 2010).

This presents an accessible overview of analytical psychology and its key theories. Jung's early influences are explored and his ideological and spiritual development traced. Subject matter ranges from his early formative years to his writings on a growing array of subjects including the esoteric, mythology, dreams and phantasy. The reader gets a real sense of the man behind the philosophical and psychological ideas he contributed to psychoanalysis.

Jacobs, M., *Still Small Voice* (London: SPCK, 2nd revised edn, 1993).

Jacobs' style of writing is uncomplicated and informative. The book offers facilitating skills and techniques; for example, how to keep boundaries and how to manage resistance. He also gives examples of how the counsellor might approach difficulties with the client. Appendix A contains useful practical exercises.

Jacobs, M., *Psychodynamic Counselling in Action* (London: Sage Publications, 1988).

This presents a comprehensive account of the counselling process from the perspective of this approach, beginning with an exploration of the first counselling session and following through to the ending session. Michael Jacobs cleverly adopts the emotional difficulties of two Dickens characters – Little Nell from *The Old Curiosity Shop* (whom he calls Hannah), and Doctor Manette from *The Tale of Two Cities* (whom he calls Karl) – to build case studies.

Jacobs, M., *The Presenting Past* (Buckingham: Open University Press, 3rd revised edn, 2006).

A truly illuminating book designed to help counsellors develop their skills. It demonstrates clearly how a counsellor translates psychodynamic theory into practice. In the original edition Jacobs uses an adopted form of Erikson's model – the Eight Ages of Man – to show how past conflicts and transferential material between counsellor and client relate to the presenting problems of the here and now. Jacobs illustrates the themes of counselling with in-depth case studies. In the revised version Jacobs further explores basic psychodynamic themes. He draws on the work of object relations therapists such as Erikson, Winnicott and Klein to highlight major development themes: trust, dependency, authority and autonomy. The updated version contains a new chapter on how major themes arise at various times during the therapy process.

Miller, A., *Banished Knowledge: Facing Childhood Injuries* (New York: Doubleday, 1990).

Alice Miller writes passionately against conventional (Western) methods of child rearing, which includes the role of education. She believes that children learn to sublimate their emotional needs to comply with parental and societal demands. This developmental oppression later leads to hatred and violence in society, which she terms 'The Vicious Circle of Contempt'. She writes from personal experience, 'the child within', and also as an individual who practised as a psychoanalyst for 20 years.

COGNITIVE BEHAVIOURAL

Alford, B. A. and Beck, A. T., *The Integrative Power of Cognitive Therapy* (The Guildford Press, 1997).

This is a good introduction and overview of cognitive therapy as developed by Beck. It is a concise, thoughtful and comprehensive guide. It looks at the early development of cognitive therapy and the problems inherent in the approach.

Beck, Aaron T., *Cognitive Therapy and the Emotional Disorders* (Penguin, new edn, 1991).

Considered a classic, the book gives the reader a good sense of the theory and workings of the approach. Beck describes how cognitive processes contribute to emotional disorders and how automatic self-defeating thoughts can be replaced with beneficial positive thought processes. He points out that cognitive processes are observable by the client through introspection, allowing the client to build self-awareness. Problem-solving techniques allow the client to correct misconceptions in their thinking. Emotional disorders such as depression, anxiety neurosis and phobias are discussed. The principles and techniques of cognitive therapy are highlighted.

Dickson, A., *A Woman in Your Own Right – Assertiveness and You* (Quartet Books, 1982).

This is a well-known book. It is written for women but it is equally informative for men. The aim of assertiveness training is to teach people how to replace dysfunctional ways of relating to others – that is, passive, aggressive, or manipulative behaviour – with clear, direct and honest modes of communication. Topics explored include: assertiveness techniques, body language, anger and assertive approaches to work, money and sexuality.

Dryden, W., *Rational Emotive Behavioural Counselling in Action* (London: Sage Publications, 3rd edn, 2004).

The book is a revised and updated account of the approach, including recent developments. The basic premise of Rational Emotive Therapy (RET or REBT) is that self-defeating irrational beliefs are the cause of client problems and these can be replaced with different thoughts, feelings and behaviours to bring about change. The book demonstrates how the techniques work in practice with a detailed case study.

Greenberger, D. and Padesky, C. A., *Mind over Mood* (Guildford Press, 1995).

This is a self-help book written by two cognitive therapists that shows the principles, applications and methodology of cognitive therapy. Aaron Beck has written the foreword. Moods are linked with thoughts. *Mind over Mood* contains action plans and thought records. Mood questionnaires help the reader to identify changes occurring in their feelings. There are also chapters on understanding depression, anxiety, anger, guilt and shame. It is an easily understood manual of self-help. It is also a useful book for the trainee counsellor as it demonstrates the 'bricks and mortar' of the therapy.

Milne, A., Wilding, C., *Cognitive Behavioural Therapy* (London: Hodder Education, 2010)

This introduces the reader to the basic skills and techniques of CBT in an easy to understand self-help format. It contains examples of how to use worksheets, how to conduct simple behavioural experiments and tasks to test out self-defeating beliefs and assumptions, and many short case examples to illustrate the available strategies. It also gives tips on how to cope with anxiety, in its many forms, and depression. It's a useful book for anyone interested in developing a basic understanding of the CBT method or self use.

Trower, P., Casey, A. and Dryden, W., *Cognitive Behavioural Counselling in Action* (London: Sage Publications, 1989).

Cognitive behavioural belief is built on three basic premises: that emotions and behaviour are determined by thought process; that emotional disorders result from negative and unrealistic thinking; and that emotional disturbance can be helped by altering the negative and unrealistic thinking. This book is an overview and three-part guide to cognitive behavioural counselling. Cognitive behavioural counselling is explained in a direct and straightforward way. The methods of teaching the model are communicated well by the authors. Methods for facilitating change and homework tasks are discussed. The final part of the book demonstrates the application of cognitive behavioural counselling and discusses its limitations.

GRIEF THERAPY

Worden, J. W., *Grief Counselling and Grief Therapy – A Handbook for the Mental Health Practitioner* (London: Brunner-Routledge, 3rd edn, 2003).

This is a very helpful book. It is down to earth and sensible; for example Worden suggests that the counsellor addresses his or her own history of losses as a means of helping and understanding the grief of others. There are questions listed to aid the reader in this task. Other chapters include guidance on helping with a 'complicated mourning', 'resolving pathological grief', and instruction on how to help those suffering special types of losses, including suicide and AIDS.

Kubler-Ross, E., *Death – The Final Stage of Growth* (London: Simon & Schuster Inc., 1997).

This offers perspectives on death from an array of sources; for example, a rabbi, doctor and nurse as well as personal accounts by terminally ill patients and their survivors. There is a funeral director's account of tending to his own father's funeral. The experience led him to become a facilitating funeral director, welcoming the participation of the bereaved in the funeral preparation and service. It is a very touching book.

Wertheimer, A., *A Special Scar – The Experiences of People Bereaved by Suicide* (London: Routledge, 2nd revised edn, 2001).

A highly regarded writer on bereavement, Alison Wertheimer is herself a survivor of suicide. The book begins with a personal account of her own experience of her sister's suicide. While writing the book she carried out interviews with 50 people who were also bereaved by the suicide of a significant other. Their stories highlight the difficulties particular to suicide. The effects, Wertheimer says, have been described as 'a personal holocaust'.

CULTURAL

d'Ardenne, P. and Mahtani, A., *Transcultural Counselling in Action* (London: Sage Publications, 2nd revised edn, 1999).

The authors have had the experience of living and working away from their own countries and cultures, which has given them first-hand insight into the problems of communicating across cultures. Both authors trained as clinical psychologists, which they felt hindered them when they worked transculturally. *Transcultural Counselling in Action* reflects the culmination of the work they have done to build effective ways of relating in the transcultural setting. Emphasis is placed on the active and reciprocal process of the work. There is a useful resource section in the appendix.

Lago, C. and Thompson, J. *Race, Culture and Counselling* (Buckingham: Oxford University Press, 2nd revised edn, 2005).

A thorough study of the complex dimensions of race and culture. A broad range of issues are discussed; including issues of race and power, the intentions and limitations of Western theories of counselling and psychotherapy, non-Western methods of helping, and valuable guidance for supervisors, trainers and counselling agencies. Well worth reading.

ONLINE COUNSELLING

Anthony, K., and Jamieson, A., *Guidelines for Online Counselling and Psychotherapy: Including Guidelines for Online Supervision* (BACP publications, 2nd edn, 2005)

Provides an overall guide to related topics such as online practice as a specialism, client suitability and contracting, professional codes and law, data protection and confidentiality, and guidelines for online supervision.

Payne, L. *et al.*, *Guidelines for Telephone Counselling and Psychotherapy* (BACP publications, 2006).

Covers the basic issues and concerns of telephone counselling, recognizing telephone counselling as a specialist area. It addresses subjects such as ethical issues, theoretical orientation, experience, training, contracting and the suitability of equipment and environment.

Goss, S. and Anthony, K. (eds) *Technology in Counselling and Psychotherapy: A Practitioner's Guide* (Basingstoke: Palgrave MacMillan, 2003).

All uses of modern technology relevant to counselling and psychotherapy are covered, including telephone technology and computer technology, the worldwide web, stand-alone software, and therapy by e-mail and chat room facilities. There is a section devoted to the workings of individual therapy online and another on the supervisory relationships online. Practical issues such as data storage and contracting are addressed and the section on telephone counselling and psychotherapy is illustrated with case studies. It concludes with discussion about the need for international research and regulation. It's a very useful book that presents material that is potentially quite complex in a straightforward, practical way.

Index

Image credits